PR ЈⱭ **OL** ЈUN 2014
SU MAY 13

OF FEB 2016
SO AUG 2017
NA SEP 2018

THE WAR IN

THE COUNTRY

THOMAS F. PAWLICK

THE
WAR
IN THE
COUNTRY

How the Fight to Save Rural Life

WILL SHAPE OUR FUTURE

GREYSTONE BOOKS

D&M PUBLISHERS INC.

Vancouver/Toronto/Berkeley

for Foxy Grandpa

Greystone Books
A division of D&M Publishers Inc.
2323 Quebec Street, Suite 201
Vancouver BC Canada V5T 4S7
www.greystonebooks.com

Library and Archives Canada Cataloguing in Publication
Pawlick, Thomas
The war in the country : how the fight to save rural life will shape our future /
Thomas F. Pawlick.
Includes bibliographical references.

ISBN 978-1-55365-340-0

1. North America—Rural conditions.
2. North America—Environmental conditions. 3. Ontario—Rural conditions.
4. Ontario—Environmental conditions. 1. Title.

HT421.P39 2009   307.72'097   C2009-902713-5

Copyediting by Pam Robertson
Cover and text design by Naomi MacDougall
Cover photographs © Lecorre Productions/
Getty Images (top) and Ben Bloom/Getty Images (bottom)
Printed and bound in Canada by Friesens
Printed on acid-free paper that is forest friendly
(100% post-consumer recycled paper) and has been processed chlorine free
Distributed in the U.S. by Publishers Group West

We gratefully acknowledge the financial support of the Canada Council for the Arts,
the British Columbia Arts Council, the Province of British Columbia through the
Book Publishing Tax Credit, and the Government of Canada through the Book
Publishing Industry Development Program (BPIDP) for our publishing activities.

Beauty strip.

We left
a ribbon of trees,
covered the clearcut
hidden behind
with billboards
and signs,
screened the fine
criss-cross of
lines, of
marred earth and
scoured ground.
Look,
don't see.

We supply
surround sound,
soothing through
speakers,
muffle the animal
gasping and
groans, grunting
and moans,
The hissing of
strange-colored
clouds and seepings.

Don't hear.
Don't try to be too
clear.
None of it is really there,
no glow,
no smell in the air,
no dark soup
underground. The
surface looks calm,
as you cruise from
town to town,
cocooned, embalmed,
don't look,
don't stare.

Don't notice.

Contents

A Different Kind of Great Dying

Microcosm: a little world, a world in miniature
WEBSTER'S COLLEGIATE DICTIONARY

FOR AT LEAST SIXTY years in the industrial north of our planet, and for perhaps twenty-five or so in the rest of the world, a kind of Great Dying has been taking place—not the mass disappearance of endangered animal and plant species usually described or predicted by environmentalists, but a different kind of dying. This one, though it has had and will continue to have an ominously destructive impact on the environment, is not so much a biological phenomenon as a cultural one.

It is a uniquely human tragedy, caused by humans, and its consequences are yours, ours—everyone's.

Our rural world is dying.

If a coroner's inquest was looking for the cause of death, its jurors would have trouble pinning down a single one. A whole complex of factors is involved, playing off of each other like so many caroming pool balls at the break, or sub-atomic particles after colliding in a physicist's accelerator.

Even pinpointing an original impetus, some force or movement that shattered stasis and started the whole thing moving—the action to which all else is reaction—is problematic.

Perhaps that first force was simply greed, or more than that. Perhaps it was, in Cyrano de Bergerac's immortal dying words, a multitude:

> Who are you? Are you a thousand? Ah, I recognize
> you, all my old enemies!
> Falsehood? [he strikes with his epée]. Ha-ha! Compromise, prejudice, cowardice! [he strikes].
> Am I bargaining with you? Never, never!
> Ah, there you are, you, stupidity! I know in the end
> you'll lay me low.[1]

And it may yet. Most urban people—and they represent the vast majority of the population (80 percent or more in most so-called developed countries)—are, if not stupid, at least ignorant of what's happening. They don't know because no one has bothered to tell them.

This is the fault of our news media, which we can with some justification label truly stupid, or at least truly irresponsible, because they could easily know, and report, but haven't done so. With a few honorable exceptions, mostly in Canada (the work of André Picard of Toronto's *Globe and Mail* springs to mind, along with that of TV Ontario), they're too busy chasing "pop divas," "celebs," and axe murderers, too focused on reporting such crucial events as the current size of Britney's breasts, or, as one major online news site recently headlined: "How to keep your makeup from melting," to do the job of informing and educating that is supposed to be part of journalism. Worst of all is U.S. television.[2]

I spent two years researching and writing a book about this, called The Invisible Farm.[3] It was aimed at journalists, trying to alert them to the situation, and was published by a well-reputed house in Chicago. But like the proverbial tree that falls in the forest with no one there to hear, it made no sound.

And what is it that people don't know?

A Perverted System

They don't know that a perverted system, conceived and implemented by power elites with minimal democratic process, has captured those government departments charged with supervising the countryside, turning them into little more than an enforcement arm whose practical function is to create conditions that tend to wipe out: a) the family farm, b) rural small businesses, c) the culture and vitality of rural small towns, and d) the security and autonomy of all rural landowners, including retirees, back-to-the-landers, and other refugees from city stress.

The goal appears to be simple and brutal: to clear most rural lands of their inhabitants (save for a few suburban, transplanted enclaves), to raze whatever is left of our centuries-old rural cultures, including those of indigenous or First Nations peoples, and zone the resulting vacuum as Industrial with a capital I, turning it over to "factory farm" operations whose methods hark back to the failed collectives of the old Soviet Communist Empire, to mining companies, or here and there to recreational real estate developers.

The goal also appears to be to weaken or eliminate the very basis of democracy at its roots; that is to say, at the level of local municipal government, where voters have traditionally had the greatest direct influence on and control over their communities. In Canada, as Roger Epp, professor of political studies at the University of Alberta's Augustana campus in Camrose, Alberta, notes, federal and provincial governments "have eroded municipal decision-making authority over intensive-livestock or confined feeding operations, in order to ensure that neither local objectors nor upstart councils can stop 'science-based' developments or harm provincial reputations as safe havens for agri-business investment." [4]

Rural people are viewed as simply "in the way," Epp writes, adding that

> from the perspective of governments and outside investors, the countryside is no longer understood in terms of rooted human settlement and livelihood. Rather, it is coming to serve two very different purposes. The prettiest places become upscale playgrounds: tourist resorts, golf courses, parks or weekend property with a view of the mountains. The rest—mostly out of sight, out of mind—are envisioned as either resource plantations or dumping grounds. They are 'empty.' [5]

This is no mere rant, or conspiracy theory, particularly where farm ownership and the targeting of small business are concerned. It has been voiced as policy by spokesmen for government as far back as the Nixon administration in the U.S., whose secretary of agriculture, Earl Butz, famously snarled at American family farmers: "Get big or get out!"

For decades, corporate and government policies have pressed relentlessly toward Butz's goal, via the infamous "cost-price squeeze." Corporations have come to control the food production system at both ends, setting prices for everything farmers need to produce a crop—farm machinery, fuel, seed, fertilizer, herbicides, and pesticides—and then setting prices at the other end as well, the "farm-gate" prices farmers are paid for their food products. So-called "input" prices have constantly risen, while output prices have dropped, till the farmer, caught in the middle, can no longer produce a crop and expect to make enough from it to cover the cost of production. Beef cattle producers today are actually getting prices *lower than* those paid to their predecessors at the height of the Great Depression, in 1936.[6] The prices for feed grain such as corn have collapsed similarly, to below those earned by farmers in 1932.[7]

The farmer is being squeezed right out of business.

And now corporate forces are taking over the middle of the system, buying up the land as farmers leave it and consolidating it into massive factory farm operations.

Recent examples of how government sees this process were articulated in Ontario government policy papers (see chapter 8) and in publications like the Alberta Ministry of Agriculture, Food, and Rural Development's *Bacon Bits,* which told readers that small, independent hog producers would soon become no more than a "residual supply group" in the "New Agriculture."[8] Perhaps most outrageously, the mindset has been exemplified by some of the younger spokesmen for the financial side of Big Agribusiness, men like Gary Blumenthal, president and CEO of World Perspectives Inc., a Washington, D.C. consulting firm specializing in major food industry clients and investors (the firm's former president had for thirty-six years been an executive with the agri-food mega-giant Cargill Inc., and one of the firm's current clients is the World Bank):

> Certainly the countries with the fewer number of farmers are actually better off. We tend to have this romantic view of agriculture as, you know, we want to protect the small farms because they're nostalgic. And it may work in countries like Canada or the U.S. where you have government subsidies or consumer subsidies... there's something to be said for that if we want to subsidize.
>
> But we need to appreciate that this is a social policy. It's not an industrial policy. We have Renaissance festivals. You can go to a Renaissance festival and you can romanticize about what the Medieval era was like, with castles and knights and serfs and, you know, broken-down peasant farmers. We don't have to subsidize to romanticize about it.[9]

Blumenthal is wrong about North American subsidies, which tend to heavily favor large industrial operations over small family farms, and the world he inaccurately dismisses as Medieval was not Medieval at all. The Medieval era lasted roughly from AD 700 to 1500, while most family farms in North America were wiped out between 1925 and 2000. But the rural scene he sees as merely nostalgic has, in fact, nearly disappeared. So many census reports and statistical tables have attested to this rural population decline, and to the consolidation of arable land into megafarms, and they have been reported in so many different publications (including two of my own[10]) that repeating them is repeating a truism. Blumenthal describes the ultimate statistical results as well as anyone:

> If we just look at Canadian average farm size over the past while, your data from the government from 1981 to 2001, the farm sizes increased by 45 percent... in the U.S., over half of all commercial production comes from just 34,000 farms. Now we have two million farms, but as you can see a relatively small percentage produce most of the agriculture.[11]

He exults in this situation, enthusing that "North American farms are in the hundreds of acres or even thousands of acres!" In other words, bigger is inevitably better. He is content that a country which, at the time Henry David Thoreau was writing *Walden,* saw the majority of its citizens engaged in agriculture or its subsidiary industries, now sees barely 1 percent of its people engaged in farming.

American poet/farmer Wendell Berry is less enthusiastic, branding the process "a work of monstrous ignorance and irresponsibility on the part of the experts and politicians, who have prescribed, encouraged and applauded the disintegration of farming communities all over the country"[12]—a disintegration that resulted in thousands, perhaps hundreds of thousands, of individual business failures, bankruptcies, divorces, family breakups, suicides, and community collapses.

Joseph Stalin's purge of rural Russia's kulaks in the 1930s had been more physically brutal—he simply shot or starved his victims—but nothing as terrible had been seen in the West since the infamous "enclosures" of Tudor Britain.[13]

Not only did the process ruin scores of North American rural families and towns, it also resulted in the near-total destruction of the nutritional value of the food being produced by Big Agribusiness—the food that urban people, too, must eat—as well as in wholesale, widespread environmental destruction, as described in detail in my previous book, *The End of Food*.[14]

Of course, the process has not gone on without opposition, and stubborn pockets of resistance are fighting back even today, in North America and around the world.

In the 1970s, the so-called "back-to-the-land movement"—which was an outgrowth partly of the 1960s countercultural revolution and partly of the ideas of earlier times, such as the Great Depression–era Catholic Land Movement in Britain in the 1930s—made a determined, idealistic effort to reverse the trend. Thousands of young people, individually and in groups, migrated out of the cities and into the countryside, hoping to launch small-scale commercial or at least subsistence farms.

In the U.S., they were inspired by the work of people like Helen and Scott Nearing, whose books *The Good Life* and *Living the Good Life*[15] became best-sellers, while every issue of *Mother Earth News* magazine—whose first issue in January 1970 heralded "a new beginning"[16]—flew off the shelves. In France, the same kinds of young people were inspired by Claudie Hunzinger's *Bambois, la vie verte*,[17] while in Japan they looked to Masanobu Fukuoka's *The One-Straw Revolution*,[18] and in Australia to the so-called "permaculture" ideas of Bill Mollison.[19] In Canada, where I joined the movement, they read *Harrowsmith* magazine,[20] whose first issue in 1976 bore the cover line "Kissing Supermarkets Goodbye." After working a small farm in Quebec for several years, I became a *Harrowsmith* editor and moved to Harrowsmith, Ontario, in early 1979. Before it changed hands in the 1980s, the magazine had a Canadian circulation of some 135,000, which gives a sense of how many people were inspired by these ideas. There is no other way to know how many took part, in the U.S., Europe, and elsewhere. No census includes a "back-to-the-land" category.

It was a wonderful, almost heroic effort, and some of those who took part in it succeeded. Here and there, though by now isolated, they still manage to keep up their homesteads, proving that their "pie in the sky" theories could actually work in practice.

But they are few and far between. Their generation was succeeded by a new one, self-styled "yuppies" (young, upwardly mobile professionals) who bought into the trickle-down economic theories of the Reagan/Thatcher/Mulroney years and dreamed not of raising golden grain fields, but mostly of making pots of money on the stock market. The already destructive government policies that had caused rural decline in the first place became more pronounced, more draconian, more favorable to the multinational food corporations, and more harsh and unbending toward struggling rural families.

Typical are farm taxation policies.

It is no longer possible in Ontario to operate a "subsistence" farm, of the kind operated in the U.S. of the 1930s by the Nearings, or by me in the 1970s in Harrowsmith, without paying a heavy tax penalty. Even if a family spends most of its time working the land where they live—and produces enough grain, vegetables, meat, eggs, milk, and firewood on it to make themselves fairly self-sufficient—the government does not regard them as actually farming. They cannot claim the lower farm rate of property tax, unless they sell commercially a minimum of $7,000 worth of their produce every year. They are instead taxed at the same rate as a wealthy urban resident who purchases a lakeside cottage to use for summer holidays, and makes no effort to do anything on the property other than sunbathe.

If this rule were applied in places like Latin America, India, or Africa, where most of the large rural population engages in subsistence farming, virtually no one there could be legally classed as a "farmer."

In Alberta, the farm property tax system was recently modified to impose a new, "split use" regime. Farmers who had for decades been paying a normal farm rate for their land are now required to pay a different rate for any part of the farm that is not actually in crop. That is, the farmhouse, any woodlots, and any ecologically sensitive plots are now taxed at the residential rate. This can result in an additional tax burden of anywhere from $2,000 to $5,000 or more for small family farms.

Nor is the rate of property tax the only example. Federal income tax regulations in Canada allow a full-time farmer to deduct the full amount of any farm business losses during a given year. However, if that same farmer, in an attempt to stave off bankruptcy after years of continuing losses, takes an off-farm job, or the farmer's spouse does so, the amount of losses allowed is sharply restricted. In some cases farmers who have lost $20,000 or more due to the cost-price squeeze, bad weather, or other factors, can only deduct a maximum of $6,000 if they've had the poor judgement to try to help themselves by taking a second job.

In short, small family farms, subsistence farms, and ecologically minded farmers who put part of their property to use to protect the environment are systematically penalized.

Thanks to such policies, by the year 2000 the process of rural decimation, at least in North America, was so far advanced as to almost constitute a fait accompli.

But the human spirit, which seems to share an almost universal conviction that life in the country is somehow more human and natural, better for families with children, and better for the environment, refused to let rural culture expire. At the very moment when multinational corporate power and government collusion with it appeared triumphant, a new, stubbornly determined rural revival movement—made up of the ragged, struggling remnants of the remaining family farmers, of diehard back-to-the-landers, of once-urban residents who had come to the country to retire, or to start anew, and of indigenous people (in Ontario, especially, the Mohawks and the Algonquins), began once again to fight back.

Once again, there is a war in the country—perhaps this time a last stand.

In Europe, it's been led by countries like France and Poland.

Under Soviet Communist domination, a vicious effort was made to drive Poland's peasant farmers off the land and collectivize Polish farming, as had been done (with disastrous results) in Russia. But Poles, united by their own longstanding religious and cultural ideals, resisted the

Communist initiative fiercely, and by the time Gorbachev was ushering in the fresh air of glasnost and perestroika, and the Soviet Empire was crumbling, Poland still boasted the highest percentage of individual family farms in Europe.[21] Poland's peasants had hung on till eventual victory.

And then the Western corporate capitalist world entered, via the World Bank and various American and European lenders, trumpeting a policy called "structural adjustment," which required "belt-tightening" and "economic efficiency" in agriculture. The peasant farmers of Poland found themselves under siege all over again, by those they thought would be their rescuers. The new interlopers ordained mergers, consolidations, winnowings-out, all in the name of an efficiency that looked good to purely mathematically inclined economists, but disastrous to ordinary rural Poles.

It wasn't long before this created its own resistance.

A Pomeranian farmer, Andrzej Lepper, whose farm fell into debt and who was on the verge of bankruptcy, formed a protest group called Samoobrona, or Self Defense. Grouping disillusioned voters in small towns and villages, along with hard-pressed family farmers, he began a series of high-profile acts of civil disobedience intended to stop the sale of Polish land to foreigners and slow the harshly uncompromising "structural adjustment" measures that were being imposed on countries of the former Soviet Empire at the behest of the European Union and lenders like the World Bank. He and his followers were arrested and charged repeatedly, but persisted until, in 2006, Lepper became minister of agriculture and rural development. He remains controversial, and the battle in Poland continues.

In France, with its deep-rooted cultural attachment to *la vie paysanne*, and its consumer devotion to high-quality cuisine and wines, efforts to consolidate small farms into large industrial-scale operations, while eliminating the protective tariffs that kept many smaller French farmers in business, also met with strong resistance. In 1987, French farmer José Bové founded the *Confederation Paysanne,* or Peasants' Confederation, and began a series of high-profile public confrontations similar to those of Samoobrona, blocking highways with tractors and farm equipment and demonstrating on the steps of government buildings. Bové himself was sentenced to prison for his role in dismantling a half-built McDonald's franchise. His movement, too, continues.

In the Third World, India has led the way, with peasant farmers rising in mass protest against efforts by corporate multinationals to establish restrictive patents on such basic commodities as rice, and to force the adoption of so-called "terminator" seed technologies. The books of Indian researcher Vandana Shiva,[22] documenting the issues, inspired millions and helped in forming the now-influential Third World Network.

In the U.S., where the process of corporate industrialization of the rural world has probably gone further than in any country other than the now-defunct Soviet Union, organizations like the National Farmers Union and National Family Farm Coalition have continued to struggle against the odds, boosted magnificently by the efforts of singer Willie Nelson, who in 1985 joined fellow musicians John Mellencamp and Canadian Neil Young to form Farm Aid, a movement partially funded by Nelson's concerts and devoted to raising awareness of rural issues and defending the family farm.

In Canada, the Canadian National Farmers Union has done great service in documenting the problems and educating the public, while the much more recently formed

Ontario Landowners Association is performing a more radical, politically effective service through public demonstrations and confrontations reminiscent of those in France, Poland, and India. Cofounder Randy Hillier (who, like Bové and Lepper, has been arrested for his activities) was recently elected a member of the Ontario Provincial Parliament. His Ontario-based group may soon be joined by a counterpart organization with similar ideals and activist fire, in the province of New Brunswick. The movement could go national.

The war isn't over, after all. The international corporate power brokers who rule today's food industry—and most of our federal, provincial, and state governments—may have declared victory prematurely.

Tighter Focus

Of course, a book that tried to document all of these worldwide, decades-long, ongoing struggles would be impossible for a single author to compile. It would have to be a virtual encyclopedia of world agriculture, running to thousands of pages. And who would read it? Certainly not many of the ordinary citizens/voters whose electoral voices and public activism are the only hope of turning things around.

A tighter focus is required.

Hence this book, which homes in on my own home ground, eastern Ontario, where I ventured as a back-to-the-lander in 1979, left again, and to which I returned in 2005. Every wild current that swirls elsewhere in our planet's rural territories runs also through this place, buffets it, endangers it, provokes and inspires it, tosses up individual tragedies and individual heroes and heroines from among its population.

They are my neighbors. Some are my friends. They are a microcosm of the world. Anyone who understands their fight will understand what is at stake in his or her own country. Americans, Mexicans, French, Poles, Kenyans, Bolivians, Russians, and Chinese will recognize themselves, or their rural neighbors, in towns like Tweed, or Napanee, or Marlbank. Hopefully, they will, as Blake said, "see a world in a grain of sand," and realize why every one of us must take sides now and fight to win the War in the Country.

How It Used To Be

You don't know what you've got, till it's gone.

JONI MITCHELL, "Big Yellow Taxi"

PICTURES COME BACK SOMETIMES, from a long way away. Like the Broadway Market in downtown Detroit, sixty years ago.

Ma used to like to shop at the Broadway because everything was fresh, just like the produce at the outdoor, awning-sheltered Western and Eastern Markets, where truck farmers and market gardeners came in from miles around all through the growing season. The markets and the small farms and gardens that supplied them had been bustling for decades. They were part of an established agricultural order, accepted and appreciated, just as the Broadway was also part of the then-thriving Great Lakes fishing industry.

There were all sorts of things on sale at the Broadway, atop white counters and behind glass displays: sausages, meats and vegetables, cheeses. But to me, the best thing about it was the fish, including lake trout right from the nearby lakes, Huron and Erie, maybe caught and shipped only a day previous. Fresh fish and seafood of all kinds, displayed on beds of crushed ice. I used to love the smell, like being out on the water.

Then, as history records, the sucking, parasitical sea lamprey invaded the Great Lakes, wiping out the trout and a way of life for thousands of fishing families in Canada and the U.S. Photos of the ugly, eel-like creatures, their razor-sharp mouth parts burrowed into the living flesh of the trout, were in all the papers, inspiring disgust.

I was surprised, but probably shouldn't have been, when those images from a vanished childhood world popped into my head, walking down the laneway in 2007 with Bruce Switzer, 81, and his brother Bud, 71, on my eastern Ontario farm. The life of rural Ontario is being drained today by a whole set of afflictions, some of them older than, and together at least as destructive as, the plague of sea lampreys.

The ugly effects were visible all around us: neglected fields and orchards, not worked regularly or responsibly for thirty years or more, overgrown with thistles, quack grass and "trash" bush—prickly ash, red cedars three to five feet tall, and out-of-control lilacs, spreading from what were once decorative borders around a farmhouse to become persistent weeds—weathered gray barns and outbuildings, gradually deteriorating, partially roofless, their loose boards flapping in the wind, and near them the hulks of rusting farm machinery, abandoned on land no one cared for anymore.

Of course, eastern Ontario is still beautiful, and not all its former farmsteads are in ruins. Some are still well cared for by the few surviving farmers, and some have been bought up by city folk for weekend getaways, or to raise horses.

These neatly kept retreats are scattered checkerboard fashion among the abandoned sites. But compared to what it once was, today's landscape is a mere echo.

The property on the Hogs Back Road where we were hiking had been purchased by my son and me about a year and a half earlier, but had once been farmed by the Switzers' father. Bruce had been a boy there. I'd invited them over, to hear a bit of the history of the place for which we were now responsible.

An incredible rush of images from his own childhood must have been going through Bruce Switzer's mind, as the three of us moved along.

A Cool Morning in June

It was a cool morning in June, following two days of rain, and both brothers wore windbreakers.

"I was born in 1925. I left here when I was ten years old," said Bruce. "But I didn't move very far away."

He paused in front of a small shed outbuilding, constructed of the gray barn board typical of earlier days. My son and I were keeping our old Massey 180 diesel tractor there. Next door to it, windows boarded up, was the 150-year-old Orange Order Hall, still surrounded by banks of bright orange tiger lilies. Once a month, a dwindling number of aging Order members come and recall past glories, hidden now behind the boarded windows.

"This [the shed] was where we stored the car," said Bruce. "We bought a car before the Depression, a Model T Ford. We only drove it maybe four years, till the Depression came." He paused for a few minutes, standing there, looking at the shed he hadn't seen in seventy-two years.

"They'd brought the car from Marlbank, the dealer. He was a salesman. Mother and Dad bought the car, and Mother learned to drive. He [the salesman] learned her to drive in an afternoon, and she took him back to Marlbank with the car. She took him home. My father always called her Daisy, and she called him Dad."

"It would have been a black Model T, I'll bet," I laughed, recalling Henry Ford's famous dictum: "They can have any color they want, as long as it's black."

"Oh yeah," said Bruce. "Shiny black, and with side curtains. We thought that it was beautiful. Leather seats. I remember taking it back to Kaladar, because we had an uncle and aunt lived back there, picking huckleberries, picking blueberries. When we got into that car, we had to fit there. There was some of us hanging out the sides. Until the Depression came on, and we parked it in the drive shed."

"Because it was too expensive to buy gas?"

"Oh yeah. That was where we parked it. And when we moved, in 1935, we towed the car [with horses] out to Westplain. We put it in and jacked it up. We never drove it again."

The worldwide economic crisis and collapse in farm prices had made it impossible for the Switzers to continue working the 150-acre farm. They took over a much smaller place, closer to town and to markets.

That was the era of the Okies, I thought to myself, the time of Steinbeck's *Grapes of Wrath*. The Dust Bowl. People wandering the roads, starving, pushing their worldly belongings in carts, Bennett Buggies as they were called in Canada, after the prime minister of the day. The Switzers put their Model T up on blocks, in their new, smaller place, and never drove it again. Never again.

We walked a bit farther down the laneway, to an opening in the lilacs.

"I remember hay growing here," said Bruce. "But all this stuff [lilacs], there was none of this stuff. Here is where we rode downhill on sleighs [in winter]. We've got to go up and find out where that old house is at." He strode on, anxiously alert now, concentrating, until we came to a spot, now totally overgrown, where a ruined stone house foundation lay in the ground, maybe five feet deep. It was the site of the house where Bruce had spent the first ten years of his life, 1925 to 1935.

"Right there," I said.

"Yeah. There's where the house sat, right there."

Every step we took on that chilly June ramble together was a step backward in time, to a world long gone, but still fresh in Bruce Switzer's mind. A world where people thought differently than they do today, interacted differently, organized their social and economic lives differently, farmed differently, sold their produce differently, conceived the whole idea of husbandry, marketing, and above all consuming in a way so markedly foreign to the way things are done today that the world in his brain may as well have been a place on the far side of the moon.

In many ways, I think, despite the truly hard physical labor it required of its inhabitants, and the disaster of the Great Depression they were fated to endure, it was a better place, a place worth rediscovering. No one can understand the lamprey-like repulsiveness of what's happening in the countryside today without some benchmark for comparison, some rudimentary idea of what was there before.

A Greek Chorus

My neighbor Claude Brown remembered that place in time too, and told me more about it as we sat on the sunporch of his waterside cottage on Lime Lake, not long after the Switzer boys' visit to my farm. His two grade school–aged granddaughters played in the shallow water nearby, laughing and splashing. Claude had gone to grade school with the Switzers. As he spoke, the words of Bruce and his brother, and many other people who have helped me understand those old days, came back, echoing and adding to the pictures he described, like a Greek chorus.

"Did they [the Switzers] tell you what their dad did off the farm?" Claude asked.

"No."

"He built I wouldn't know how many miles of fence in this country. He built patent fence by the mile. All the fences on this place he and my father built together. All over. Patent fence. With the rails and stakes. Most of those fences down there would be Wes's fences."

Brown, an 83-year-old man with a deep, sort of muffled voice, saw that other world again in his mind, while his two grandchildren played. Half the fences he referred to were now dilapidated, falling down, around pastures where nothing grazed anymore but white-tailed deer. Cedar wood doesn't rot, like other woods do, seeming to last forever, but the fencing wire used to hold the rails together has to be replaced now and again, and there was no one around anymore to replace that rusted wire. My own farm must have at least a mile or so of cedar fence still standing, marking off the now overgrown fields. We'd made a start at repairing them, but had a long way to go.

"Do you know where the stop sign is [on the Hogs Back Road]?"

"Yes."

"That was Francis Somerville, a bachelor, and he owned all the land on the south side of the road, right down till you see the farmhouse away this side, the third one up here. Davises lived there. Birds lived in the next one and we lived here. Jarmins here [pointing], and I'm not sure who lived where Robin Tyner is now. And there was Hendersons on each one of the corners. Switzers was on the right. We went to school together…"

"I always wanted to go to school," Bruce Switzer had said, "from the time I could walk, I guess. And Mother told me, 'When you get six, you can go to school.' Well I turned six in March, and they wouldn't let me go to school. I had to wait till September. Well sir, did I ever get upset. I cried. And I'd go upstairs and look out the bedroom window and I'd watch the other kids go to school. The Browns lived up on the Hogs Back, you know, Helen and Claude Brown, and Bernie is Claude's boy, Bernie and Stella, and they'd come down and go with George, and go over and go with Ted, and then go to school. They'd come over to our place, and then they'd walk down across the field that he's plowing there. Unless there was hay, and then they had to go around the field, go out and then down through the pasture. It was all open. I would go up there and I'd cry and I'd cry to go to school."

1931. A little boy at a farmhouse window. All that's left of that house now are the crumbling remnants of its limestone block foundation, half buried in thick, tangled lilacs.

"This is the horse stable," said Bruce, whose father kept Clydesdales for work. "We lost one in the well back here. A workhorse. Jerry, his name was Jerry. Big, big horse. Fell in the well. I could find the well, but he couldn't, because he fell to death." Jerry must have been well loved, as animals often are on a small farm. He must have been a friend. The look in Bruce's eyes hinted at it. They piled up limestone rocks to cover the well, a cairn/monument to Jerry.

We came to the barn, perhaps one of the oldest structures on the property. One wall, the one facing the prevailing wind, had several boards missing or loose. My son and I planned on replacing them, on putting the old barn back into service. The Switzers and I had gone inside.

"Here's where we kept sheep," said Bruce. "And we put the hay in here and we fed the hay out of here. We put the sheep in, for them to have little lambs, right in here. This is the granary. This is the grain bin. Isn't this amazing!"

He was like a kid on Christmas morning, running around the base of the Christmas tree, finding presents. "Oh well, look, the beams are [still] good in here. These are good beams. Unbelievable!"

"It was all mixed farms then," said Claude Brown, when we met later. "We always had a couple of sows, nearly always. Everybody had a few hens, and probably eight to ten cows, up to fifteen. My father had four horses. Every farm sent a couple of cans of milk, 30-gallon milk cans.

"There was a cheese factory here in Marlbank. The one that drew them [milk cans] with the horses lived down below you, just where Tyner's Road goes to the right. He had a team and wagon, went around every day. The cheese factory was just at the edge of town. You didn't get much for the milk, but then it didn't cost you much for groceries. My mother would make butter in the wintertime, and she'd have a few made to take in to sell. I can remember Father giving her two dollars and she'd get a week's groceries."

The milk was sold raw, unpasteurized.

"Did anybody ever get tuberculosis in those days? Have you ever heard of that?" I asked, thinking of the current angry controversy over the sale of raw milk in the province, a controversy which has seen government pitted against small farmers, putting many out of business.

"It wasn't a common disease. They'd put it [the milk] in the vat and they'd put that rennet into it. It was cheese, not milk. If they started in the morning, it was cheese by four o'clock." More splashing, and the laughter of little girls...

"Well, look at this, Bud! And the rafter's made out of poles. Probably tamarack. The pulley and the track [for conveying hay] is still there." Bruce Switzer, enthusiastic, had pointed at a huge beam in our barn. "It's really amazing how they cut them, and get them up in there. Them old guys could do that stuff. They was rock solid. They had a bee in, fifty men would come. They worked. They fed them good. They grew all the food they wanted to eat.

"These guys knew what they were doing. They say that they were dumb and all that, but they were smart. To build a barn like this? Look how they put them big things up there. Look at that! Look at that! Ropes, pulleys, windlasses."

Most of those "old guys" were transplanted Irish, both Catholics and feuding Protestants, Orangemen and budding Fenians, or their first-Canadian-generation children. In Ireland, those first pioneers had been deadly enemies. Here, they still didn't like each other much, but they limited their battles to the odd fistfight, realizing that in their new wilderness environment, life depended on neighbors working together.

Eventually, their children ended up marrying each other, the old feuds forgotten.

The Switzers, whose ancestors came originally from Switzerland, had at one point migrated to Ireland, and then come to the New World with their Celtic neighbors.

Bruce's foot had hit something on the barn floor: "An old horseshoe. A horseshoe they put there!"

I picked it up, for good luck.

Farm Census

In Hastings County, at the time Bruce Switzer and Claude Brown were growing up, there were 4,840 full-time, professional farmers in the area, not counting perhaps another thousand part-time or subsistence farmers, and home gardeners, who often kept chickens and the odd hog as well, or tended small orchards.

The rolling land they worked was underlaid mostly by light gray limestone, which visibly poked up to the surface everywhere. Some 600 million years ago, the region had been a shallow, warm ocean, crammed with sea life—clam-like brachiopods and lobster-like trilobites—whose skeletons sank to the bottom, laying down layer after layer. The outline of their bodies is often still visible in fossil form. Crossing from one pasture to another with Bruce and Bud, I spotted a trilobite in the gray rock beneath our feet.

Soil formed over limestone is usually slightly alkaline or neutral, and good for cropping. People had it better here than their counterparts who tried to settle just a little farther to the east and north, where the granite of the Canadian Shield dominates, and where the acidic soil is even more shallow. The dividing line between the ancient seabed and the much older Shield is easily seen from the highway, in places like central Frontenac County, where the gray, stratified outcrops of limestone change abruptly to jutting pink-and-black-spotted granite.

Some people in the area in those days farmed part-time and worked off-farm at places like the "pea vinery" at Chapman's Corners, south of Tweed. At the vinery, crops of peas grown locally were stripped of stems and husks, then sent off to canneries in Belleville for finishing.

Food was everywhere. Fresh food, nourishing, raised by people who most food buyers could meet personally. If anything was wrong, the buyer knew exactly where to go and who to see to complain about it. There was nowhere for the grower/seller to hide, no anonymity.

In nearby Napanee, to the south, there was a thriving and industrious farmers' market, perhaps founded as far back as the 1850s (the official date is 1864), while in smaller towns like Marlbank (Tweed Municipality) there were individual country stores, and innumerable growers who had established delivery routes for regular customers throughout the rural area.

Evan Morton, curator of the Tweed and Area Heritage Centre, described it for me:

"Just growing up here, what you'd have would be people going around peddling, like honey, or something else. It was individuals that peddled their produce. You had people with berries. They'd go around and just knock on people's doors. You had certain families that year after year after year would supply your meat or your eggs. They would come by and have a regular route. You didn't have to worry about going to a central market. People picked wild blueberries in the hills around Kaladar and sold them along routes or at roadside stands. Now most of the berries at those stands are imported, commercially produced...

"We never went hungry or cold," added Marlbank's Mildred Foster, 66. "We had ten cows, twelve cows. My mother made butter. Dad drew the milk to Marlbank, to the cheese factory. My grandfather drew there, my father drew there, with the horses."

Echoing Foster, Claude Brown adds later: "We ate well. We never went to bed hungry [during the Great Depression]. No need to. We had lots of food, and we was dressed as well as everybody else, and we didn't know the difference. We thought that was the way the world was..."

The cheese factory in Marlbank, like those in hundreds of other small Ontario towns, made cheddar cheese, cheddar for whose quality the province eventually became world famous. In Hungerford Township alone, there were independent cheese factories at Marlbank, Otter Creek, Goose Creek/Maple Ridge, Murphy's/Larkin, Clare River, Forest Mills, Pine Grove, Rock, Victoria, Bogart, Hungerford/Alexander, Tweed, Cedar, Roblin, Stoco, Premier, Kervine, Thomasburg, and Moira Valley—nineteen factories. And the industry created small spin-offs.

"When my grandfather died in '31, father had two sisters," said Claude Brown. "And Granddad had left them a little bit of money and he had to [get it for them]. He got a hundred cord of heading off a ranch we had back here. What I mean by heading, I don't know if you've heard of it, it was just basswood, made out of basswood, and it's sawed for cheese box heads, for the boxes. There was a little mill in Marlbank that sawed these boxes, about 36 or 38 inches long. He sold it to the mill, made money to pay off the sisters."

Basswood heading, felled by hand without the aid of any still-to-be-invented chainsaws, was cut and shipped, to box cheddar cheese and assure a family inheritance. The work took strong arms, strong men with hard bodies, men used to work. You wouldn't want to tick one of them off, for fear one of those strong fists might connect with your jaw.

Mildred Foster recalled buying those boxed cheeses: "We'd go to Forest Mills and get two or three of those great big brown things of cheese. Big round ones. I think they called it a wheel at that time. Sometimes we'd get more, enough for the winter."

Trees had many other uses.

"We had a big [maple] sap bush," recalled Bruce Switzer. "We tapped two to three hundred trees. I've seen Dad work day and night boiling sap, and then we hired people to help us. Oh, we put out a lot of maple syrup, a lot. We took it to Napanee in milk cans. There was a farmers' market."

"We tapped about 450 trees," said Claude Brown. "Sold a lot of syrup for a dollar a gallon. Now you can't buy a cupful for a dollar. My father had a route out towards Tyendinaga. He went every year. He took four cream cans, those eight-gallon cream cans, of syrup, and put them in the trunk of the old car. They'd dip 'em out. Took a quart measure with him..."

And there was firewood.

"Most people had customers," said Bruce Switzer. "If you was good, if you was a good supplier, had good wood and give them a reasonable price, you took it there year after year. You took it right to their house. It cost you a little bit [of commission] to sell in the [Napanee] market. They'd cut it for a dollar a cord.

"Arthur and I cut ninety cords in one month, bush cords [a stack 4 feet by 8 feet by 4 feet, or 128 cubic feet]. It was for Perry Armstrong and it was soft maple. I was just got married, and [Arthur] just got out of the army, and Perry wanted one hundred cords cut. He said, 'You won't have to cut no brush; you won't have to pile no wood, you won't have to split no wood. You cut her down and cut her up.' And he was there every day with a team. He got his chores done in the morning, and the ice was just there and about that much snow. It was starting the full month of January. We was up at daylight, was in there in daylight. Drive the car right in on the ice. I had a Model A Ford. We cut them down, I helped him cut them down, with a saw four feet long. We stayed there till dark, and we was there before daylight."

Bruce's older brother Arthur, at the time a just-returned veteran of the Second World War, was proof against the cold. As Bud recalled: "Arthur got out of the army in '45, so it must have been '46. In the dead of winter, Arthur would go into the woods with Dad to cut wood, with no socks and rubber boots. And when Alton [a younger brother] came home from [the market in] Napanee, they'd have a load ready for the next morning."

People nowadays have a hard time imagining what it was like to work that hard, and to think it normal. But after fighting in Europe against the Nazi menace, or in the Pacific, and coming home alive and in one piece, young farm boys must have thought it a relief to be back home, working in the woods, even in rubber boots with no socks.

For decades, farm people from around the area had made the trip in to the farmers' market in Napanee, on Market Square, or to see individual customers there, at first in wagons pulled by horses, and later in automobiles or trucks. The Switzers brought their firewood in on a wagon pulled by a team of Clydesdale horses.

"When they was going over those railroad tracks in Napanee and you had a full cord of wood on, you needed a good team to cross," said Bud. "Dad had a bunch of bags, and he soaked them in kerosene and he carried them with him. When Dad got to the tracks he'd lay these things down and they'd just skid across. [At the market] you wouldn't unload unless you had to. But if I come along, and said I want to buy that cord of wood and you take it up to my place, you'd get fifty cents, go up there and unload. If not, you piled it in the market and the market people sold it and give you your money."

In addition to maple syrup and firewood, the Switzers brought livestock to the market. "We'd ship pigs," said Bruce. "They was white. Yorkshires. Hogs and chickens went into the Napanee market. Buyers from Canada Packers and Swift and who else would come to Napanee on Poultry Day. In the fall they had two Poultry Days, maybe a month apart or two weeks apart. And you dressed your chickens, you left the guts in, you just took the feathers off, and they come and they paid you so much a pound. We had them gray Barred Rocks mostly. And we tried some Blue Andalusians, they were about this tall. And then we got some Black Minorkies [Minorcas], had feathers on their legs. But we couldn't do nothing with any of them. We had great luck with the Barred Rocks."

In Napanee, there were not only Poultry Days, but Turkey Days. "You'd kill the turkeys the day before and they weren't dressed, you just plucked them," said Brown. "Take them down there the next day. A buyer would come up from Montreal, more than one of them. There was no refrigeration at home, and the next day maybe he'd buy them at ten o'clock in the morning, maybe two o'clock in the afternoon. They were carried over to this room and threw in a heap, pretty near to the ceiling. That night they'd put them in a van and go to Montreal. And I never heard of anybody dying. They didn't spoil."

A photograph, taken on a Poultry Day in 1906, shows only a part of Napanee's Market Square, but more than thirty horse-drawn vendors' wagons are visible. There must have been at least a hundred on that day. In later years, there were more. And not every farmer went to Napanee every time he had something to sell.

The Browns also kept Barred Rocks, and pigs as well, explained Claude. "We usually kept them [pigs] to 200 pounds. My father took them to Marlbank. There used to be the stockyards there. We didn't have that many hens. You could take eggs to [the general store in] Marlbank and they didn't have to be graded. The storekeeper would give you a few cents a dozen, and he'd sell it back out to the people that lived in the village and didn't have birds, maybe a couple or three cents a dozen."

Families got their baby chicks to raise from larger poultry growers/incubators, like the Lakeview Poultry Farm in Tweed, which in 1927 took orders for 7,000 baby chicks from neighboring small farms. Foster's cold storage lockers, also in Tweed, kept pork, beef, and game meat on ice for longer periods, until the era of the individual home freezer began, enabling families to keep their meat at home.

Not All Work

Life then wasn't all hard physical work, questionable sanitation, and business transactions, of course.

"They used to have barn dances at Pete Perry's, every Saturday," said Mildred Foster. "They'd go in, past the cows. Guys would sit up in the hayloft, drunk on whiskey. There were all kinds of bands." They played good, old-fashioned country music, heavy on the fiddles, and danced till dawn.

"They also had concerts in the Orange Order Hall, right beside where you are now. They had Valentine's parties, everything there." Sometimes they had "uplifting" lectures, or readings by local poets and essayists. Today, the hall stands unused, except for that single meeting, the last Friday of every month, to which the dying breed of Order members (most now in their sixties or seventies) come. A couple of them drop by every few weeks in summer, to mow the lawn around the building, or to clear a path in the snow in winter. I greet them with friendliness each time, as they gather to beat the drum for King Billy, even though my own Irish ancestors were firebrand Fenian Catholics and my mother was related by blood to the Republican hero Michael Collins.

There were sports, in the old days, like curling, usually on outdoor rinks on the pond next to the local mill or later near the small hydro dam. And of course, there was the all-Canadian game of hockey, at which Ontario farm boys, much like Saskatchewan's great Gordie Howe, got their earliest lessons in skating, checking, and passing the puck.

On Sunday, there were preachers. The Switzers' house was about 100 yards west of the Lime Lake Methodist Church, built in 1906, my present home.

"Right in our house we could hear the preacher preaching," recalled Bruce. "And they preached the real Gospel. They didn't fiddle around, whispering to one another. They told it like it was. You didn't have to come inside [the church building] in the summer. There was some of them old Methodists, they were born-again preachers."

The red brick church itself had been built by its congregation, in the same way they built barns: all the neighbors gathering for the bee, dividing up the tasks. The men framed the beams and studs and laid brick, while women prepared food. The Amish people, living now around Aylmer, Ontario, maintain this tradition.

People were attentive to the natural world around them, which helped them supplement their diets, not only with wild berries but with walnuts, butternuts, and, of course, wild game meat and fish. Everyone hunted deer, ducks, and partridge.

"We'd find a bee tree," said Bruce Switzer. "It didn't matter whose property it was on. If you found a bee tree you marked it and put your initials in it. And the regulations were, you could take it, take the honey."

Walking with me in one of the woodlots on his old farm, he stopped suddenly, grinning, and pointed at a clump of small wildflowers on the ground. "Honeysuckles! They're sweet on the top. You can bite the end off them. See them little things? We used to eat them." He bent, and carefully picked a handful. "Mmmmm! I love 'em."

It was, in every sense, a community, mostly self-sufficient and largely in tune with its environment.

Even the local Indians, Mohawks and Algonquins, were part of it, although by the Switzers' time they existed mostly on the periphery. Ill-treated by government officials and land speculators, they had been, in fact, the province's first farmers, skilled in indigenous plant selection. Before their lands were stolen, they'd taught the white settlers how to grow corn (maize), squash, and kidney beans.

But the fatal combination of racism and greed that accompanied European settlement saw most native people pushed off the best land, first by clear-cutting loggers and then by the swarm of impoverished, mostly Irish refugees who followed the lumber barons. Both Irish and natives were victims of those who wielded power in the new society, but at the time they failed to appreciate their economic kinship.

"We didn't see them [regularly] like we see them now," said Bruce Switzer. "In the spring they'd come around selling fish. You could buy a fish from them for a buck, a great big pickerel. They were allowed to spear fish. They'd come through in an old car and sell you fish a buck apiece. Great big pickerel like this."

"They was good people," added Bud Switzer.

My own friend Harold Perry, 76 (see chapters 6 and 7), an Algonquin who grew up in the same era as the Switzers, recalls how his family trapped, smoked hides and fish, and hunted to survive. "I would take a single-shot .22 rifle to school and shoot partridge on the way to school and [more often] the way back. There were a lot of partridge then, and we lived right from hand to mouth. If we didn't get any fish or partridge we didn't eat. That was the way it was. But we were good at it. We ate."

"Our lifestyle was altogether different [from the present]," Bruce Switzer continued. "Everything didn't have to be done today. They cleared off an acre this year, or two acres, clearing trees and rocks. They could afford the time. And over thirty or forty years, can you imagine that many stones? At one time they moved a crusher in and crushed all that rock. They put them through a crusher and sold it to the county [for maintaining gravel roads]." Everything was done with horses, simple (though often ingenious) machinery, and the muscles of men.

Nothing was wasted. Everything was used. Everything fit. There was time for everything, even childhood squabbles.

Bruce paused on the laneway, looking toward the site of his old house. "If you got all this brush cut, I think if you look you'll find a jackknife. I got mad at my brother Arthur, and he'd got a jackknife, see, for fishing. And I took it and I reached up and hid it up on a beam. And he could never find it after. He looked and looked."

Getting Rid of Them

And then, in the space of a few years, the world that the Switzers and Browns, the Yorks, Busbys, Davises, Birds, Fosters, and Tyners, the Algonquins and Mohawks knew began to disappear. The process had, of course, started earlier, when some of the families that had settled on the most marginal land (like the rocky terrain around the Switzer farm) realized it wasn't the best and moved away. But it really started to gain momentum around the end of the first quarter of the century. It took roughly two decades for the bulk of the rural society the Switzers were a part of to be destroyed, although bits and pieces still cling here and there today.

A number of things killed it.

Competition from big business in the U.S., which became concentrated in fewer and fewer hands as corporations consolidated and began to establish continent-wide supply chains, played a large part.

The canning plants in Belleville, which had provided a market for local vegetable growers, as well as part-time, off-farm work, were among the first to go. "People worked at the canneries every summer," said Morton. "Then Del Monte from California bought them up, just to get rid of them." The pea vinery would have died as a result.

As the corporate structure grew and gained in market power, farm-gate prices—what farmers were actually paid for their crops—plunged. The infamous "cost-price squeeze" began. While farm-gate prices—what the large, corporate food-processing companies and supermarket chains paid their suppliers—fell, or stayed stagnant, the cost of every farm "input" (tractors and equipment, seed, fuel, fertilizer, interest on bank loans) rose steadily, until more and more farmers found they were earning less on their crops and livestock than it cost to grow them. The corporate structure profited at both ends, selling inputs high and buying farm produce low.

Government tax policies, and subsidies that favored large farm operations over smaller ones—alluded to briefly in chapter 1— added to the pressure on small growers. The government rules and predatory corporate price structures were worst in the U.S., but also struck Canada.

"I think the milk was the biggest change," said Claude Brown. "Every farm had sent a couple of 30-gallon cans of milk to the cheese factory. When we (Claude and his wife Audrey) first got married, we bought 195 acres over here

at Pine Grove. But I couldn't make a living. We started out
with Durhams. We had ten or eleven cows. But you couldn't
make a living with ten cows anymore. Now, I don't think
there's a cow that's milked between here and Roslin. I know
there isn't any between here and Marlbank. You couldn't
buy a quart of [fresh] milk between here and I don't know
where."

To survive, Brown took a job driving transport for the
Strathcona paper company, and worked as a trucker for the
rest of his career, until retirement. Ironically, Strathcona
made cardboard boxes, which were used by the big processors to ship their goods.

Meanwhile, the supermarket chains had also entered the
scene, and slowly began to strangle the traditional network
of country stores (where clerks would gather merchandise
for the customer, and usually provide a helping of free local
gossip while doing so) and farmers' markets, where local
growers could sell their food directly, without a middleman.

"I remember when the A&P store was down on Main
Street in Napanee years ago," said Bruce Switzer. "A&P
store was about the first one. Loblaws, and then they
branched out."

According to *Webster's Dictionary*, a supermarket is: "A
large, self-service retail store that sells food and other house-
hold goods." The online *Wikipedia* entry on the subject is
worth quoting at some length:

> The typical supermarket occupies a large floor space
> on a single level and is situated in a residential area in
> order to be convenient to customers. Its basic appeal
> is the availability of a broad selection of goods under a

single roof at low prices. Other advantages include ease of parking and, frequently, the convenience of shopping hours that extend far into the evening...Supermarkets are often parts of a chain that owns or controls (sometimes by franchise) other supermarkets in the same or other towns; this increases the opportunities for economies of scale.

Supermarkets usually offer products at low prices by reducing margins. Certain products (typically staples such as bread, milk and sugar) are often sold as loss leaders, that is, with negative margins. To maintain a profit, supermarkets attempt to make up for the low margins with a high overall volume of sales, and with sales of higher-margin items...Many supermarket chains are trying to reduce labor costs further by shifting to self-service check-out machines, where a group of four or five machines is supervised by a single assistant.[1]

The entry adds that such chains expanded "as the North American economy sank further into the Great Depression and consumers became price-sensitive to a degree never seen before." Increasingly, the large chain stores no longer sourced their merchandise from local suppliers, but from a few centralized, large producers, which formed part of their national networks. As the years went on, those large producers became ever larger, and ever fewer.

The effect in Hastings County was dramatic. According to the Census of Agriculture, the area's 1931 population of 4,840 farmers dropped to 2,603 by 1961, and stood at a mere 1,190 by 2001—a drop of more than 75 percent. In neighboring Lennox and Addington County, the story was similar. In 1901, the number of acres under cultivation there was

336,277. By 1981 the total had dropped by 62.5 percent, to 126,424.[2] It's even lower today.

Claude Brown frowned when he was asked how many full-time farmers were in the immediate area, of perhaps thirty surveyed lots, when he was young. "You could count every single place, all up and down the road here, they raised a family."

Now there are only three, and one of them has an off-farm job. He has no milk cows, only beef cattle. Across from me, a pair of sisters, retired schoolteachers, have bought up a few acres, completely renovated a house, and turned the surrounding land into a sort of suburban perfection, with a laid-down-sod lawn so carefully manicured that it could be used for a putting green. When I met them for the first time, they noted that they wanted no vegetable garden, only flower beds. Only this year did they relent, and plant something nourishing.

For all the corporate economists' vaunted claims about the benefits of such "efficiency," overall farm production hasn't increased much in the area. "There's probably just as many cows being milked between here and Napanee [today] as there was seventy-five years ago," said Brown. "They're just all on two or three farms"—down near Hay Bay, where there is good bottom land. Hundreds, even thousands of families put out of business, not to increase production, but to constantly lower the price corporations have to pay their suppliers—and thus increase corporate profits.

For a number of years, there was no longer a farmers' market in Napanee. Recently, there have been attempts to revive past glories. So far, however, the results have been spotty at best—a couple of tables under an awning next to the Giant Tiger discount store parking lot. A couple more downtown, near Gibbard's furniture factory, which recently went up for sale.

Market Square stands empty, as do an increasing number of what once were well-kept farm fields. "It's all going back to bush," lamented my neighbor Doug York, whose family has farmed in the area for more than 150 years. "It's a shame, when you think how hard they worked to clear it and farm it, to see it all going."

Walking with the Switzer brothers across our land, I was struck by the difference between Bruce's memories and what was there now. Formerly lush pastures were now overgrown with prickly ash and red cedar; partridge and deer love *white* cedar, which offers shelter from the wind and good browse, but red cedar does them no good. The thorny prickly ash is of no use to wildlife, except perhaps the odd rabbit that may find refuge from a red fox in its briarpatch.

True, larger wildlife like moose, and predators like wolves and cougars, had suffered from the original European settlement, and the wild turkey—too delicious for those hungry settlers to resist—was actually wiped out. But white-tailed deer prospered amongst those Irish immigrants' cornfields, along with abundant small game. It's an ill wind that blows no good. Compared to the wastelands that are today's factory farms, and the lethal landscapes created by mining, it was an environmentally friendly world.

The result of all the economic "efficiency" that destroyed it was good for neither man nor beast, an ill wind that blew no one—except a few already-rich corporate executives— any good.

And what, exactly, has succeeded the world of Claude Brown and the Switzers?

Great Expectations

Pasarian: "Bill's point is, if we control the food people
eat it's tantamount to making slaves of them."

Paul Buher: "Ah-ah. Customers!"

DIALOGUE FROM *Damien: Omen II*

CALL HER BETSY. IT'S not her real name, but she is afraid
that if she mentions her name, and one of her former
neighbors reads it, it could reignite the bitter divisions and
rancor that ensued when her family's mixed farm in rural
Ontario was faced with the appearance next door of what
Canadians call an intensive livestock operation (ILO), and
Americans call a confined animal feeding operation (CAFO).

That is to say, an industrial, or factory, livestock farm.

"We're really reluctant to talk about it, because we've
sold the property [her own farm] and we've moved on," said
Betsy. "We're trying to put it behind us, because it was huge
and cost us a lot. It was a very difficult time, and we've paid
in a lot of ways, not just financially.

"It ruins communities."

Using the word "farm" to describe what started to bloom and grow up next door to Betsy is actually misleading. ILOS/CAFOS are no more farms, in the traditional sense, than Walmart is Mom and Pop's corner store. It's more accurate to refer to these enterprises as manufacturing plants, like foundries, or stamping plants, except that their raw materials are, technically at least, alive.

In the United States, and on the Canadian prairies, their sheer size can be staggering. U.S. operations may contain as many as 50,000 hogs on a single "farm," or 20,000 to 30,000 beef cattle in a feedlot. Poultry farm numbers are even more surreal, in some cases climbing to hundreds of thousands of birds per manufacturing plant, with each of several buildings on the property routinely housing 20,000 or more birds each.

Sludge and Stench

"I was raised on a mixed farm," Betsy said. "We [her parents] had pigs and cattle. My husband's farm had dairy. We also had a horse barn, and the dairy farm was across the road. They [her parents] were milking about eighty cattle there."

Then her neighbor, whose line fence was barely 1,000 feet from her house, decided to start an ILO. Within only a few months, the lives of Betsy's family, and their livestock, would become unbearable, filled with sludge and stench.

"It was referred to as a 1,000-head barn, but not of course 1,000 head in it. It was at least 1,200 or more in it. It was a finishing operation [where hogs are fattened prior to slaughter]. He put up one barn, which no one fought because everyone was farmers. They felt that was the Right to Farm.[1]

"The second barn went up very shortly and we had huge concerns. We were directly [on the weather side] of the wind, at about 1,000 feet, and he had liquid manure under the barns."

It is fairly standard for the storage tanks under a barn with 1,200 to 1,600 hogs to hold a million or more gallons of liquid manure, for a minimum of 240 days, after which it must be disposed of by spreading it on or injecting it into farm fields as fertilizer. One large eastern Ontario hog plant has an outdoor storage lagoon with 4.5 million gallons of manure. The barns usually have slatted concrete floors, through which the pigs' dung falls into the tanks below. As this sludge liquefies and decomposes, it can give off as many as three hundred different kinds of toxic or malodorous gases, from hydrogen sulfide (H_2S) and ammonia (NH_3), to a whole range of often carcinogenic amines: trimethylamine, monomethylamine, isopropylamine, ethylamine, n-butylamine, amylamine, dimethylamine, diethylamine, and so on. The mix may also include carbon dioxide, methane, aldehydes, ketones, amines, amides, mercaptans, thioacids, and disulphides.[2] These gases rise back up into the barn and have to be carried away by ventilator fans so the pigs won't have to breathe them.

"The air in the barn is replaced every so many minutes to keep the gases away from the hogs," said Betsy. "If those fans go out, you're talking maybe twenty minutes before the hogs are dying from the fumes. They have to pump the air outside because it just rises from those pits."

In fact, the gases are so toxic that they have been lethal to hog farm workers. Two farmhands died in California in 2003, choked to death by hydrogen sulfide fumes.[3]

"Ultimately, even if you keep your windows closed, the air outside becomes the air inside. There's no getting away from it," Betsy recalled.

The stench was stifling, on an order of magnitude far beyond what a born-and-raised farm wife was used to inhaling from the manure of a mere eighty dairy cattle. And it was carried not only via the barn ventilation systems, but from the eventual spreading of the liquid manure on the surface of the fields around the barns, where it was used for fertilizer.

"We had a [second] farm that grew up to have a mill, a feed plant on the other side of us that got to be huge. Because the hog farmer didn't have enough acreage [to legally spread] his manure, the mill used it on their [land], so this liquid manure would be spread all around us. We could no longer have the clothesline. We didn't enjoy the outdoors very much. And if the smell got in the house, it stayed there, contained in the house."

The effects of such gases on human health are potentially myriad, ranging from the directly physical toxicity of sulfur dioxide, the dangers of the various carcinogens, and the triggering of allergies or asthma, to the more indirect effects of the unpleasant odors, including their psychological effects. Writes biologist Bill Paton of Manitoba's University of Brandon:

> Unpleasant odors can... trigger possibly harmful reflexes, modifying olfactory function and other physiological reactions. Annoyance and depression can result from exposure to odors along with nausea, vomiting, headache, shallow breathing, coughing, sleep disturbances, and loss of appetite...
>
> A more recent study reports more tension, depression and anger, reduced vigor, and more confusion among the exposed group.[4]

An Ontario Ministry of Agriculture, Food and Rural Affairs (OMAFRA) factsheet on worker health goes further, noting that:

> Many people cannot stay in a pig barn for very long without the onset of serious coughing and chest tightness after the visit. Often, we think that it will not happen to us and that the people who have reactions are not "tough enough."
>
> However, this is not funny at all for the farmers who have to sell their farm or stay away from the barn because they developed respiratory problems such as chronic bronchitis or occupational asthma or even worse, farmers lung disease.[5]

According to the fact sheet, "10 to 30 percent of all patients diagnosed as having farmers lung disease will die within five to six years from the time of diagnosis."[6] Those who don't die will nevertheless sustain permanent lung damage.

Rather than subject his pigs and farmhands to this, Betsy's neighbor sent it over to her.

Nor were odors her only problem. Water quality can also be damaged, by the spreading or injection of too much manure over a given area, or by contamination from leaking underground concrete manure tanks or above-ground storage lagoons. "They say there's only two types of concrete wall, one that's cracked and one that's going to crack," said Betsy. "Coliform [bacteria] was really the issue that we would have. We tested [the well] and we had counts of 220 [bacteria colonies]."

In most jurisdictions in the U.S. and Canada, drinking water must have zero coliform colonies per 100 mL to be considered safe. (A fecal coliform count of 200/100 mL is the maximum allowable level in water for swimming.) Betsy's well had 220 times the acceptable amount.

Fecal coliform bacteria come from only one source: shit. What can happen if one regularly drinks water with such a high level of contamination? The coliform colonies themselves are only indicators of other things that may be in the water with them, but those other things can include pathogens that cause cholera, typhoid, hepatitis, meningitis, skin rashes, eye and ear infections, and nausea, as well as deadly E. coli infections.

"We had no proof where the coliforms came from," said Betsy. "But before the hog farm, our well was normal."

Besides their own personal discomfort, Betsy's family had another indicator of trouble.

"Because the cattle were at the home farm [upwind and uphill from the ILO], it wasn't bad. But our horses had issues. In horses, it always manifests itself in the feet. They would react in what would be seen as a founder. They would be lame and stiff."

Founder, or laminitis, whose cause is uncertain, is an inflammation of the sensitive part of the interior of the hoof. The disease, which usually affects the two front feet most seriously, is accompanied by intense pain. It can cause severe lameness and permanent damage to the foot. Notes Jack Coggins, in *The Horseman's Bible:* "Horses afflicted with founder may be partially cured but will seldom be fit for anything but the lightest work." [7]

"We had four horses, and every one of them ended up with the same symptoms," said Betsy. "The smallest ones, my Shetlands, it's become chronic. And even though we've moved and we see improvement, it's very, very slow and I'm not sure we'll ever bring them around. The first week we were here at our new property, it was like they were new animals. They dropped backward on me again, but my farrier had come that same week we moved and could not believe they were the same animals. It was that drastic [a change] in just that short time."

Eventually, Betsy and her husband had to react to all of this.

"When the first barn went up, you just looked at it as the right to farm," she said. "The second you question, and the third you start to scream. You know, come on, on 100 acres [the size of her neighbor's original land base]!"

The couple made a complaint to the provincial Normal Farm Practices Protection Board, charging that their neighbor's practices were not normal and should not be protected.

"It was the first time that they'd had farmers against farmers," she said. "And that's really sad." Despite a mass of evidence, the board ruled against the couple. Although they could prove damage, they couldn't prove definitively that the damage was caused by any single, specific, or direct emission from the pig farm. Betsy remains convinced that the decision was essentially political.

"What we believe now is that there's no way we would have been allowed to win, because he would have had to remove one of the barns. And there were many communities in Ontario watching, and had these barns had to come down probably there would have been many others. And of course, cleaning these up, the government couldn't afford what it would cost. They could be sued because they [the farms] were granted building permits without proper information. We knew that at the point of two hog barns on his [their neighbor's] property, his debt load was $1.3 million.

"The farmer won the hearing, but he then filled in the excavation for his third barn and never built his third barn. Which says to us, this really smells, literally. Somehow things were taken care of [for him], but [we believe] he was also told, 'Don't you dare push the envelope here.'"

Needless to say, by the time a decision was rendered, the hog farmer was no longer on speaking terms with Betsy and her husband, nor were many others. A rift had been driven through the entire community, between those who had supported the hog factory and those who hadn't. And that rift remains.

As chapter 4 will show, however, Betsy's community got off fairly lightly. Elsewhere, the advent of the factory farm has sparked far worse trouble, from lawsuits to arson, assault, and even shootings. But that's getting ahead of the story. Some background is in order.

THE FACTORY FARM had its genesis in the cost-price squeeze, which at first forced smaller farmers to sell out to bigger neighbors, and then forced those bigger neighbors to become ever-bigger, in order to maintain a diminishing profit margin by effecting what economists like to call "economies of scale." Rather than having one hundred farms and one hundred farmers producing ten or twenty hogs or cows each, one farm and one farmer—using more and more expensive machinery and adopting mass-production tactics more suitable to the Ford Rouge plant in Detroit than to the rural environment—would attempt to produce 1,000 or 2,000, or eventually 50,000 animals. Only thus could the one remaining farmer in a country municipality afford to stay in business, given the steadily lowering farm-gate price offered by the corporate-dominated market for his output.

In the U.S., the biggest of these farms were eventually either bought outright by their corporate customers, or locked into contracts with them that allowed the producer little autonomy. Many—in the U.S., most—of them are now owned by a handful of companies, like Smithfield, which as long ago as 1983 already owned or controlled 1,600 pork supplier factories in the state of North Carolina alone, each branch factory housing thousands of animals.[8] By 2002, the top five pork packers in the U.S.—Smithfield, Tyson, ConAgra (Swift), Cargill (Excel), and Farmland—"accounted for at least 75 percent of all processing," as well as for the lion's share of on-farm—or rather in-plant—pork production.[9] They were also the top five in beef and had by then made significant inroads north of the border. By 2005, Cargill and Tyson were the two largest meat packers in Canada. (Among the largest Canadian-owned packers was the McCain family–dominated Maple Leaf Foods, which controls both the Schneiders and Dempster's brands.) The continent's major corporate players were close to achieving what conservative economists see as the perfect result: dominant market control at both the input and output ends, and thus control of both prices and profits.

Their empires, which continue to grow, were the product of nearly unbridled corporate power, the desperation of individual farm families to stay in business, the ignorance or indifference of government bureaucrats, and the increasing domination of markets and the terms of trade by rules set by the World Trade Organization (wTo).

In Canada, the existence of agricultural marketing boards, which function as de facto farmers' unions able to negotiate farm-gate prices, put a moderating brake on the process, so that the wholesale destruction of the American family farm was only partially accomplished north of the border. But not for long. (Much more on the boards' part in the story is in chapter 5.)

Life in the Barns I: Hogs

The yearly and daily routines at an ILO are much like those at any manufacturing plant, with the exception that, unlike the production line in, say, an auto plant, where the parts are of steel or plastic, its components are living creatures. A great deal of their lives, though not necessarily all, involves suffering, sometimes intense suffering, while their overall experience as manufacturing components is profoundly unnatural. If the operators of the factory become careless, or get too greedy and start to cut corners (as an ex–hog farm worker will describe a few pages later), those lives can become horrible.

Hog plants are fairly typical of most large animal manufacturing. They range from massively comprehensive "farrow-to-finish" (birth to slaughter) operations, to somewhat smaller specialty plants that focus on only one or two stages of production, such as *farrowing* (where sows give birth to piglets), *gilt* selection (where unbred sows or gilts are prepared for breeding), *weaner* production (where piglets are weaned, usually around five weeks, then sold to other plants to finish), and *finishing* operations (where males not wanted for breeding, and females not selected as gilts, are fattened for slaughter). The specialty plants perform functions similar to what a parts supplier would in other kinds of manufacturing—say a manufacturer of ball bearings who supplied the Ford Rouge plant's wheel assembly line.

Animal population numbers are sometimes hard to state, since they change throughout the production year. In the U.S. a major farrow-to-finish operation may have 50,000 to 100,000—or even more—pigs on the property on a given date. Canadian plants tend to be slightly smaller. For example, Hay Bay Genetics Inc., near Napanee, Ontario, normally houses around 2,700 breeding sows, which produce 59,000 to 61,000 piglets annually. Half to two thirds of the piglets are sold as weaners at 55 pounds, and the rest, usually between 18 and 20 percent, are raised to market weight of 250 pounds, then either kept for breeding stock or sent to slaughter. Thus the plant could have as many as 14,700 pigs (2,700 sows and 12,000 finishers) on the premises at one time.

A typical specialty hog-finishing operation might house 1,200 to 1,600 animals per barn, and include two to four barns, for a total of 4,800 to 6,400 animals. A farrowing barn might hold a similar number, from 1,200 to 1,500 sows. Some house up to 2,500. Individual barns range from 32 by 40 feet to 60 by 100 feet.

The pigs in many of these barns are kept in pens or crates of varying sizes, divided off by steel-tube frames that can be disassembled and reassembled in varying dimensions for varying uses. For example, in Ontario, the provincial government recommends that "a 1.5 by 4.8 meter pen (five by 16 feet) will accommodate 20 feeder pigs up to a weight of 45 kilograms (100 pounds)." [10] As a "rule of thumb," one square foot is recommended for "every 25 pounds of pig." [11] Gestation stalls, where pregnant sows spend between 116 and 120 days before giving birth, are usually two by seven feet, sometimes slightly more. Sows in these stalls, which will be banned as inhumane in Europe by the year 2013, are unable to walk or turn around for the entire period of their confinement.

To form an idea of what these spaces are like, imagine twenty grade school–aged human children confined day and night, for weeks on end, to a 5-by-16-foot space. Or a pregnant woman confined for nine months in a space so small she could not turn around in it. Pigs, of course, are not humans, but they are amongst the most intelligent of mammals, on a par with dogs.

"As a farmer, I cannot tolerate the gestation stalls," said factory farm critic Fred Tait, of the National Farmers Union (NFU). "A hog is a fairly intelligent animal, and if you watch their behavior they do this repetitive chewing of the bars of that crate. There are different theories for it, because of course the hogs can't talk. One is it's the frustration from being confined. The other is it's a diversion from the pain in their legs, from standing in that cramped quarter all the time. You couldn't put any other animal, like a dog, in that sort of confinement or you'd be fined for cruelty."

The floors of most barns are made of pre-cast concrete with slatted holes in them to let the pigs' manure and urine fall or drain into the liquid manure tanks below. The hogs never walk on grass, or even dirt. Lighting in the barns is artificial (fluorescent). The pigs never see the sun.

They cannot root in the soil for tubers or insects, or graze on fresh greens as they would in nature, or on the family farm of fifty years ago.

"We have a dry sow ration, we have a nursing sow ration, and we have eight stages in the weaner barn," says hog producer Eric Davis of Hay Bay Genetics. "It's based on corn. It's got corn and wheat, corn and barley, whatever the economics are at the time, whatever is available." Fellow hog producer Mark Slack, in nearby Tweed Municipality, feeds his 1,600 finishing animals a ration "geared towards maximum weight. In a finishing operation there's about five phases of feed, sometimes six. The base composition will be a corn/soybean base, or corn/soybean/wheat."

Unlike many producers, Slack says he does not give his hogs artificial growth promoters, or non-therapeutic antibiotics. But many larger North American producers routinely lace their feed with both. In the European Union, in contrast, use of non-therapeutic antibiotics in animal feed has been banned outright.

A WOMAN WHO spent ten years as a hog farm worker, specializing in farrowing and gilt selection, described for me a much less fastidious Ontario operation:

"Ours was a 2,500-sow unit, where we bred, gestation, and we had a farrowing unit. We had open gestation [not using gestation crates]. A sow unit ain't that bad, compared to, like, a fattening barn. There was twenty-four, actually twenty-five pens where sixty-five pigs [in each pen] could eat. It was on computer chips. That's how they ate, they computer chip controlled all the eating... It was all concrete slat floors [in the pens]... Everything's lit. There's lots of [fluorescent] light, but there's no windows...

"They seem happy when they're in an open pen and can run around and socialize. But they have their pecking order. They do have a queen bee. They try to find the queen bee within a couple of days. There's a lot of fighting within a couple of days, and then they're fine once they find the one that's the boss of the whole, like, herd…You always kept the gilts [sows that had never been bred] together in a separate gestation pen, because there'd be too much fighting, because of the weight of the pigs, if we let them in with the other sows."

Although fighting to establish a pecking order is natural in hogs, it can carry a price tag if the animals fight on slatted concrete floors, rather than on the straw or pasture of traditional farms.

"We had a lot of bad feet," the ex–hog farm worker continued. "Like, infection of dew claws that were ripped off. It was hard, because they would get caught in those slats. You know, like the dew claws on the back of the feet? Sometimes they would rip off and they could get infections. Sometimes, if they were fighting, they would, their hip would dislocate and stuff like that. You'd see that."

If an injured sow did not respond quickly to medication, it would be culled. So would any animal that escaped from the barn, even for five minutes, because of the chance that it could pass on infections picked up outdoors if returned to the herd. Factory-bred hogs, unlike their more hardy, traditionally raised counterparts, have developed little resistance to common diseases, and any infection will spread like wildfire in the cramped conditions of industrial barns.

So hyper-fearful of infection are producers that most operations will allow no visitors into the barns. Employees who must enter are required to strip, shower, then put on a special set of in-barn-only clothes before entering. When they leave, the clothes are left behind. "They had a washer that they had inside to wash them," explained the ex-worker.

How were sows culled? "They'd shoot them. It was like a long, steel thing and shot, like, blank bullets in the head with a steel rod, and that would kill them. It was always above the eyes, in the middle. You'd have to hit a certain spot in the brain, or you'd have to do it a couple times." Experienced workers were deft, however, and rarely missed the first time. Most hogs died instantly, and thus relatively painlessly.

"I was the head farrowing tech. I delivered babies," the ex-worker continued, adding that the original plant owner, Premium Pork (now bankrupt and out of business), provided roughly six months of employee training, including training in swine medicine. "I did all these courses. I was taught by a vet from [a nearby city]. He showed me exactly how to C-section. I was the only one that was ever taught how to do a proper procedure."

On many of the largest hog farms, to save time, sows are routinely given Cesarean sections, rather than waiting for them to give birth naturally. At this worker's plant, however, C-sections were seen as a last resort, because once the procedure was done, the sow had to be culled.

A C-section would be done only when there was something really wrong.

"If the cervix was blocked totally and you can't reach the babies [to pull them out by hand], then I would give a C-section. If the mother was panting, and you knew that there was something wrong. You'd have to shoot it before. You'd shoot it and you'd have three minutes to get the babies out. Because, you know, if they're not delivering and you can save eighteen to twenty-three babies that's worth forty dollars apiece, you'd want to save those eighteen babies, you know what I mean?"

Normally, she said, sows would give birth fairly easily, perhaps with a bit of "internal," or helping the animal by putting on surgical gloves and pulling some of the piglets out. Within five days of giving birth, a healthy sow would be bred again. They recover "very fast." An average sow would be bred eight times, before being culled. Thus the average sow's lifespan would be about two years.

The ex-worker regards the operation as it was during her first few years, under Premium Pork, as "good" overall, but once Premium went out of business and another owner took over the plant, things went downhill fast.

"He [the new owner] was a very cheap man and he didn't want that many people. In the barn, you're supposed to operate with eleven and a half people, and he only wanted eight people. And the care wouldn't be as good as if you had eleven people. And now I hear, because I have a friend that does work there now, he says they're down to six people, from eleven...because if you have more than six [the government requires that] you have to have a health and safety person on staff.

"So you know how much care those animals are getting."

That care included "daily routines, that you'd have to feed them and in the sow units, like the breaking units, you'd have to feed them and scrape behind them. And farrowing you'd have to feed them and look after the babies and you'd have to clip their teeth and their tails and stuff like that, and keep surveillance on them to make sure they weren't injured."

Probably the most important job, however, was farrowing (birthing).

"I was there all the time, like, you know, midwifing. I would even come in after hours if I heard, if there was a problem with the sows. I would make a special trip there just to help the mother out, like to deliver babies. And you know, if you don't have that many people to keep an eye on the animals..."

Upset with the new owner's practices, this worker—the plant's only veterinary-trained farrowing technician—eventually quit. "With Premium they always gave raises. But when [the new owner] came over he was a kind of a cheap man. He wanted you more. Holidays, you had a week and that was it. And you had to be there on shift days. It was hard to get time off at Christmas. You had to work holidays...After [the new owner] took over, there was no training at all."

According to a former co-worker of hers, contacted subsequently, no staff were actually fired. "It's just that they quit, right? So he didn't rehire people, so they would cut the number under [six]."

"Why would he care about having a health and safety officer (HSO)?" I asked.

"He's run into a lot of problems there. A lot of the workers were complaining about sprays [some animal medications are administered by spraying]. They didn't know what they were." The drugs being administered, via sprays, injection, or inclusion in feed, might include antibiotics such as Liquamycin, or steroids such as Predef, a potent corticosteroid.

If the owner had an HSO, there may have been questions, and "he would probably have had to pay someone a little extra money to do it [work as an HSO]."

When the ex-worker left, the only other farrowing person on staff had less training than she'd had, and "he don't believe in internals at all. Internals means to go in and make sure, pull out the babies. If you see the mother having trouble, we'd go in with an arm glove and check her and pull out the baby if there was trouble, pull it free. But he won't. He believes in Planate and Lutalyse. If they haven't gone within fifteen days [of the projected birth date] you'd Lutalyse 'em...We'd even use oxytocin. Once they started to give birth, you'd give a shot of oxytocin and they'd push all the babies out."

Planate and Lutalyse are prostaglandins used to stimulate birth. The *Oxford Minidictionary of Chemistry* defines prostaglandin as "any of a group of organic compounds derived from essential fatty acids...They act at *very low* [italics mine] concentrations to cause the contraction of smooth muscle; natural and synthetic prostaglandins are used to induce abortion or labor in humans and domestic animals."[12] According to the *Oxford Minidictionary of Biology,* oxytocin is: "A hormone, secreted by the posterior pituitary gland in mammals, that stimulates the ejection of milk in lactating females and the contraction of the uterus during parturition."[13]

According to the ex–hog worker, they were administered "by direct syringe, like a needle through the neck." Frequently, a sow so treated, because it had shown itself prone to difficulty in birthing, would be sent to slaughter afterward.

Could these birth-inducing drugs, potent even at low doses, remain in the meat after slaughter, and thus pose a danger to pregnant women who eat it? Could they find their way into barn waste and manure, and eventually into the water table? What about the antibiotics and steroids?

"Those are good questions," said veterinarian Dr. Shiv Chopra, formerly with the Canadian federal watchdog agency Health Canada. "On the Liquamycin, because it's an antibiotic, the idea is not residue [in the meat itself], because the government defines a maximum residue limit. They can determine if it's present. The problem is that [if used too frequently, or at low doses] they produce antibiotic-resistant pathogens. And all these hormones and antibiotics are also coming out as excreta and getting into the water supply. And you will find them in flowing rivers.

"Any drug that Health Canada approves must be assigned a maximum residue limit, or MRL, and that must be published in the *Canada Gazette,* under Part Two, Table Three. If you go there *you will not find a single hormone listed* [author's emphasis]. There is no safe dose. You cannot determine a safe level. There is no test. So [by using hormones in food production] they are breaking the law. The Europeans have banned non-therapeutic use of antibiotics. They are banning, as of 2009, all non-therapeutic use of hormones. They are not willing to tolerate any hormones whatsoever, in any amount, in the food industry."

The ex–hog worker recalled other things being put into the pigs.

"We used to [under Premium Pork] get our feeds from Masterfeeds. But [the new owner] made his own feeds. He bought a mill and all that stuff. And I found that Masterfeeds was way better. They used to put antibiotics in the feed. There was a lot of disease. The only thing we had [under Premium] was some mild cases."

Then the new owner took over.

"He'd even put, like, fat and stuff in there, in the feed. He wouldn't tell us exactly. He was experimenting all the time, and it was not good." With the new owner's feed recipes came outbreaks of coccidiosis [a form of scours, or diarrhea], Porcine Reproductive and Respiratory Syndrome [a viral infection], and ileitis [chronic inflammation of the intestines].

"When we had coccidiosis, you could smell it a mile away, the scours would smell bad on the piglets. And then they had ileitis. That's a bad one. They start having blood in their stool and it kills them."

Would the owner not have been better off to stick to Masterfeeds?

"It cost too much money. I think there's a lot of neglect (now) towards the babies getting born and stuff like that. This is the cost of cutting it back, having less people and having less experienced people. He's a very cheap man. If he could get away with just immigrants from another country that you could pay six or seven dollars, he'd get away with it. Let's just put it that way."

Asked why he doesn't, she replied, with unconscious irony:

"Because they don't last, for some reason."

As an anti-ILO Canadian NFU activist noted, this is exactly what has happened on some American and Western Canadian hog farms, as well as in the meat-packing plants that buy their products. Speaking of a nearby packing plant, and one of the farms that supply it, she said:

"Now they [the packing plant] are bringing in people. They tried Maritimers, they tried people from the Ukraine. They tried Mexicans there too. But now it's people from El Salvador, China, and African countries coming to work and settle. They're going on the second shift now, so they need all these extra workers. I don't know what they're going to do for housing all of them. They have been known to stack trailers on top of one another, like a sort of rabbit hutch design. We have Mexicans coming here. They put a ten-year-old child in the pig barn [that supplies the packing plant] to be a laborer, and not attending school. The ten-year-old was the oldest [of eight children] and he went into the pig barn to work."

Her husband echoes her description: "In the packing industry, because of its downscaling of wages, currently the labor is from El Salvador. The Mexicans wouldn't stay, largely. They just went back...The sad part of this is, these people are coming here to work in that plant for two years and they'll get Canadian citizenship. So we have a labor contract that says if you can endure this underpaid, brutal job for two years we'll give you Canadian citizenship as a reward. I never thought this country would come to that.

"We're seeing people come out of there with carpal tunnel syndrome. I know a young fellow that's worked there [in a meat packing plant]. He'll have his two years in in December, and now he's getting to a point where he's starting to lose the use of his hands, and he's got numbness in his wrists. He's working in a hog plant. This is the way these people come out. We're going to be graduating people out of there as disabled Canadian citizens. They're standing on a line and they're making these specific cuts on a hog carcass all shift, repeat, repeat, repeat, deboning or cutting up the carcass. It's bad. It's very bad."

ANOTHER EFFECT OF the industrial hog industry is a general loss of breed variety. Of the world's estimated population of some 825 million domestic pigs,[14] including hundreds of individual breeds, the vast majority of hog-producing plants use only one or two. Most industrially produced hogs are so-called "common white pigs," usually crossbred from the Yorkshire and Landrace breeds. A very few use Durochs.

Absent from the corporate breeding plans are Cornish pigs, Tamworths, Berkshires, Gloucestershire Old Spots, British Lops, Large Blacks, Choctaw, American Mulefoot, Guinea, Vietnamese Potbelly, and hundreds more swine breeds, each one presenting unique characteristics that make them adapted to producing meat with a wide choice of gourmet flavors, as well as genetic traits that make them especially adaptable to a myriad soil, plant, and climate regions.

If the corporate industrial model gains total dominance of the industry, many, perhaps most, of these breeds will vanish forever.

The water and air pollution effects of large-animal ILOs are not limited to their next-door neighbors, such as Betsy, but often spread far beyond the immediate vicinity. Hay Bay Genetics, mentioned earlier, has been described as having "a relatively good reputation"[15] in the industry. Nevertheless, the company, its then-president Ron Davis, and farm manager Mark Davis were convicted in Ontario Provincial Court in February 2002 on three counts of violating pollution prevention sections of the Fisheries Act by discharging a deleterious substance into nearby Hay Bay, which links to the larger Bay of Quinte. The court also ruled that Hay Bay and its officers had failed to comply with a directive issued by Environment Canada to reverse or lessen the harmful effects of storm sewer runoff from their property.

The company was fined $35,000, while incurring an estimated $200,000 in costs. The company subsequently appealed the judgement. The appeal court reversed the conviction of Ron Davis. It upheld that of Mark Davis, but changed his sentence from a $5,000 fine to an absolute discharge. The fine for Hay Bay Genetics, a multi-million-dollar business, was reduced from $5,000 to $500. The money due the local conservation authority was reduced from $30,000 to $19,500. All monies were paid.

The company's activities were also cited in a 1998 bid by the North Marysburgh Ratepayers Association, in Prince Edward County, for a property tax rollback. The group, made up of eighteen rural families, claimed the proximity of Hay Bay's 2,500-sow unit had caused a sharp drop in their property values.

Responding to the rash of citizen complaints, lawsuits, and protests, the corporate hog industry has begun looking for ways to hide or mask its odorous by-products. Industry publications, like *Manure Manager, Hog Country,* and *Manure Matters,* are full of articles and advertisements touting the planting of tree shelterbelts to intercept odor plumes before they get to neighbors' land, injecting liquid manure into the ground rather than spreading it on the surface, or adding various additives to the pigs' feed that can chemically bind or minimize compounds that cause odor.

Critics scoff that this cosmetic approach is like trying to put a Band-Aid on cancer.

Life in the Barns II: Poultry
Routines in factory chicken plants are fairly typical of how most smaller livestock, from turkeys to rabbits, are produced industrially. The numbers are, if anything, more startling than those for hog plants.

The barns of The Egg Basket/River Valley Poultry, a plant near Newburgh, Ontario, contain some 347,000 birds and the farm ships an entire 18-wheel transport load of eggs every day. Despite its size, it is only the third-largest egg producer in the province. It has several barns, some with 20,000 or more birds inside.

Not far away, near Napanee, Kaiser Lake Farms is a bit smaller. Run by Eric Kaiser and his son Max, the plant at the time Max was being interviewed had 33,800 day-old baby chicks in two pullet barns, and 25,300 laying hens in the layer barns.

Baby chicks are usually purchased day-old from specialized hatcheries, then raised to the age of nineteen weeks, until ready to begin laying eggs. A pullet is a female in its first year of laying. Due to the assembly-line requirements of an industrial operation, in which the birds are jammed together in crowded cages, the baby chicks must be debeaked before starting their manufacturing cycle. If the beaks are left on, the nervous, crowded birds would peck at each other, causing injuries and slowing egg output. The work is done in dim light, which calms the birds.

"These lights here, they use about one and a half lumens," explained Max Kaiser, during a tour of one of his pullet barns. "When we used to trim the beaks [ourselves] we would keep them fully dim like this because the chickens are calmer when you're working with them. Because we use incandescents, when you dim them they become a little bit darker in color, a little bit redder, and that's good to keep the chickens calm. Blue light makes them very active. Red light makes them calm. They see infrared light too, so even a white chicken, we look at a white chicken and we see it white. Chickens see a lot of intricate patterns on them, they have very intricate patterns on their feathers, but we can't see them with our eyes.

"We had a little light bulb on the rig itself, just a Christmas tree light, a white one so you could see what you were doing. They're in the cage. One fellah's in front of you and you pull the chicken out and you hand it to the guy sitting on the beak trimmer and he just *ka-chunk* and puts it back in the next cage. The guys who do it professionally and that's all they do, two guys with beak trimmers could be through this barn in about two and a half days, because that's all they do, all the time."

A working lifetime spent slicing the upper beaks off of thousands, millions of tiny baby chickens.

"But now they have a laser treatment at the hatchery. So they hit them a day old. It's much less invasive and we have lower mortality because of it. Because if you go in there and grab those chickens out and snip their beaks off [under the old method], they're going to back off their feed for a few days. It's also stress for them, and if they had any underlying medical problems, every time you handle them that stress could trigger whatever is in there. The birds we have now [Lohmanns] have a genetic tendency for a disease called Merrick's disease. So anytime you throw a stress at them like that, especially if you're trimming the beaks and causing them to back off feed, you get a spike in mortality for the next week, very big."

It's not surprising that the chicks "back off" eating for a week, or die. The Brambell Committee, a group of veterinarians and others appointed by the British Parliament to investigate problems in intensive farming, concluded: "There is no physiological basis for the assertion that the operation is similar to the clipping of human fingernails. Between the horn and bone of [the beak] is a thin layer of highly sensitive soft tissue, resembling the quick of the human nail. The hot knife blade used in de-beaking cuts through this complex horn, bone and sensitive tissue causing severe pain."[16] There is some evidence that debeaked birds experience something akin to the persistent "phantom limb" syndrome observed in human war amputees.

As for the weakness for Merrick's disease, it is tolerated by producers because the breed, second only to White Leghorns in popularity, has a higher laying capacity and better eggshell quality. "Actually, before we had that breed, prior to that, I had never seen Merrick's disease myself," added Max. "Dad had seen it back in his father's farm, back in the '50s and '60s, but I had never seen it here until we started getting [the Lohmanns]. So if trimming the beaks [at the hatchery with a laser] is all it takes, and we don't lose even half a percent now, fine. They're pretty high-performance animals so you've got to keep them in this bubble."

Just as on the large animal operations, the "bubble" includes the ubiquitous, factory farm focus on "biosecurity." Visitors aren't allowed into the barns, and employees must dip their shoes or boots in a pan filled with disinfectant before entering.

"We had avian influenza here a number of years ago," recalled Max. "We can't afford to give them the protection to stave off whatever a wild bird might drop on them. None of the guys who work for us has pet birds. None of us hunt waterfowl or any fowl. The wild turkey hunt's on right now but I'm not going to do it. It's not worth the risk."

In order to be allowed to generate the amount of manure produced by its livestock, a factory farm must have a minimum amount of acreage in crops, where the waste can be spread as fertilizer, or have contracts with other farmers whose land can be used for the purpose. The ratio of "spreadable" crop land to manure volume is regulated by the province's Nutrient Management Act, passed partly in response to a wave of complaints about water pollution by ILOs.

Kaiser has some 900 acres in crops, which he farms using the no-till (for no tillage, that is, no plowing) system. Since the no-till system does not include covering previous crops or weeds by turning them over with a plow and burying them, some other way must be found to get rid of weeds and make way for a new crop. Kaiser depends heavily on chemical spraying, for example when he wants to plant a new crop to follow alfalfa.

"Its [alfalfa's] root structure is deep. It's strong, and you just spray it up good, and it might take two applications. If you're going to go in, say, in the spring and plant corn, I would spray it in late October or mid-October. We spray it with Roundup. You might throw in some 2,4-D. If you put down a little bit of 2,4-D with the Roundup, you'll get a better kill on some of those things like alfalfa. If you're prepared to go back in the spring as well and spray before planting, another shot of Roundup, you'll get a second shot at killing. And then a conventional corn herbicide program will keep anything else from coming up."

Kaiser also grows pick-your-own strawberries, partly as a friendly public relations gesture to his non-farming neighbors.

"With the strawberries, we mow them off in summer with the bush hog, and then we used to rototill between the rows. I don't do that anymore. I have spray hoods and I spray between the rows with Gramoxone, which kills anything that's on the surface."

The result is that Kaiser's fields look like something out of a Disney movie, or a manicured golf course—absolutely uniform perfection, every field totally weed-free and the divisions between fields as straight as the cut of a razor.

But at what price?

All of the herbicides sprayed by Kaiser, of course, are legal and approved for farm use by the provincial government. He is breaking no laws when he sprays, and his no-till system even fosters soil conservation and moisture retention in the soil. By the standards of conventional, factory farming, he is following good farming practice. But...

Roundup, a systemic, broad-spectrum herbicide produced by Monsanto, contains glyphosate ($C_3H_8NO_5P$) as its active ingredient. Although the U.S. Environmental Protection Agency (EPA) classes glyphosate as posing no risk to human health, numerous environmental groups dispute this. Twice, the EPA has found scientists deliberately falsifying test results at research laboratories hired by Monsanto to study glyphosate. In one of these incidents, the laboratory owner and several employees were indicted on felony counts. The owner was sentenced to five years in prison and fined $50,000.[17]

Recent research indicates that "glyphosate induces a variety of functional abnormalities in fetuses and pregnant rats. Also in recent mammalian research, glyphosate has been found to interfere with an enzyme involved in testosterone production in mouse cell culture and to interfere with an estrogen biosynthesis enzyme in cultures of human placental cells. In controlled residue studies, the World Health Organization (WHO) found 'significant residues' in wheat with residues not lost during baking."[18] There "are concerns about the effects of glyphosate on possible human reproductive dysfunction."[19]

Studies of Roundup's effects on amphibians "indicate it is toxic to them," and the EPA has "concluded that many endangered species of plants, as well as the Houston toad, may be at risk from glyphosate use."[20]

A chlorinated phenoxy herbicide, 2,4-D is absorbed into a plant through the plant's surface, after which it circulates through the plant, causing abnormal growth and blocking the passage of liquids and nutrients. The roots starve and the plant dies. According to the Sierra Club of Canada:

> The herbicide does not affect target weeds alone. It can cause low growth rates, reproductive problems, changes in appearance and behavior, or death in non-target species.
>
> Additionally, the spraying of 2,4-D often contaminates ground water systems [about 91.7 percent of 2,4-D will eventually end up in water]. This contamination threatens the vegetation and the animal life that consumes it. The chemical will also be carried by run-off into the local river systems, thereby jeopardizing the health of aquatic life as well...
>
> Documented [human] health problems related to 2,4-D include reproductive damage (i.e. sterility), respiratory difficulties, atrophy, nausea, loss of appetite, skin rashes, eye irritation, and chronic headaches. Non-Hodgkins lymphoma has also been associated with 2,4-D exposure. Furthermore, there is evidence of teratogenicity (birth defects) and mutagenicity (mutation of cells) provided by studies involving 2,4-D and lab animals.[21]

Gramoxone, whose active ingredient is paraquat, is manufactured by Syngenta and is widely used in North America as a non-selective herbicide. Paraquat is the trade name for a quaternary ammonium herbicide, first introduced in 1961. In July of 2007, a European Union court banned its use on grounds that it does not meet EU health standards.[22]

Says *Wikipedia:*

> According to the [U.S.] Center for Disease Control, ingesting paraquat causes symptoms such as liver, lung, heart, and kidney failure within several days to several weeks. Those who suffer large exposures are unlikely to survive. Chronic exposure can lead to lung damage, kidney failure, heart failure, and oesophageal strictures.[23]

None of these herbicides, of course, is banned in Canada, and a grower, if he follows the manufacturer's instructions for use, would not be putting them on his fields in pure or acute concentrations. Nevertheless...

Finally, there are the conditions under which animals produced via the industrial system, whether hogs, beef cattle, or broiler chickens, are shipped from the "farms" to the processing plants for slaughter. Under the thirty-year-old federal laws that currently govern animal transport in Canada, beef cattle "can be transported for 52 hours without water, feed or rest, regardless of the condition of the animal or summer temperatures... In the case of pigs, it is 41 hours."[24] The federal Canadian Food Inspection Agency (CFIA) is considering changes to the laws, but these are unlikely to be published soon, and may do little to make conditions in the trucks more humane.

Is This Trip Necessary?
Making a rare exception to the biosecurity no-visitors rule, Max Kaiser allowed entry to one of the family's barns, where 27,000 fully-feathered five-week-old chickens were housed,

twenty-four to a wire cage. The din of clucking, peeping, and rustling was so loud it was difficult to hear Kaiser speak. He was explaining the paddle mechanism that sweeps away the birds' manure as it falls through the bottom of the cage rows.

But the thought that occurred to his visitor wasn't about paddles and manure. It was about the close, stuffy feeling of the air inside the barn, the din of all those thousands of birds, kept in such unnatural conditions, and the obvious question:

As Second World War soldiers used to say, "Is this trip necessary?"

Has all of this voluntary self-sacrifice—giving up hunting (once an integral part of rural life), refusing to let your kids keep pets like parakeets or canaries, all of the heroic sanitation measures to avoid catastrophic disease outbreaks (outbreaks which could not occur on anything like such a scale in a system of small farms with small flocks or herds), the investment of millions of dollars in infrastructure, incurring of massive debt loads, and all of the hyper-efficient organization—resulted in a better product?

In other words, is it worth the trouble and expense the grower at the bottom of the industry pyramid is going to? Is it worth the air and water pollution and the pain of the brutalized animals involved? Is it worth carpal tunnel syndrome and ten-year-olds working in the corporate barns out on the Prairies? Is it worth the loss of breed diversity?

In terms of top-of-the-pyramid corporate profits, probably yes. Food industry CEOs are getting richer. But in terms of the delivery of nutritious, healthy fare to the food-buying public, the answer seems to be, no, it's not worth it.

As my previous book, *The End of Food*,[25] demonstrated, the nutritional content of most corporate, supermarket-sold food has been falling steadily for the past fifty years, while the number and amount of toxic contaminants in that food has been rising just as steadily. Meats are no exception, as the book, citing nutritional tables published by the U.S. and Canadian governments, points out:

> According to the USDA tables, chicken—which many of us eat in an attempt to avoid steroid-rich red meats—is in deep trouble. Skinless, roasted white chicken meat has lost 51.6 percent of its vitamin A since 1963. Dark meat has lost 52 percent. White meat has also lost 39.9 percent of its potassium, while dark meat has lost 25.2 percent.
>
> And what has chicken gained? Light meat, 32.6 percent fat, and 20.3 percent sodium; dark meat, 54.4 percent fat and 8.1 percent sodium. Let's hear it for fat and salt.[26]

The book also points out that the eggs from free-range chickens (birds which are not caged and are allowed to forage outdoors) "contain up to 30 percent more vitamin E, 50 percent more folic acid, and 30 percent more vitamin B12 than factory eggs."[27]

Similar decreases have been recorded for pork and for beef, while the number of toxic compounds found in meats has skyrocketed. Everything from acrylamide, to arsenic, to bovine growth hormone (BGH) is mixing in the witches' brew that is industrial food.

And what about those lonely, individual farmers who, not yet driven out of business like their former neighbors by the cost-price squeeze, have taken the advice of government extension agents and Farm Credit advisors and banked their survival on taking the ILO/CAFO route? Has becoming managers of mass-production factories saved them? Are their profits booming?

It can cost between $340 and $400 "per hog space" to construct an industrial hog plant, and once built that structure is already in decline. As Betsy, quoted earlier, explains: "These [industrial] farms don't last. Fifteen years and a lot of things, because of the gases, need to be replaced."

Eric Davis, of Hay Bay Genetics, noted there are many overhead costs. "If you look at your base costs of, say, a finisher barn at $300 per pig place [now an outdated amount] and you depreciate it at 25 percent over a twenty-year period, you've got $4 per pig place in depreciation. At 7 percent interest, you have basically $7 a pig in interest costs, [to total] $11. You take repair and maintenance of somewhere between $1 and $2 per pig, you're at $13. Then take your heat and your hydro at $2, you're at $15 a pig. Then you have to take your labor off, so you're probably at $17 per pig." And so on, and so on.

Davis didn't reveal his actual profit margin, but some producers claim it often barely reaches $1 per hog space, depending on market price fluctuations.

"We've got a million bucks invested [in infrastructure]," said hog producer Mark Slack.

"Plus we've got a million and a half bucks for the land." And getting a bank to provide financing for even such a moderately sized industrial plant effectively requires that the producer be backed by a larger player.

"When you get into this, if you're aligned with a larger producer somewhere, that's probably the only way you're going to get a loan. What they're assuming is that if the big guy is successful then there will be a greater chance of you being successful. Because if you're following the same program and same protocols, then you will be following their lead. The decisions are made on Bay Street [Canada's Wall Street] by people in white ivory towers.

"We went with what was called a large integrator. You want to be aligned with someone who is willing to supply you with animals. We built a gilt selection barn for them. But they ran into, I'm trying to say this politely, they ran into financial difficulty during the last downturn in the hog cycle and became victims of the [then] undervalued Canadian dollar. They were Premium Pork. We had borrowed money on their contract, and we never saw an animal. They filed bankruptcy before we finished building."

"So you never got anything back?"

"No. So it ended up, we bought animals off of Hay Bay Genetics until we could find another group to go with." Today, he added, "we are tied with the largest hog integrator in Quebec, called Coop Fédérée. They supply us the animals. They had supplied us feed up until this last group. They have a manager in our area and he looks after several thousand animals."

He added that the hog marketing board, which was once an effective bargainer on behalf of farmers, is no longer able to influence prices because it no longer employs a quota system. "Hog price [now] is determined by the price of hogs in the U.S. We used to be [able to sell at the] best [price] option, but now we're set up with the Chicago Mercantile Exchange."

Canadian marketing boards are divided between those that have quota, and those that don't. Members of the former type of board purchase a set amount of quota—that is, yearly volume of grain, eggs, or livestock that they are allowed to produce. All of their production is sold via the board, which negotiates price with the large multinational food corporations. This is referred to as "single-desk" selling. The price takes into account the producer's costs and makes sure these are covered by the selling price of the product. Boards that do not have a quota system are far weaker, and often serve as little more than political lobby groups.[28]

Currently, dairy products and eggs are regulated by boards that have quota systems, referred to as "supply-managed" systems. The hog board under which Ontario producers are grouped is not a quota board, and thus its members have virtually no influence over the price their hogs bring in the marketplace.

To get an idea of how weak the individual's position is under such a board, one has only to look at the example of the neighboring province of Manitoba. In 1996, the province's Conservative government arbitrarily eliminated single-desk selling of hogs, despite opposition to the move by some 76 percent of Manitoba hog farmers.[29] While there had been 2,969 producers in the province in 1991, by 2001 only 1,379 were left, a drop of 54 percent in ten years.[30] At the low prices dictated by meat packers, most growers couldn't even break even.

Of the remaining producers, only 11 percent—152 farms—produced 82 percent of the hogs sold.

In the year 2015, thanks to heavy lobbying by the corporate sector, the European Union's Common Agricultural Policy (CAP) will officially end all supply management, quota systems in its member countries. A similar scenario is planned for Canada, soon thereafter.

The decision to go this route has been made by faceless, appointed bureaucrats, responsive to industry pressure and not to any electorate. The policy lead for it was taken first by the World Trade Organization (WTO) but regional groups and national governments have been quick to fall in line. The recent attempt by the Conservative Canadian federal government to weaken the Canadian Wheat Board was only the first shot across the bow of Canada's beleaguered board system. When the quota system goes, the remaining family farms in this country will face doom.

Mark Slack offers his analysis:

"In my opinion, an example is Parmalat. They're an international company, one of the largest milk processors in the world, even though they've gone through some major restructuring in Italy. And you know, in some boardroom in Europe, under Canada's heading, there is [corporate] profit per liter, and the profit per liter is low. The reason it's low is because we have quota. We have restricted production to artificially inflate the price. And the only pressure I think any of those politicians feel is from lobbyists hired by people like Parmalat to do very simply one thing: increase the profit in their industry...And what they would like to do is to narrow the farmer's margins and increase their own margins. And the way to do that is to get rid of quota." Because Slack is tied with a cooperative, his contracts are likely slightly better than those obtained by many other producers.

"They [farmers who go the ILO route] enter into it with great expectations," said Betsy. "And each time their contracts are renewed, the profits are going down. They try to increase the size of their operations to increase the profit margin. They start out with decent contracts, but then it goes down, down, down."

To which the NFU's Fred Tait added:

"It [industrial farming] displaced farmers from an industry and replaced them with investors from corporations. It doesn't take more than a decade for [industrial farms] to become politically unsustainable. Eventually, they'll move offshore. It looks to me as if it will be to Brazil, Argentina, because of the production capacity of grain and the availability of labor."

In fact, farm production may not only move out of Canada and the U.S., seeking cheaper labor in the Third World, but those farms that remain in North America may no longer be in Canadian or American hands. Since the recent boom in ethanol-based bio-fuels began, so-called "sovereign wealth investment funds," which operate on behalf of foreign governments, have become active in speculating in farm land in other countries. China is said to be one of the major players in this regard.[31]

"We're going to have all these white elephants [barns] sitting," said Betsy. "And how do we know the manure tanks aren't leaking? We don't know."

"In Manitoba, the province, through the Agricultural Credit Corporation, has underwritten the loans that created the industry. So the public are holding the bag on this one," said Tait.

"It's beyond the whole generation of where you believed that if you were good to your land, your land would be good to you," concluded Betsy. "We're way past that, with no consideration to the next generation."

(**4**)

The Insurgents and the Surge

The worst are full of passionate intensity.
W.B. YEATS, "The Second Coming"

Who is the hero, who the villain?
VIETATO FUMARE, *We, just down from the trees*

MARK SLACK DOES NOT make an easy villain, although there is no shortage of people in his part of eastern Ontario who think he is one. Now in his early forties, he still looks like a fresh-faced, farm-boy student at the University of Guelph, from which he graduated—quite a few years ago now—with a degree in agriculture.

Slack did grow up on a farm, and has just enough of the youthful, big-dreams aura about him to make it impossible to see him as a sold-out, corporate bad guy. A few minutes talking to him and you realize that to take him that way would be a caricature.

And yet, from the summer of 2000 until today, he has been at the center of a string of battles, first in the village of Erinsville, then in neighboring Tyendinaga Township, and finally in Tweed Municipality—battles that pitted neighbor against neighbor, farmer against cottager, farmer against farmer, lawyer against lawyer, politician against voter, and provincial against local government. At the core of all these fights has been Slack's stubborn determination to launch an industrial hog production plant. Some think his effort an epic of selfishness, others a heroic example of entrepreneurship.

"He was like a dog with bone," said a neighbor.

Driving up the Kinlin Road on a cold but sunny day in early March 2007, en route to his farm, protest signs decorate the trees and fence posts on his neighbors' land: "YES Family Farms; NO Mega Hog Factories." Talk to the people who posted those signs and the hard feelings generated by the most recent fight are easily apparent, simmering beneath the surface of what may well be no more than a lull. But pull into the driveway at Slack's new-looking, two-story frame farmhouse, and the picture becomes bucolic. Outside the house is a swimming pool (empty), and a hockey rink for the kids. Blue jays squawk aggressively in feeders hanging from the trees, knocking seeds off onto the snow-covered lawn, while three snowmen stand on watch on the other side of the drive. A black Labrador dog, limping on three paws, comes wagging up to greet the visitor.

Mark Slack's wife, Sarah, opens the door, and glances at the dog.

"She was running through the snow with icy crust on it, and she must have broken through and either pulled a muscle or twisted it, or something," she explains.

Slack himself is not home yet, although the appointment was made some time ago, and the visitor is invited—oddly—to wait in his car. Oddly, because it is a breach of country etiquette not to invite a guest you knew was coming inside, and offer coffee, on a cold day in late winter. The guest is left sitting in the car for half an hour, briefly running the engine and turning on the heater to take off the chill. Finally, still not invited in, he is told Slack isn't likely to turn up, and he leaves.

Another day, another appointment, and this time Slack is in. Once again, there is no offer of coffee, no sense of rural hospitality. Everything is strictly business. Slack sits down on the other side of the dining room table, while the tape recorder runs.

"I went to Guelph," said Slack. "So did my wife. It's a good Ag school. I stayed up for a summer and got a job working for a cash cropper who had 300 sows and farrow pigs on two different sites. The first summer, because I have a mechanical aptitude, I ended up going into the barns and working with fixing fans and augers and things like those. And one of the managers moved on, so I was put in his position, managing one of the farms. That place is where it started.

"Sarah and I didn't meet in university. But she got a job for the same guy, running the other operation. And then we met and we got married, and Sarah ended up managing one of the farrow-to-finish operations for about nine years. It was one of the things I had desired to have just after we got married, was to have a finishing operation. I mean it's something we've had to work towards and sacrifice for, but at the end of the day I'd say we're very pleased with it."

Neighbors Not Pleased

Many of Slack's neighbors, throughout his years of controversial struggle, developed the opposite view. Even those who ended up not being his neighbors, like the ratepayers' group in Erinsville, near Beaver Lake, that first fought him to a standstill in 2000 and prevented him from locating in their area. Mark Oliver and Barb Pogue, until June of 2007 co-owners of the 128-year-old Lakeview Tavern, near the boat launch, were among the earliest members of the Beaver Lake Preservation Association. Sitting around the kitchen table in their house overlooking the lake, they recalled those early skirmishes.

"The first location [where Slack tried to set up] was just up at the corner, at Young's Road up on Highway 41," said Oliver, who in addition to running the tavern was a schoolteacher. "That was prior to us being in the fight, really. There was a group of women that sort of put it on the radar, Virginia Storring and Jill Smith and Colette Drisdale. They were the first to raise awareness in the communities. Anyway, the procedure went along. He put in an offer on some farmland there. He got a permit and everything to start building, before people kind of clued in.

"Somebody got the building inspector out there, to show the inspector where he had approved the building permit for this pig farm to be built. The building permit was later rescinded."

Actually, it was the Quinte Region Conservation Authority that made the initial decision, by canceling Slack's septic permit.

"This was a fortuitous thing, with the septic," said Stone Mills Township councillor John Wise at the time. "The community said to the township 'we don't want this thing here' and the township said 'we agree with you, that it does pose a significant risk, but legally our hands are tied.' Then we had this mistake with the septic system . . . It's a septic system just for the human employees and a permit was issued for it in error. And when the permit was withdrawn, the township was able to withdraw the building permit." [1]

"You've got a circle of command that are looking for a way out, an Achilles heel, with absolutely zero tolerance," an angry Slack complained when the township's decision was announced. [2]

It was the first permit on the first lot that he picked, in Stone Mills Township, and it was gone.

Slack then tried again in nearby Tyendinaga Township, but was rebuffed there, as well. And while he was preoccupied in Tyendinaga, Oliver recalls, the Stone Mills council "had gone to work and developed an agricultural bylaw that related to intensive farming. They had to make it so that it was applicable not just to this particular situation, but to any and all intensive livestock operations, whether it be beef, poultry, or whatever. They had in that bylaw a requirement for a hydrogeological survey to be done."

Fresh from his second defeat in Tyendinaga, Slack came back to Stone Mills again, testing the new bylaw, and the Beaver Lake group swung into action.

"We were able to gain a lot of support from ratepayers here on the lake," said Oliver. "And we started a fairly extensive water-testing program, because we wanted to have a baseline of information available of what the lake was like before this operation started. We were testing for everything that might be indicative of pig manure leaching into the lake: cadmium, copper, the metals, as well as for coliform and fecal materials. We were doing that at fourteen or fifteen locations around the lake, three or four times a summer."

Ratepayers' groups have been among the earliest and most determined of opponents of industrial farms, in many provinces and U.S. states. For example, the Concerned Daly Ratepayers Inc., of Daly, Manitoba, fought a battle remarkably similar to the one with Slack, in 2001–02.

Feelings ran high at the time among Stone Mills residents. Steven Alls, and Pastor Brian Hart, of the Church of the Assumption of the Blessed Virgin Mary, in Erinsville, were planning a project aimed at rejuvenating the village. Dubbed the Irish Village ecotourism project, it would have reconstructed an energy-efficient, environmentally benign pioneer hamlet, sort of a mini Upper Canada Village (one of Canada's premier international tourist attractions), to serve as a tourist draw and market site for local craftspeople.

"I watched six months' work and lots of people's dreams go up in smoke," said Alls. "Who wants to walk around a tourist site with a hog farm right behind?"[3]

"My husband was a farmer," said retired schoolteacher Marie Kennedy at the time. "He worked like a slave. He loved farming and worked hard at it to provide for his family. Now, I'm afraid none of the ten children and the grandchildren will want to come home. Not with the smell. They say you can smell it for twelve miles."

Baker Dave Greenland in nearby Tamworth added: "Much of our business depends on tourism. I don't see how we will survive if the hog farm comes in. Look, I'm a baker. No clean water, no baking."[4]

"The second location [in Stone Mills] was just, if you continue north just past the Erinsville Catholic Church, the first road turn left, and that was property that belonged to his family, very close to Erinsville," said Oliver. "The cottagers' association had a meeting at the Lakeview Tavern that I went to. That was when the previous people owned that. They planned on holding an information session at the Erinsville school, open to the public, and they asked me to chair it. Being a schoolteacher, I guess they figured I wouldn't be nervous about being in front of people. And that was the beginning of my involvement.

"They put posters up, and I think an ad in the paper, and it [the school meeting] was packed, easily several hundred people. There were even people outside. We [had to] set up a loudspeaker outside."

What people were concerned about, what made them come out in such numbers, was the possibility that pollutants from the hogs' manure would find their way into the lake or into their drinking water, causing possible health problems and hurting property values—especially for cottagers.

At the meeting, Slack and his wife countered their opponents' emotion with an emotional appeal of their own: "Mark and Sarah have a dream," Slack told more than two hundred protestors at a public meeting on his proposal. "We just want to make a living and raise our kids."[5] Surveying the audience at the meeting, Sarah Slack complained, "Is it [local opposition] going to start again?"[6]

Many in the audience were not impressed: "I just don't see why they want to locate in Erinsville," said Dovie McLaughlin. "It's selfish to disrupt so many people's lives."[7]

"The location of this pig farm was such that the groundwater could drain from it into the lake," said Oliver. "And that was our cue to get up and get going. Our concern was based on all the literature we were coming across that demonstrated, we thought pretty consistently, that these things were environmental disasters. And so we started looking into our bylaw that we had in the township, and at the [provincial] ministry regulations.

"We were worrying about these nutrient management agreements [provincial Nutrient Management Plans, required under the Nutrient Management Act], and we discovered he had received approval from the Ministry of Natural Resources by submitting these nutrient management documents that have agreements with other farmers [to spread surplus manure]. We got copies of the plans, and they had lot and concession numbers and tax roll numbers on them and we called the clerk... and there were issues with some of them. We checked the ownership on one, and it was property that belonged to a lady who had been an opponent of factory farms. She was just livid."

Some of the same farms and lots were still included when Slack later submitted his plans in nearby Tweed Municipality. In a note to the Tweed clerk, opponents pointed out that:

"We noticed some significant discrepancies and omissions:

"1) The agreement for Lot 20, Conc. 10 [Stone Mills] is for property that is owned by Alan and Palmier Stevenson-Young. These people are opposed to Mr. Slack's hog operation and told us that they did not sign an agreement with him to spread manure on their property and never would. Further, the roll number indicated on this manure agreement... does not match the correct roll number.

"2) The agreement for Lot 18, Conc. 2 + Lot 17, Conc. 2 + Lot 17, Conc. 1 [Stone Mills] also has the wrong roll number...

"3) The agreement for Lot 17/18, Conc. 2 [Tweed] also has the wrong roll number...

"The number of tillable acres is omitted on two of these three agreements..." [8]

The mix-up over lots could have been an innocent mistake, but it hurt Slack. The Stone Mills council was supportive of hog factory opponents, and the second request for approval of the planned hog operation was also rejected. "There was a problem with the hydrogeological study," said Oliver.

Slack, however, was not deterred.

"Obstacles are what you see if you take your eye off the goal," he likes to say. He decided to try yet again, this time just to the west, in the municipality of Tweed.

Again, a citizens' group formed to block him. They called themselves Farms Not Factories (FNF). All across Canada and the U.S. today there are groups like them, from the locally oriented Concerned Daly Ratepayers Inc. in Manitoba, to state or provincially oriented groups like the Wisconsin Stewardship Network and the Ohio Environmental Council, to Hog Watch Manitoba and Alberta's Society for Environmentally Responsible Livestock Operations. There are also umbrella groups, like the U.S.-based GRACE Factory Farm Project, which provide a clearing house for information. Some were already in operation when the Tweed group started and some came after, but they had a common sense of outrage, and felt a common weakness in face of the seeming power of their opponents. Slack, of course, was not a corporate bigwig, and hadn't very much power, but many in his area felt he was a stalking horse for others, that bigger fish would inevitably follow him onto the scene.

Five of the original FNF members gathered to talk to their journalist visitor one evening in the farmhouse kitchen of Sue Vander Wey. It was obvious that every one of them had been scarred in some way by the ongoing battle.

"Some of the Tamworth [a village in Stone Mills Township] people actually gave a warning to Tweed, to look what this guy is up to," said retired University of Toronto physics professor Joe Vise.

"[They said] he was headed this way, that there were some issues around that type of operation," added Lisa Schneider, a library technician in a Tweed elementary school. She and her husband live in a house they built themselves, by hand, just down the road from Slack. Their lights are powered by solar electric panels and they heat with wood year-round, trying to leave as little of an imprint as possible on the environment. Vise also uses solar power, and even heats with solar hot water. Vander Wey is the widow of a full-time farmer, while the two others present, John Wilson and Denice Wilkins, live in a passive solar home on 160 acres nearby, and also own 35 acres in the village on which they raise pick-your-own blueberries.

As in Stone Mills, Slack had already gotten a building permit, approved in 2002 by the local building inspector. As before, the local municipal council was, at least initially, inclined to listen to the citizens' group's protests, but like their neighboring council felt their hands were tied due to the permit having already been granted. It was at this point that residents formed the FNF group and decided to launch an information campaign. A few entries from a chronology of events, drawn up by Sue Vander Wey, gives a sample of what followed:

Dec. 3, 2002—100 concerned citizens attend Tweed Council meeting. Council agrees to ask [provincial] Ministry of the Environment (MOE) for an environmental assessment.

Jan. 9, 2003—48 residents meet at Heritage Centre to discuss what can be done about hog operation.

Jan. 13–16, Council seeks legal advice concerning building permit.

Jan. 15—Slack meets with 15 local farmers to solicit support.

Jan. 21—Council informs public that MOE has declined to do a review.

Jan. 22—200 people attend public information meeting at the Legion Hall.

Jan. 28–30—Legal advice to Tweed Council states it would be difficult to get an injunction to stop building permit.

Feb. 18—378 signed letters [opposing the hog plant] are presented at Council meeting. Council asks Chief Building Officer to rescind building permit, stating Council's research on Intensive Hog Operations (IHOs) had caused concerns about residents and the environment.

Feb. 22—Family Fun Fundraiser raises funds to oppose Slack. Slack files an appeal in Ontario Superior Court against building permit revocation.

March 3—Council passes an interim bylaw to prohibit IHOs in the municipality for one year.

March 26—Ontario Superior Court reinstates conditional construction permit as originally granted.

April 1—FNF requests that Council appeal court decision.

April 12—Public meeting at Heritage Centre; bridges and load limits become an issue.[9]

The roads leading to Slack's property, which was topographically on a sort of island, had several small bridges, across which trucks carrying construction materials for building his plant were required to pass. Once construction was completed, other trucks, carrying feed, and eventually hogs, would also have to cross the same bridges. The bridges were rated with 10-ton load safety limits, above which physical damage, including possible collapse, might be done to the bridge structures. The trucks traveling to Slack's farm were routinely exceeding the limit.

"They were 10-ton bridges," said Schneider.

"And he's bringing in 40, 50, 60-ton trucks" said Wilson.

One day, a car might be driving across and it might collapse under it, or worse:

"Our concern was more toward the school bus" explained Vander Wey.

One of the bridges, the focus of most of the traffic, lacked a posted load limit sign.

"It was on this teeny-tiny little windery road, and they'd done some minor refurbishing of it and forgot to put the load limit sign back up," said Schneider. "So then we spent several thousand dollars to hire [an engineering firm] to come and assess it. And sure enough, yes, it was a 10-ton bridge. And so we took that to Council, made the presentation.

"And they said, 'Oh no [the load limit would not be enforced], we'll have to look into that [before taking action].'"

The Farms Not Factories group, meanwhile, had protest signs printed and distributed to area residents who opposed the hog plant. But shortly after the signs began turning up on local lawns and farm fields, vandals began burning them, as well as knocking down the rural road mailboxes of those who'd posted the signs.

"My signs were burned," said Joe Vise.

"They were taken and burned," agreed Denice Wilkins.

Lisa Schneider proffers a color snapshot: "This is Mr. Slack at the end of our driveway, in the dark, about to take one of our signs. He was reaching like this when my husband snapped. My husband stood there at the edge of our driveway and just sat patiently to see what was happening, night after night, and waited to see who it was. He didn't actually expect it to be Mr. Slack. And Slack said, 'You just made a big mistake, buddy,' or something like that, and Ed began backing up toward the house. And Slack got back in his truck and drove away."

The photo is inconclusive. It shows a frowning Mark Slack on foot on a road, advancing toward the camera. What he might have said, or been doing before the photo was taken, is not apparent. Another photo in the same batch shows a burnt protest sign, but there is no evidence as to who may have burned it. Slack denies any wrongdoing (see below).

He said/she said.

There were also claims of numerous road incidents.

"Mr. Slack repeatedly swerved his truck at my vehicle," claimed Schneider. "It was repeatedly. It was a harassment thing. [He was in] the big red truck with the slotted tool box. I did go to the police about it. I made a report." The Madoc post of the Ontario Provincial Police (OPP), where the report was made, would have had conflicting stories, and no witnesses to corroborate the complaint if they followed it up.

The group claimed there was another incident, this time with a witness.

"We were standing by the ditch where we were testing the water. We had a girl down to help. And he [Slack] speeded up [his truck] and he was spraying gravel at us." No one reported the matter to police.

Asked whether the three incidents happened, Slack replied: "No, no, and no. Somebody did burn a sign, though."

"Kids?"

"Yeah. They were having a lot of fun with it."

Other incidents, not involving Slack himself, were corroborated, especially when FNF members began picketing one of the bridges where overweight trucks were crossing. "We faced off at that bridge," said Wilson. "We had demonstrations, and the police were there." *Tweed News* reporter Maril Swan described one, involving Lafarge Cement trucks and FNF pickets who were handing out literature to the truck drivers:

> ...the Farms Not Factories group warned the cement company that they were endangering their drivers by allowing them to drive loaded cement trucks

over the Otter Creek bridge to the site of the proposed hog farm...

Among the printed material is a report stating the bridge should be posted for 10 tons. The cement trucks weigh more than that empty, and over 40 tons loaded with cement. [FNF member] Lyell Shields stated that Lafarge trucks were crossing the bridge about every five minutes while the cement pouring was being done.

While The Tweed News was at the site, four empty cement trucks rumbled over the small bridge. Will Verhulst of FNF waved the drivers to stop so he could hand up the information sheets...The picket continued peacefully until a local farmer, Harold Prevost, confronted Farms Not Factories members and vowed he would keep the bridge open so the cement trucks could cross. FNF was not blocking the bridge, but standing about 50 feet back from it. Bylaw Enforcement Officer Don Barnett called the Madoc OPP when it looked like a problem was developing. Prevost tore down a hand written load limit sign made by FNF which they had placed on the bridge, then left the scene.[10]

Prevost, who strongly supported Slack's venture, began turning up at Tweed council meetings, wearing a peaked cap with a pink hog snout on it.

At one point, recalled the Beaver Lake Preservation Association's Barb Pogue, a Slack supporter turned up at the Lakeview Tavern after closing. "We had locked the door and were cleaning up, and he was trying to get in and he was quite drunk and was banging on the doors. We didn't open and he eventually ended up over at the Tamworth Hotel, caused havoc, and was thrown out, and the police arrested him. We heard after that it was one of those fellahs from Tweed that came over."

The heavy trucks continued traveling up and down the roads to Slack's property. "One of them had to back up two kilometers on the Kinlin Road because it couldn't make the curve on one of those tiny bridges," recalled Schneider. Another gravel truck, belonging to a local contractor, ended up in the ditch.

"One night we were driving home, it was actually from the all-candidates meeting during the provincial election," said Wilkins. "It was that night. And we came around the corner right near Slack, and sure enough there was the truck, in the ditch.

"We called the police that night."

"We all got there at about dawn, around six, seven o'clock," added John Wilson. "We started videotaping him. He [the contractor] arrived with his high-ho, pulled the truck out of the ditch and was trying to take it back to Slack, so it would be off the road. But he pulled it over to the side. The police came with their scales, to weigh his truck, which was empty but was still over the load limit, and supposedly [were] going to charge him."

"Then what happened is [the contractor] said it was us, that he swerved and ended up in the ditch because one of us was shining our lights so he couldn't see, blocking the bridge," said Wilkins. "It was all our fault! He made it all up!"

Fortunately for the accused FNF members, they could prove that they were at the all-candidates meeting, actually talking to Liberal candidate Leona Dombrowsky, at the time the contractor claimed they were on the bridge obstructing traffic. The matter was dropped, and neither the contractor nor FNF was charged.

Numerous other incidents, ranging from attempts to provoke fistfights to unidentified men on tractors shining their lights into FNF supporters' windows at two AM, followed each other. And not all were aimed at the FNF. One of the most serious episodes was aimed at Slack

"We had a gentleman walk up our driveway and shoot the windows out of our tractor," said Slack.

"Why would he do that?" I asked.

"He would do that because the idea of one of these barns is greater than the reality of them. We [industrial livestock operators] deal with ratepayers' groups. I mean all over the place. One of the reasons that Maple Leaf did not reinvest in Ontario [but moved instead to the Prairies] is because ratepayers' groups in Hamilton kicked up such a fuss for them putting in a new killing plant. And these fools have no idea where their food comes from, and these fools are ignorant of agriculture and ignorant of agricultural production, and yet they are the reason it is the way it is.

"We had a group form and try to stop us, and they used every intimidation they could use. They bombarded council."

"Did he [the tractor shooter] get charged?"

"He did get charged. Yeah. But the people that hired him didn't."

Although no link was found between the shooter and Slack's opponents, articles in some farm papers began referring to the FNF as "terrorists."

On the streets of the town of Tweed itself, people took sides in the dispute, and made their choices clear. "It created an atmosphere where things tended to fester," said one FNF member. "You walk down the street and people cross to the other side to avoid you. Personally, we'd like to put that behind us."

"What makes it so terrible being in a small community is that, if you fight some battle in the city, you're fighting against all kinds of people you don't know, you'll never know. They're not your neighbors, you'll never see them again and it doesn't matter," said Wilkins. "When you're in a small community, everybody knows everybody else, everybody's related to everybody else."

"It's divisive for a very long time," added Schneider.

Unable to tolerate the tension, some people simply sold their property and moved away.

Creating Stereotypes

Each side tended to stereotype the other.

"They're very tribal," one FNF member agreed. "They're a tribe, and in a sense maybe we became a tribe. I mean, we had all kinds of people, but in a sense we start to 'them and us.' There is a groundswell sometimes, of feeling that is partly true but partly irrational. And that is the 'from-aways' coming to tell us what to do with our land, right? That's always a big issue. There was a big groundswell against us."

"But we've been here for decades, many of us, and we're not like cottagers," said Sue Vander Wey.

"We tried to tell the farmers that we were really on their side," continued Denice Wilkins. "But we were not here for generations. They would say, 'Oh these darn people coming and telling us what we can do and what we can't do. If they don't like the smell of manure they shouldn't live in the country.'"

"They" became the operative word.

"They are your typical leftover hippies, work for the CBC kind of people, who had never set foot in the [hockey] arena," said Mark Slack of his opponents. "Our potential environmental impact was touted that there would be dead babies, empty storefronts, and the Bay of Quinte would be poisoned. There is no logic to the argument. Any hog barns are met with just this *insurgence* of, this wave of ignorance!"

By the time he'd launched his initiative in Tweed, Slack had already learned what he took to be valuable lessons about dealing with ratepayers' groups.

"With my experience, the best way to approach them is not to approach them. They're trying to change your mind, and they called for us to have public meetings and so on and so forth, and we'd been through it all once before, because we had a building permit revoked on our property in the neighboring township. And at the public meeting [there], nobody was interested in hearing what we were doing. They only were interested in us hearing their opinion.

"So my advice would be, no public meetings. They're pointless."

Of course, this served only to make his opponents more angry than before.

"That was one of the most frustrating things in the entire situation," said Lisa Schneider. "He would never speak to the people in Tweed. He would never come to a meeting. He wouldn't speak to anyone: he wouldn't speak to reporters, he wouldn't speak to people on the street, he wouldn't come to a meeting, he wouldn't answer the questions that were posed in the newspaper. It was just a blank wall of silence, and that was really frustrating.

"At least if he would sort of bring out his point of view, we could have intellectualized and maybe understood part of it.

But we were just hitting blank walls with questions that we couldn't find answers to."

Meanwhile, the controversy over the bridges continued, but before it could be settled a whole new dimension was added to the battle: an election was held in November 2003, and a new municipal council and a new reeve (president of the municipal council) were elected. The result was a situation that the ratepayers of Daly, Manitoba—whose local council at one point ignored public opinion and favored a pig farm application—would recognize.

The new reeve, Vance Drain, was himself the owner of an industrial livestock operation, in his case Drain Poultry Ltd., a plant with thousands of birds, and FNF members feared he would sympathize with Slack. Their fears were understandable, given Drain's September 20, 2001 testimony to the provincial Standing Committee on Justice and Social Policy, then holding hearings on Bill 81, which led to the passing of the Ontario Nutrient Management Act regulating disposal of animal manure and other wastes.

Liberal Steve Peters, then opposition agriculture critic (a Conservative government was in power at the time), was in attendance. He was later (2003) appointed minister of agriculture in the Liberal government that came in afterward.

According to the Official Report of Debates (Hansard), Drain complained about local townships "legislating the farmer out of business" and "mounting pressures from new residents to limit or control manure, fertilizer, herbicides and pesticides." Noting that he spread the manure from his chickens on twenty to thirty area farms per year, he lamented the likelihood of legislation being passed under which "larger farms will be forced to submit plans that will be accessible to everyone, and the media could then publicize or sensationalize the plan details, making for a public relations nightmare for the farmer. Environmentalists or activists could use this report for ammunition against the farmer."

He came back to the secrecy issue again and again in his testimony, stressing: "I have a real concern that it becomes public...I believe it will happen that somebody can sit on a keyboard somewhere in an office and type in a few letters, get your nutrient management plan, and spend the time, if they want to, for sensationalism, because maybe that's where they make their money, sitting outside your place, you do some stupid little thing wrong and it gets sensationalized all over the place, and you really will go broke."

Others testifying at the same hearings included fellow eastern Ontario industrial livestock producers Eric Kaiser (father of Max Kaiser, quoted in chapter 3) and Pauline and Elwyn Embury of River Valley Poultry (also mentioned in chapter 3). Kaiser complained that "fear of public outcry in regard to nutrient pollution is creating a new group to harass. The message is clear: pass the buck, blame the farmers, farmers are criminals who need to be legislated." He added that "you have a small percentage of the population, who are 'rurbanites' driving the policy." (More on this segment of the rural population in chapters 7, 9, and 10.)

Pauline Embury regretted that "farmers who have wanted to expand their business in the past two years have been forced to comply with township bylaws." She added that she, too, was uncomfortable with nutrient management plans being accessible. "The whole issue of public scrutiny— I'm not against people knowing what we're doing. We run a very clean operation. But I think it [the possibility of disclosure] puts people on edge." Elwyn Embury attempted to blur the line between factory and family farms. Asked how he would classify his operation, he replied: "I think a family farm is run by the family. An intensive farm would be run by a corporation that would invest in the operation and they're not on the farm every day." By this criterion, Ford Motor Company would be just another family business.

Later, Slack would take a leaf from the Emburys' book, calling his plant Slack Family Farms.

If Slack saw his opponents as insurgents, Farms Not Factories faced what looked to them like a counter-surge when the new council came in. According to Joe Vise, its members—a majority of whom were farmers—had a different agenda than their predecessors. "They circled the wagons," he said. "And it was with the guns pointed outwards." Lisa Schneider believed that "Vance Drain was determined to let, to make this guy [Slack] have his farm."

To which Slack himself added: "Vance was a definite asset. Vance was cautious and he was incredibly fair. He did not give us anything that we didn't deserve, and he took away from us nothing that shouldn't have been taken away...You have to remember, they [factory farm opponents] don't know what they want. They only know what they don't want. You can't have that running a council."

Drain doesn't think the council, under him, was biased. "The rules are the rules," he said. "You can read them one way and you can read them another way. Animal rights people, PETA [People for the Ethical Treatment of Animals], you name them, they have their goal. Some people would like to see 3,000 hogs running around in a field instead of in a place that you can control it."

"How did you deal with that on council?" I asked him.

"You deal with the rules."

In keeping with Drain's previously expressed penchant for secrecy in matters involving Nutrient Management Plans, the new council delayed when FNF members asked for details of Slack's plans, hoping to check lot numbers and names, to see if they were genuine and really represented landowners willing to let the pig waste be spread on their properties. But when copies of these Nutrient Transfer Agreements were eventually provided, they were filled with strikeovers in heavy black ink, blocking out names and numbers, and masking details.

Efforts to force compliance with bridge load limits en route to Slack's property continued. "People started to call the police and say look, there's a 40-ton truck here out on this road," recalled Schneider.

"At first the Madoc OPP didn't want to investigate it," said Vise. "They eventually did."

"If council had insisted that the bridge load limits be enforced, then the police would have been much more active," added John Wilson. "At first Leona Dombrowsky [then the local Liberal candidate for the provincial legislature] appeared to be on our side. When we told her the trucks were going over the load limit, she went to the OPP, on a Sunday afternoon, and said, 'Why aren't you enforcing this?' This was when she was running for office."

"And then she [got elected and] became minister for the environment," said Vise.

"And that was it," said Wilson.

"The end of that," agreed Wilkins.

FNF members were convinced that the provincial government was not objective, but was instead committed to fostering the growth of ILOs. Indeed, a January 17, 2005, letter (see below) from Steve Peters, by then minister of agriculture in a new Liberal government, appeared to support this view. If this was the case, then Dombrowsky's new attitude, once elected, could be seen as simply toeing the party line. In June 2005, Dombrowsky herself was appointed minster of agriculture, succeeding Peters.

The FNF presented its study of the bridge load limits to council on February 17, but no official action was taken. Finally, on April 16, the council—despite having a professional engineering study already in hand—voted to do its own study, and hired Greer Galloway Group Inc., of Belleville, to conduct it.

"They went and spent our money, taxpayers' money, to go and hire someone to do it [the engineering study] again," said Schneider. "And it didn't get done until Slack had brought in all his trucks to build the place, and then it was, 'Yeah, you were right.'"

While the council's load limit study was wending its leisurely way toward completion, and its eventual conclusion that the bridge in question was indeed a 10-ton bridge, load limit signs on five local bridges were removed or vandalized, several of them being dumped in rivers. Construction of the new hog facility continued, as trucks rumbled up and down the narrow rural roads.

On June 17, an anti–hog plant petition with nearly 1,200 signatures was presented to council, but council members voted to cancel the next meeting, putting off public discussion of the petition for another month.

Council also rejected an FNF application for a permit to hold a raffle for a side of beef, to help defray the group's legal costs, on grounds that the FNF—whose goal was to prevent air or water pollution of their community—was not a recognized community service organization. A permit was obtained from Stone Mills Township instead.

By now, the Tweed council had voted to reinstate Slack's building permit. It had also brought forward a proposed bylaw to severely limit public delegations making presentations to council, a measure citizens quickly dubbed the "muzzling bylaw."

"Whenever we discovered something new or something onerous about factory farming, we would make a presentation," said Wilson. "Many of us made personal presentations. And council basically said, 'That's it, we don't want to hear any more about this.'"

"A person could not, within a year I think it was, talk more than once on a given subject," added Vise.

The actual wording stipulated that "a delegation shall address council on a specific topic only once," that "an individual making a presentation to council shall not pose questions during or at the end of the presentation unless invited to do so by the chair," and that "a delegation shall address council not exceeding 10 minutes unless granted extra time by the chair." [11]

"They actually had an egg timer, and it would go off and you had to stop," said Wilkins.

On July 20, the same day that the 1,200-name petition was at last presented to council, members voted to pass the muzzling law. It did not sit well with many voters. As one noted in a letter to the editor of *The Tweed News:*

> The fact that two or three members of council are farmers creates a situation for conflict and perhaps requires some introspection rather than an attitude of "they're not going to win..."

It might help to remember that running a municipal
council is not quite like running a farm. With a farm
you make the decision and the animals have no choice
but to live with it. The electorate are not mute animals
and this is supposed to be a democratic process...
If you can't take the heat, get out.[12]

A later bylaw prohibited any noise or demonstrations
during council discussions.

"You couldn't applaud or make any noise in council," said
Wilson.

"One guy said 'here, here,' and they tried to kick us out,"
said Schneider. "We decided not to go. And then, *bang-bang,*
they pounded the table and adjourned the meeting."

"Shut down the meeting," agreed Schneider.

"Adjourned the whole meeting, canceled it," said Wilson,
shaking his head. "And they actually passed another bylaw
that specifically prohibited us from making any presentations about hog factories."

No one thought at the time to test these muzzling
bylaws as possible violations of the Canadian federal Char-
ter of Rights and Freedoms, which guarantees freedom of
speech. The hog plant's opponents had enough on their
plate, legally speaking. On June 23, 2004, five opponents—
Lawrence O'Coin, Ernest Allore, Lyell Shields, Günther
Huettlin, and John Genore—filed a notice of appeal in the
Superior Court of Justice in Belleville, against Tweed's chief
building officer and the Tweed council, asking that the reinstatement of Slack's building permit be reversed. Shortly
afterward, Slack joined the suit as a respondent. Both the
FNF and the Beaver Lake Preservation Association backed
the suit.

On August 27, the suit was heard before Judge Albert Roy, but a final judgement wasn't rendered until October 6. In the interim, work continued on Slack's plant, and on September 14, he held an open house, attended by Tweed council members, to show off his new facility.

The court decision found in favor of the appellants and against reinstatement of Slack's building permit, recognized the legitimacy of the appellants' concerns, and chided the chief building officer for not making a satisfactory Nutrient Management Plan a condition of granting the permit before construction began. The hog plant's opponents had won, but it was a purely symbolic victory. Slack's first barn was already in place.

"Virtually no court will tell somebody to take a facility like that and tear it down," said Vise.

"Which is what he knew, of course, and he built anyway, as a fait accompli," said Schneider.

In fact, provincial legislation had already frustrated any future, local legal or legislative efforts to oppose factory farms. Ontario had passed a law similar to those in several other provinces, such as Alberta, where the Agricultural Operations Practices Act effectively removed factory farm decision-making power from municipalities and put it in the hands of the provincial government.[13] Ontario's Nutrient Management Act, Section 61(1), took control over intensive livestock operations out of municipal hands, while the Farming and Food Production Protection Act put jurisdiction over farm practices firmly under provincial control. Local people and local councils no longer had anything to say about what the industrial food plant next door might choose to do.

And even if they did, details of what that plant might be doing were no longer theirs to discover, at least not very easily. Heeding the advice of industrial farmers like Drain and Embury, the legislature decided to write the regulations attached to the Nutrient Management Act—Regulation 267/03, Sections 28(1), 29(1), and 30(1)—in such a way as to make various parts of the process of getting approval for spreading manure both complex, and accessible to outsiders only with difficulty. An ILO operator must develop not only a building program that will qualify under municipal construction permit rules, but must also develop both a provincially overseen Nutrient Management Strategy and a Nutrient Management Plan. The strategy goes on file with the ministry, but the more detailed plan—which contains details on how much manure is to be spread and how often spreading will take place—does not. It is kept on file only by the operator. "Typically the plans we don't see," explained provincial environment officer Peter Doris. "If you're putting on 3,000 or 10,000 gallons per acre we don't see that unless you're putting on biosolids [from a municipal sewage treatment plant] as well."

Only operators with 1,800 or more hogs need to have a plan; those with fewer animals need only the strategy, which doesn't go into detail regarding spreading. Inquirers seeking information on a strategy and/or plan must file a Freedom of Information request under the Freedom of Information Act to access the program, but may not be able to access the plan. Key details—such as the amount of manure being spread by an operator, its volume per acre, and the frequency with which manure is spread—are not released at all. Ordinary citizens no longer have access.

Vance Drain, after serving one term as reeve during the hog controversy, declined to run again and now devotes his time to his poultry plant and other businesses.

In the end, however, the Farms Not Factories group feel they won at least something. Like Betsy's neighbor's project (mentioned in chapter 3), Slack's original plans were scaled back considerably, and they believe that was at least partly a result of their efforts.

"Because of the whole controversy that we stirred up, [we think] the size of the barn was brought down quite a bit smaller than he had originally intended," said Wilkins. The original plan, which matched one posted on the Premium Pork website, called for a larger barn and an outdoor lagoon for manure storage. The eventual barn was smaller, and featured under-barn, enclosed storage. FNF members believe this may actually have simplified matters for Slack. "The Nutrient Management Act that came in gave him, if he was small enough, more freedom than if he got bigger," said Joe Vise.

As Doris's explanation of the 1,800-animal limit indicated, the FNF may have guessed right on this. So far, no additional barns have been built, and Slack indicates none will be.

"Plans to expand, for me there is none," he said. "We are under the size that's required by the Ontario government to have our Nutrient Management Plan approved by the director." This may both help and hurt him, when the provincial funding available for ILOs over a certain size is considered (see below).

When all of the costs incurred in fighting Slack's project are factored in, however, the FNF's small gains tend to pale in comparison.

First, they have not stopped the overall movement toward factory farming in Tweed.

"Factory farming is safe in Tweed," said Wilson. "If you want to have more factory farms, you can. Come here. Tweed is a good place to build a factory farm."

"The big worry of our group is that this is the beginning, and what happens here will be a message to more industrial farms," said Vise.

And there was a dollar cost.

"Over the course of this thing, we [FNF members and their supporters in the community] spent easily $60,000 to $70,000," said Wilkins. The legal case against reinstatement of Slack's building permit ate up a large chunk of the total, and FNF members are still angry about what happened after judgement was rendered, regarding the payment of court costs. Under terms of the judgement rendered by Judge Albert, Slack and the municipality of Tweed were each required to pay half of the total court costs of $12,000. The municipality paid its half in full.

"Slack never paid, and he got away with it," said Vise.

In fact, on May 27, 2005, Slack was subjected to a debtor's examination in court to determine his ability to pay, at which he claimed to be losing money on his operation and unable to cover his share of the court costs. He explained what happened:

"When they started their suit, everything that I owned and everything that was me, the land, equipment and everything else, was rolled into an incorporated business called Slack Family Farms Inc. And they sued Mark Slack. Mark Slack had nothing. If Mark Slack has nothing then Mark Slack doesn't have the ability to pay. Everything I had was

rolled into the farm. So all I owned was shares in the corporation that, according to the constitution of the corporation,
could not be sold or traded."

"At the time," recalls FNF member Frank Szarka, "we considered pressing for the court to start a contempt of court
action over this, but then a letter from Agriculture Minister
Peters appeared that seemed to be saying between the lines
that if we did [start an action], we'd have the provincial government against us. We just decided to drop it."

In the undated letter, received on January 17, 2005,
Peters wrote: "we see no reason to take any action against
Mr. Slack." He added, by way of admonition: "Intensive live-
stock operations are a fact of life in rural Ontario."

Indeed, the province's commitment to encouraging ILOs,
if anyone doubted it, was made still clearer in October 2005,
when the Ontario Ministry of Agriculture, Food and Rural
Affairs, now under Leona Dombrowsky herself, announced
it was making $23.7 million available "to approximately
1,200 existing *large* [italics the author's] livestock operators [e.g., livestock operations with more than 300 nutrient
units]" to cover the costs of compliance with the Nutrient
Management Act in disposing of their manure.[14]

"Nutrient units" are listed in government tables. To find
out how many units a farmer has, one divides the number
of animals in an operation by the number in the table. For
pig-finishing operations, the number is six. Thus a hog
farmer with 1,800 finisher pigs (divided by six, for 300 units),
or more, would qualify for this bonanza. The number for
sows with litters is 3.5, so a farmer with 1,050 sows would
also qualify. (Ironically, Slack's current operation of 1,600
hogs—times six, so 266.6 nutrient units)—would also have
put him under the qualifying minimum to obtain a slice of

the $23.7 million provincial ILO-aid pie in 2005, if that was the number of hogs in his barn at the time.)

A smaller farmer with, say, 20 or even 100 hogs, would not qualify, and would get nothing. The province obviously favors ILOs over their smaller competitors.

FNF members say the municipality, by May of 2004, had already spent more than $38,000 of taxpayers' money for legal fees, engineering studies, and road and bridge upgrades required to allow traffic to reach Slack's facility.[15] Before the controversy ended, Councillor Stan Meeks admitted that more than $100,000 had been spent, although none went directly to Slack himself or to his actual plant.

The hog factory's opponents, however, see their dollar outlays and taxpayers' financial expenses as secondary to the emotional costs of the fight.

"It's hard on relationships," said Lisa Schneider. "It's hard on people's health. There were times that I didn't eat dinner with my husband. He was at the same table, but I would come home from work and be on the phone for three or four hours and crash after that. Get up and the next day we'd do it again, and do it again, and do it again. We were nervous wrecks."

"And the sleepless nights, because that's all you could think about," added John Wilson. "You're writing letters to the editor in your dreams, in your head."

"It consumed our lives," said Denice Wilkins.

"We'll never be the same," said Sue Vander Wey.

"Two of our closest friends, and most stalwart fighters in this battle, literally sold and moved away," said Wilson. "And so it changed the quality of our neighborhood. It turned other neighbors against us who we thought were friends, or at least acquaintances. Suddenly they're bad-mouthing us."

"It's difficult for everybody in town," explained Schneider. "Like the people who own the businesses here, they don't want other people arguing in there, or even asking them, 'How do you feel on this?' Because half the customers feel one way and half the other way. Like the public librarian: she was very much against it because she had done a lot of reading about it. But her job is to present whatever material is available on both sides. That's what she's required to do. But that made it hard for her because people would say, 'What the hell are all those pig videos doing here?' So [it went] all through the town."

In 2007, they were asked: "Is it over?"

"Just the other day I was walking," Schneider said, "and it [the stench from Slack's plant] made it extremely unpleasant, to try to walk on my own property. If he had been the size [originally planned], with the open lagoons, it would be unliveable at my house."

"It's up to us to be constantly monitoring our own water [because no provisions were made for the municipality to do so], and then [if anything is wrong] to prove that it's being caused by the hog factory," said Wilson. "It has to be our interest to do that."

"Who knows what the country is going to look like in fifteen years?" worries Vander Wey. "I have no idea. But I have my daughter, and I know she's grown up loving this place. But will there be a viable life for the kids?"

And Slack?

"These guys are relentless," he said. "I don't know what the end is, but I'm still convinced they're waiting for a disaster.

"They're going to have to wait a lifetime for it."

Unwanted in Eden

Sir, Hell is paved with good intentions.

SAMUEL JOHNSON, in James Boswell's *The Life of Samuel Johnson*[1]

THE PRECEDING CHAPTERS HAVE shown the kind of farms governments, at least at the national or provincial level (though not nearly as consistently at the local level), seem to like: namely, industrial-scale factory farms. And the stock of such enterprises rises even higher if they have visible contract or partnership links to the overall national/international corporate sector that finances the election campaigns of so many of those who govern us.

But what about the farms governments *don't* seem to like, those that would be most likely to appear (to put it in agricultural terms) on their Manure List?

Many people in eastern Ontario are convinced these would have to include traditional small family farms, truck or market garden farms, subsistence farms, hobby farms, and any general support or marketing mechanisms that might tend to bolster them. Government disfavor toward such targets, many believe, is expressed through a variety of mechanisms, some direct, some indirect, and some almost maddeningly complex. These mechanisms could involve anything from taxes, fees, and health, environmental, or other regulations, to the exigencies of that most Canadian of institutions, the agricultural marketing board.

Marketing boards are a good place to start, partly to deal with the hardest bit first, and partly to show how easily even the best of good intentions can go awry (how crazily far awry will be shown by the individual stories of some of the system's victims, just a few pages below).

In original form, any given marketing board served as something close to a farmers' union, grouping producers into a single association and using their numbers—and the sheer volume of what they produced—as a lever to gain better prices for their members' products. Just as unions grouped workers together and made their united labor subject to bargaining by employers, so the boards forced the large corporate food-processing and -distributing companies that dominate the international markets to negotiate fair prices for agricultural commodities—that is to say, prices high enough for individual farmers, after investing their cash and labor, to make a living.[2]

And such leverage was badly needed. The financial dislocations caused by the post–First World War slump in farm prices, and later on by the general disaster of the Great Depression of the 1930s, sparked passage of the pioneer legislation establishing the earliest marketing boards in Canada, Australia, New Zealand, and Great Britain.

The Canadian Wheat Board is an example. During the twentieth century's first decade, Western wheat farmers were faced with a monopoly at every single shipping location.

The Canadian Pacific Railway (CPR) refused to allow farmers to load their own produce at its platforms, thereby forcing them to deal with private elevator companies—and accept without question the elevator company's terms on dockage and grading. A farmer might haul his wheat 30 or 40 miles with a team of horses, only to discover on arrival that elevator price offerings had dropped below the cost of production. He could choose to sell at a loss, or haul the wheat home again. Either way, he lost money.

But the war brought change. The Winnipeg Grain Exchange closed for three years, and to assure a steady amount of grain for the war effort, the federal government put all wheat marketing in the hands of the Board of Grain Supervisors, whose price offerings throughout the war averaged seventy cents per bushel more than exchange prices in 1916.[3] Farmers got a taste of the benefits that compulsory public marketing can bring.

To provide a transition from war to peace, a temporary Canadian Wheat Board was set up after the war, which farmers hoped might become permanent. Unfortunately it didn't, and, not long after it was wound down and the exchange resumed control, the bottom dropped out of the world wheat market. Prices fell by nearly two thirds. Farmers, many facing bankruptcy, responded by trying to set up voluntary marketing pools of their own to compete with the exchange and better its prices. But then came the coup de grace: the Great Depression struck. In the 1930–31 crop year, the pools lost $25 million and nearly collapsed.

It wasn't until 1935 that Ottawa could be persuaded to intervene and establish a voluntary version of the original Canadian Wheat Board. By this time the Terrible Decade was at its worst. Many prairie farmers, like their Oklahoma counterparts immortalized in John Steinbeck's *The Grapes of Wrath*, had joined the dispossessed. Evicted from their land, carrying their worldly belongings in Bennett Buggy pushcarts (named after the prime minister of the day), they trudged down the road looking for work. Many starved.

Sales through the Wheat Board, which could at least provide a measure of price stability, didn't become compulsory until 1943, spurred in part by the need—once again—to assure a steady grain supply during the war effort. After the Second World War, the infamous cost-price squeeze (mentioned in chapter 1) had begun again and was forcing families off the land at rates comparable to that of the '30s. The pressure to regulate the industry and maintain stable farm prices became irresistible.

Compulsory boards, some federal and some provincial, were established all across the country, regulating the production and sale of most agricultural products. Similar movements took place in other Commonwealth countries, and in parts of Western Europe. Individual producers were assigned a quota for what they grew, allowing them to produce a set amount of whatever commodity they specialized in, based on their actual production capacity. What they grew under their quotas had to be marketed by their boards, most under what was termed a "single-desk system," with all members getting the same price.

For awhile at least, things were better. Prices weren't spectacular, but at least they weren't gyrating chaotically as they had previously. It helped that similar board systems in other nations were also influencing world prices. Farmers could plan ahead, draw up reasonable budgets. Some families could actually earn a modest profit and live by farming alone. Others could do so with the help of off-farm income from some other, part-time, job, while farming remained the main income source.

If you listened hard enough, you could almost hear a sigh of relief.

Then the Serpent appeared in the Garden, coiled like the S in a dollar sign, flicking its forked tongue.

Original Sin

The original sin in this case was that people began to see quota not as a tool, a means to an end, but as a commodity having a value in itself. Quota was worth something, and before anyone knew what was happening, a movement was afoot to permit it to be bought and sold.

Something analogous had happened earlier with some of the leading non-farm labor unions. Their members began to see union membership as a commodity, to be handed on from parents to children, or bought and sold through the mechanism of expensive apprenticeship programs.

In farming, quota became part of the price of entry into the industry, along with the cost of tractors and machinery, barns and infrastructure, livestock and seed. And as the price of quota was bid upward, the entry fee became steeper and steeper, rising into the hundreds of thousands and, finally, millions of dollars. Instead of being a bulwark against the cost-price squeeze, quota became a part of it, making the squeeze all that much tighter. Eventually the cost of quota in some sectors rocketed so high that anyone wanting to farm—but who was not already a millionaire, or in a position to inherit quota from parents—would have to

take out such a large bank loan as to make themselves virtually lifetime debt-serfs.

Worse than that, those who had managed to amass large
amounts of quota started to dominate their own boards,
making it harder for potential competitors to enter, multi-
plying rules and regulations, and pressuring governments
to further protect their positions. Bureaucrats and politicians paid them particular heed.

Played out in real life, the results could be devastating,
with the full police powers of the state being used ruth-
lessly—just as they were in Harold Perry's rice wars of the
1980s or Shawn Brant's quarry battle of 2007. Canada's
native peoples are not the only ones against whom brute
force and the threat of jail are considered to be acceptable
tools.

Poultry farmer Shawn Carmichael's personal horror
story proves it.

Carmichael started young—and small—but it didn't take
long for him to be seen as a threat. He began with only 500
birds:

"It started out as a high school project," he said. "The
original ones I started with were ISA Browns [laying hens].[4]
Actually, before that I started out with 100 birds, but they
were meat birds. And then one thing led to another. The ISA
Browns had a little darker shell on them, a deep brown shell,
with dark yolks. People like the looks. With an egg 90 percent is the appearance, right? Now if they taste like crap they
won't buy them again, of course. But there was never a time
where I ever had extra eggs. Every week we sold out."

In those days, a farmer didn't need quota to have 500
birds.

"The cut off point was 500. Once you went above 500, there was a little gray area there. If it was 500 on a property, you were fine. I could have 500 on my place and 500 on my father's place. So technically 1,000 birds would have been the cut off."

Carmichael's birds were free-range.[5] "They were allowed to go outside. They had the option of going out but they could also stay in the barn. They were very healthy. And the quality of what we were feeding, everything was kept in what was called the closed-loop system. No inputs were brought onto the farm. It was kept on the farm. What was produced on the farm was fed back to the birds. Everything was in a closed loop. Same with the chicks. We bought little chicks and over the years we knew exactly what we were producing. So, like anything, if you look after it, it will look after you. You put garbage in, you get garbage out.

"Basically their diet was soybeans, corn, barley. We grew everything here, although we did buy in a mineral mix. And that mineral mix is basically all your vitamins and that's it. We had a portable hammer mill that we would grind the feed in. [We had] about 600 acres. We did a bit of cash cropping too."

The operation was not certified organic. "We never did go down that road," said Carmichael. "I got [interested in] it in the mid-eighties when it was starting to gather steam. And at the time I was really big on it and thought to go into it, but I just found they were starting to go askew. What I found was, especially when they got into the certification bodies, that they just kept lowering the rules, lowering the quality. I can remember there was a fellah, certifier out of Lindsay. He's a stand-up guy, and he was a certifier and he got sick of it because they just kept dumbing the rules down. And at the end of the day you might have had a stamp that said you were organic, but to me it didn't mean crap.

"What really mattered for me was the certification of the person, when I went and met my customers on a weekly basis. If they had any questions or concerns, they knew you, it was all going to come to that door on Friday at eleven o'clock. They didn't need a paper certification. They asked me. And that certified it for them. My customers knew that, so that was guarantee enough for them. We operated for fifteen years that way, [and eventually expanded] above 500. We were up to 15,000."

At that point, the board tried to make Carmichael buy quota. "We locked horns early on, OK, and early on, they agreed to disagree. They tried [to force him to buy quota]. And I told them if they forced me it would be met with. And I think that at the end of the day they felt that, let's just agree to disagree with this guy. He's just a little guy and at the end of the day it's just not going to be worth it. And rightfully so, after what all happened. I think they would wish they had of stuck to that plan.

"The silly thing was they weren't prepared for what they were going to meet that day, the day of the raid, the day they actually showed up at the farm here. And they looked so bad that day. And it was such a stupid move."

SWATted by the Crime Team

"The day of the raid, they got the CFIA involved, the Canadian Food Inspection Agency. The marketing board never had the balls to pony up to the job. So they called the feds to do the job for them. This is 2006. We had around 15,000

birds then. So the CFIA didn't want to do the actual dirty
work, but they would do the paperwork. So they called
a RAC team, a Rural Agricultural Crime Team, which is a
division of the Ontario Provincial Police. They actually followed me around Ottawa…" It was as if Farmer Carmichael
was a criminal, or some sort of "rustler."

"They followed me around, and I have all of the documentation from disclosure from the court case, because
I had to know all the evidence they had against me. And I
was floored when I saw this stuff. Couldn't believe it. I didn't
even know I was being followed around. They never came
right onto the property, but they ran surveillance on the
back road here. They would set up there and watch me all
day. Photographed me, photographed the car…"

Carmichael thought it was more than would have been
done in pursuit of a drug-smuggling operation. "Even
worse," he believes. "They wouldn't have pursued somebody
like they pursued me. They followed me around Ottawa,
followed me on all my deliveries, took inventory of the eggs
I was taking into the stores, would go into the stores, purchase the eggs, take them back to the lab, test them. Just
absolute, Gestapo nuts! Unbelievable.

"And then, typical bureaucrats, they actually flew down
to Nova Scotia, to where I bought my cartons. I had a supplier here who I bought my cartons from in Ottawa, but
they're manufactured in Nova Scotia. So they actually flew
down to Nova Scotia to meet with the plant manager down
there to verify that I was buying egg cartons."

The scene came to mind of Officer Obie in Arlo Guthrie's "Alice's Restaurant," painstakingly investigating and
photographing Arlo's load of garbage. Carmichael had no

idea why the cardboard cartons should matter, "other than that they get a nice, comfy trip to the east coast, on the taxpayer's dollar."

He continued: "So anyway, they had built up all this evidence against me, that proved that I was illegally producing eggs. And then, of course, they had to go to a judge and shop around and get a warrant. Now naturally a judge isn't going to just hand out a warrant to go into somebody's farm because they're producing eggs. That's too off the wall. So what they did was what they do quite often. They go judge shopping, and they find one they can convince and they get a warrant. So they ended up going all the way to St. Catherine's and they found a judge there and got him to sign a warrant so they could raid the farm.

"And that day they showed up here with the whole SWAT team. Bulletproof vests, sidearms. The only thing missing that day was the choppers. The only thing missing. About thirty officers here that day that descended on the farm. A little over a dozen patrol cars. I caught them on video, and the one fellah said to the other one, 'What's your budget for today?' and he said, 'Oh, $10,000, but we've blown that one all to hell.' So they came here and you can understand it was quite traumatic at the time.

"I have six young children. It was extremely traumatic for them and for my wife. It took us about two hours just to get over the shock. They brought in a transport, started loading the birds up on the transport, loaded up all the eggs I had in the coolers, throwing them around. Loaded them all up into a separate truck, come into the house, started going through all my files, took all my files, even went into the kids' bedrooms.

"And then at that point I said, OK, I've got to do something or they're going to drive me right into the ground like a fence post. They told me that I wasn't under arrest but I couldn't leave the house. And I said, well, you got two choices. You can either arrest me or I'm leaving the house. So they kind of stood in front of me, and I said, 'Get out of the way, or arrest me, one or the other.' They knew that they couldn't arrest me. They had nothing, no grounds to arrest me. They had a warrant for search and seizure, not to arrest. So I went out. The paperwork that I've got to back this up would make movies like you wouldn't believe. So on the way out I got on the cell phone and I called Randy [Hillier, of the small farm activists' Lanark Landowners Association, now a member of the Ontario provincial legislature; for more on the association, see chapter 10] and I said, 'Randy, this is what's going on.' He said, 'OK, hang tight, keep them there, we're on our way.' So I went out, and as soon as they heard me say 'Randy,' these bureaucrats, it was unbelievable, they dropped literally what they were doing and started running for their cars.

"The name 'Landowners' just sent shivers up their spine. So I said, 'I can't let them get out of here because the show hasn't started yet.' So I ran to the tractor. And of course all of them were going, we've got quite a long laneway here, all of them were heading down the laneway, right? By this time there was three media guys here, so they were catching it. Because I called them just about an hour afterwards. So it ended up being a footrace. I headed out in the field with the tractor and it was a footrace to see who was going to get to the end of the laneway, the tractor or their vehicles. And at the last minute, it was hilarious, because I was bombing down the fields and this frigging bureaucrat was looking out across from his vehicle at me, and he's thinking he's going to beat me to the end of the laneway. And we got to the end of the laneway, and I pulled the tractor up on top and that was it. Shut her down.

"[He] couldn't get out. They were all in the laneway. None of them could get out. So one of the police come over, and I opened the door, and he says, 'You're going to have to move the tractor.' So I said, 'No, the tractor's staying right where it is.' Well he said, 'You're going to have to make a choice, Shawn.' And I said, 'No, I think you're going to make the choice. But the tractor is not moving.' I put my hands out and I said, 'Put the cuffs on.' Meanwhile, a fellah from the [Ottawa] *Citizen,* a fellah from the [Ottawa] *Sun,* and this fellah from one of the farm papers were standing right there. They knew, we can't arrest this guy. First of all they know that they're on private property. They can't charge somebody with trespassing on [their own] private prop- erty. So there's no legal grounds that they could arrest me on. They couldn't arrest me for nuisance because I wasn't causing one. So he said, 'Shawn, I really want you to think about this,' and I said, 'No, the thinking's done. You're either going to arrest me or you're going to get the fuck off the tractor.' So he steps down off the tractor and he goes over and he talks to a couple of other officers and he comes back and he says, 'I really want you to think about this.' I said 'No, the thinking's done,' pulled the key out and stuck it in my pocket and started to get off the tractor. So they finally real- ized nobody's going. I said, 'We're running the show here. Nobody's leaving until we say so.' So at that point there was about twenty Landowners who had shown up. They were still coming. So then the OPP decided, OK, we've got to establish a perimeter. So they shut the road down at both concessions, so that nobody could get in or out. And their idea was to try and control the scene.

"So anyway, they're loading up all my birds, OK? This is one of their biggest fallbacks, they brought an 18-wheeler. But the problem was an 18-wheeler would only hold about 7,500 birds, and there was 15,000. They had no idea what was here, right? It was about seven o'clock. So they said 'Shit, we haven't got enough space to put these birds. What are we going to do?' So they tried to call in a second truck, but the truck was coming through Norwood, which is north of Toronto, so they said, 'There's no way we can get down there and be in and out of there by nightfall.'

"So what did they do, they make this stupid mistake by saying, 'OK, we're taking these birds. That's all there is to it. We're going to clean this guy out.' So they decided let's put twice as many birds in the cage. At the end of the day, you know what happened. The birds died."

Not a few people, witnessing such a scene, would have been tempted to start slugging policemen. "There was a couple that it almost come close to that," admitted Carmichael. "So anyway, I think it was about noon when we kind of had control of things, just waiting for Randy to show up and to try to get some more Landowners here to try to open up negotiations. Because at that point they shoved all of us to the end of the laneway, and I was there near the tractor. But they would no longer let anybody near the barns," even though they were Carmichael's own barns on his own property.

"That's when the camps were established," he continued. "They were kind of down here at the barns and that was their camp, and the laneway was our camp. And so Randy was out about one, two o'clock—that's when we started negotiating with them. And our first negotiation was, because they were adamant that they were taking everything—livestock, products, files, everything—and they were rolling out of here. So we said, 'No, the livestock we're going to save. The eggs are going to go back in the coolers.' And we would give them one case and some chickens for their evidence. And we would let a court decide as to my guilt. They were not going to be judge, jury, and executioner that day.

"So, long story short, of course they wouldn't agree to it. So I said, 'Nobody's leaving until we are satisfied.' We had the laneway blocked. And by this time there were a lot of media that were showing up. And I was saying to their chief negotiator, 'Every minute we sit here there's another bird dying. Do you want that on your head?' And he said, 'Oh no, the birds aren't dying.' So I said, 'OK, let us have a look.' And he let us go down to the barns, and I'm telling you I've never seen someone completely go off the deep end like he did, Randy [Hillier].

"Once he saw the condition of those birds he just lost it. I thought he was going to be in an all-out brawl with all of the police that were here. So anyway, we took the dead birds back in the laneway, and laid them in the laneway for all the media to see. And once the rest of the Landowners saw that, the decision was made that, OK, we're going to close down the laneway and we're going to unload that truck. And I think most of them figured that, if they're going to start shooting at us it was worth it. They were not going to let that happen. So we got three quarters of the way down the laneway and the chief policeman asked us to stop and he said, 'Listen, you can't do this.' And we said, 'It's too late for negotiating. You won't accept our position so we're going to unload that truck.' And the head of the RAC team there, he was screaming that they're breaking the law, you know, we have a warrant. And finally the chief of the negotiations there for the OPP, he was in the presence of mind enough to realize, he turned to us and he said, 'We're out of here. There's a possibility of violence. I'm not going to let that happen here today.' Seemed to have a fairly decent head on his shoulders.

"That was the funny thing. At three o'clock, there was quite a few officers down at our end we were talking to and we said, 'You got a choice. You can do what's right here today, or you can carry out the work of the devil.' And they told us that they did not want to be involved. It was basically Caledonia, all over again. The problem was there was this RAC team that was just way out of line. So finally he realized that it was that close to violence. And he said to them, the RAC guy, 'OK, you guys step aside, they're going to unload that truck and that's all there is to it.' And that's when they actually came to us and said, 'OK, tell us what to do. You guys are in control now.' And we said OK.

Carmichael and the Landowners had pulled the SWAT team's teeth.

"It was the first time that anybody had ever stood the marketing board on their head and turned it the other way. Because they've done this before. I'm not the first guy they've done this to. And every other time they've gotten away with it. Every other time, they'd roll in, drive you into the ground like a fence post, and roll out again. That was the problem. They should know better than to roll into eastern Ontario, where the Landowners group was strong. That was what they totally underestimated. And I think the other thing was they thought 'OK, we're just dealing with another dumb farmer, and we can roll over him.'

"I guess the best thing about it was the light that it shone on the marketing boards. The biggest thing that came out of it was the *Reader's Digest* article. It blew them out of the water, just blew them out of the water. They had the audacity to turn around and say that *Reader's Digest* was a mediocre type of tabloid magazine. And this Brian Kaplan that wrote the article, he didn't hold back at all. He pulled no punches. He explained so the average Canadian out there could understand about marketing boards and the way they operate."

Buying the required quota for his birds would have been impossible, explains Carmichael, noting that the price would have been two million: "Two million dollars! Why would I be farming? If I had $2 million I wouldn't be getting up seven days a week to farm. [For meat birds, as opposed to egg producers, the minium start-up quota in 2006 was 75,152 birds, costing $850,000.[6]] The sad reality is that people are locked in it now. They're in debt to their eyeballs. They've indebted not only their children but their grand-children into it. To me, why are you doing this? It just does not make any sense whatsoever. And the industry is suffering terribly for it. When an industry becomes heavily weighted in debt, sooner or later it collapses. Because it can't service the debt anymore."

Nor can it attract new entrants, as students at Everdale Organic Farm and Environmental Learning Centre, a training program for young farmers located in Hillsburgh, Ontario,[7] made plain in an interview. The students, every one of them highly motivated and several coming originally from urban backgrounds, were unanimous that none could afford to enter a quota-governed branch of the industry.

"Stewarding the land was what I was drawn to," said Brenda Hsueh, 33. "I'd like to raise sheep and goats, and do dairy products and textiles. They're under the [government] radar now, and I'd like to get them running before the radar gets turned on. But we [Everdale students] are trying to avoid the quota industries."

Avoid the quota industries, and escape the notice of government. Such are the aims of young people today—particularly university graduates, like most of Everdale's student body, who want to enter farming.

The standoff at Carmichael's farm, meanwhile, was far from the end of the matter. The legal battle continued, and eventually degenerated into charges of physical violence, not on Carmichael's part, but that of the government.

"We went into Ottawa to deliver a subpoena to the CFIA, and these are federal bureaucrats. One of them took a swing at me [the later complaint indicated it was a commissionaire]. I still remember sitting in the police station, filing charges against these bureaucrats, all for trying to deliver a subpoena to their head office. There was so many turning events that happened to me throughout the whole thing, it was so bizarre. I could write two or three novels."

According to the *Ottawa Citizen,* police "refused to lay charges" in the alleged assault case.[8]

In the end, the whole battle with the boards proved futile. "They put us out of business," said Carmichael. "At the end of the day, that's the legislation, and the powers that they have. It's the law. But that doesn't mean the law is just."

"They even launched a second raid into here. And that ended in them walking into an empty barn where they thought there was all these chickens. Ended up having egg on their face again. But I ended up getting charged for the dangerous driving of a combine. It was pretty bizarre...It's unfortunate. When you make them look bad, they just dig their heels in...We landed in the Senate on the first of May last year [2006], and were able to talk to the Senate about the issues. It was this huge victory for us. We won in federal court our case against the CFIA..."

Carmichael estimates he's lost "hundreds of thousands" of dollars in the fight, while the toll on his family has been high.

"That's something you can't measure. Like, my children were all here when they originally swooped down on us with the SWAT team. And to this day, my son can't go to an assembly at school for fear of being in an enclosed place. He just totally fears these places. He's six. I wish more people would stand up. But unfortunately, most people just seem to walk around in a daze. They just accept it, and say there's nothing I can do about it. When actually there's something they can." And now that the dust has settled, how is the family coping?

"We're getting by, doing a bit of cash cropping..."

Sadly, Carmichael's story is not unusual in Ontario. For years, similar things have been happening all across the province, to people producing nearly every type of agricultural commodity, from milk to hogs. Nor is the part that government manipulation of marketing boards plays in wiping out small producers limited to Ontario. In Manitoba, as noted in chapter 3, governmental emasculation of that province's hog marketing board in 1996 by eliminating its single-desk selling powers wiped out 54 percent of Manitoba hog farmers.

But the situation in poultry—not only in Ontario, but equally so in British Columbia, where board rules are quite similar (see below)—remains one of the best illustrations of the overall problem in the farm product quota industries. The number, complexity, and sheer pettiness of the attacks on small-scale poultry producers, the absurdity of the excuses given for these attacks, and the nature and extent of the damage they do, put the problem in stark relief. They also make it only too clear who ultimately benefits—and it's certainly not the egg- or meat-buying consumer looking for quality in food.

Larry Robinson, of the Ontario Small Farm Producers Association, and Ken Frey, of Frey's Hatchery Ltd., elaborate:

"[When] the broiler breeder industry started off, there was no value to quota," said Frey. "If you sold your farm and you had broiler breeder quota into it, they went out and did an appraisal of your property and if they felt there was anything in there for quota, they said, 'OK purchaser, you may buy it but we will not give you the right to have that quota. That quota gets handed back to the board.' But after six, eight years, there was too much lobbying behind it, 'let's make quota valued.' The chicken board had rules in place that you could only own so much quota. Well, they had lawyers that all they did was move quota around in companies, to different companies, so the chicken board couldn't find out. And the board realized they're paying a pile of lawyers' fees just to try to track these guys down, and they [concluded], 'We're always a step behind them. So we'll just get rid of the rule. It'll cost us less.'"

Once the door was opened to buying and selling quota, the largest producers quickly gained control. "There are approximately 1,100 quota holders for meat chickens in Ontario," said Robinson, "and nobody's anywhere near the start-up minimum [of 125,000 birds]. They're way over it. Except for twelve small producers—out of 1,100—who they gave exemptions, and are holding them up as a banner of how they're flexible."

The same kind of dominance by large producers is also the rule in British Columbia, as poultry farmer Maria Castro, of Nanaimo, testified. A specialist in rare birds, Castro is a former director of Rare Breeds Canada.

"They should have never have allowed quota to be bought and sold," she said. "But now, people have invested. It's very difficult to change now. It's becoming more and more a closed shop. The biggest guys buy out the ones that fail along the way, and they have more and more quota concentration in a smaller and smaller pool of people. There are so many vested interests.

"At the moment, it's not supply management [where the amount of a commodity available to the market dictates price]. It's a cartel [a syndicate or conspiracy formed to fix prices]. There's so much money involved, huge, huge financial stakes.

"What happens now is, only the quota-holding producers are allowed to vote for [candidates for membership of the executive of] the marketing board. They're the only ones that actually get representation. But then the board makes the orders that affect everybody who grows. We have a situation where a very small group of people is allowed to make the rules for everybody else. It's undemocratic."

As control passed to the large producers, the regulations governing quota, production, health and safety, sales, and every other aspect of the industry multiplied. Any small-scale grower wanting to enter the industry was confronted not only with the impossible cost of quota, but with the difficulty of obtaining it.

"With turkey and chickens, you have to find a producer willing to sell you quota," said Robinson. "But the [Ontario] board won't even give you the names of the people who are producing. You're in a catch-22 situation. You have to get it from an individual who's selling, but they won't give you the names of any individuals under the Privacy Act. So you can't find any producers."

If an industry entrant should try to get started without quota, he or she will be faced with a welter of complications resembling what University of Waterloo sociology professor Kenneth Westhues has dubbed "Kafka circuits,"[9] a seemingly endless series of bureaucratic hurdles that force their victims to run around in circles, getting nowhere. The rules have changed repeatedly, and are still changing, but at various times have crossed well over into the realm of the surreal.

"At one time, it was legal for you to buy a meat chicken from me, raise it, kill it, cook it, and eat it," said Frey. "But if you took a piece of that meat and put it in a sandwich and walked out and put it in your car and drove off your property, you were breaking the law. The marketing board made a law that you cannot eat any part of that chicken anywhere other than your own home." A grower "couldn't even give it to his kids to take to school for lunch," without the possibility that police would come to the school, burst into the cafeteria, and arrest the child for eating "contraband."

As for eggs, Robinson said: "Ungraded eggs or any other product that's supposed to be sold from the farm, it's only legal to sell it from the home door, in front. Not from any stand outside, not from an outbuilding or anything else. It's never allowed from anywhere but the door of the house."

The term "graded egg" has been ingeniously exploited by the boards, both legally and in public relations terms, Robinson explains: "[Grading is] the size of the egg, and it's looking for cracks in the shell; it's looking for blood spots [in the yolk]. It's cosmetic and it's size." In short, mere physical appearance.

"Grading eggs is not a health issue. It has nothing to do with health and safety," he adds.

According to board regulations, every egg producer who sells eggs must first grade them, and this requires a separate "grading facility." The number of chickens and eggs produced is immaterial. All must meet this requirement, as well as adhere to a multitude of other regulations.

"If you go on the website for these things, you'll find that there's thirty-eight pages of rules for grading eggs," said Robinson. "I've read through it and I don't know what you'd have to have, the patience of Job. One of the hundreds of rules is that you cannot chew gum while you're grading eggs. The building has to be separate from all other buildings. It can't be attached to a barn or a shed or any other building. It has to have its own entranceway. It has to have a set size drain, set size windows. There have to be separate rooms, one for grading and one for storing. Storage has to be cold storage. And what is bizarre is, if the egg is ungraded it has to be in a set temperature, and if it's graded it has to be in a different temperature, a few degrees different. It's supposed to then be in another room. Once it's graded it has to be in its own room."

Robinson recounts the tale of how grading rules hurt another egg producer, also a member of the Small Farm Producers Association: "He had a AAA rating, which is the highest you can get, and your rating dictates what price you can charge for your eggs. They came there [to inspect] and he said they saw a little crack in the paint in the corner on the ceiling in his grading room. And they knocked him down to AA. Once you're knocked down to AA, then it's going to be visited twice a year. The next month they came back and they knocked him down to a single A because his balance beam on his scale was aluminum and it was corroding a little bit. The next month they came and took away his last A because, as he said, 'Wouldn't you know it! What kind of unbelievable luck'—he was washing eggs, and the sink plugged just as the guy came in. He had that sink unplugged in five minutes, but the guy marked him down. And each time you lose, you're one year before you can appeal to get it back. You're [operating] at a loss for a full year."

Large, industrial-scale producers don't have such problems, he explains. "The big producers, first of all, have the facility and equipment and all the things they're supposed to have, because they can afford it, because they're producing hundreds of thousands. But the little guy can't afford that system. And the big producers [also] have enough clout and enough power—one of them is producing 60 percent of the eggs for Ontario—that they can't just ram in and shut them down. I've also known quite a number of inspectors over the years, and they've made it clear that when you work in a sector where you're going to a big plant, one guy told me, he said *no inspector has survived ratting out or telling on a big slaughterhouse.*"

A former inspector in the meat industry, who asked that his name not be revealed, corroborated this claim. In a recorded telephone interview with the author, he said that citing a major industrial meat producer with violations would likely cost an inspector his or her job.

As for having someone else do the grading of your eggs, instead of doing it yourself and meeting all thirty-eight pages of regulations, that too is impossible. "The government, if it requires grading, should be responsible for providing grading facilities for small growers," said Robinson. "And there are none. So you've got a law that says you can't market without grading, but there's no place to get them graded." Unless, of course, you meet all thirty-eight pages of rules, and never have a crack in your paint.

The same is true in B.C., according to Castro. "The [B.C.] chicken marketing board I can deal with," she said. "But the egg marketing board is horrible. The way the rules of the board are applied, they act like a bunch of Nazis. There is the whole business of grading, trying to prevent people from selling ungraded eggs. But there are no grading stations! They unfortunately manage to persuade most of the public health people that this is a health issue, when it's not. And they don't make any distinction between birds that are breeding birds and birds that are of various ages. They're very restrictive and inflexible."

Goodbye Free-range, Heritage Breeds

The system also poses a direct threat not only to small growers and specialty hatcheries, but also to the very idea of raising free-range birds—whose meat and eggs have been shown to be superior to those of battery-raised poultry—as well as to the goal of preserving the genetic heritage of rare breeds.

"One of our customers, who has been with us for a number of years, decided he would jump through the hoops and get quota a year ago," said Robinson. "So he applied. He was going to raise organically grown, outdoors, free-range birds. And they came and told him he had to have, even though they were supposed to be free-range, he had to have a complete set-up of acceptable indoor facilities, in case there was a disease outbreak or something, so they could be kept indoors."

In other words, he had to set up a non-free-range facility that he doesn't use, in order to have permission to do a free-range operation.

"He just told them to chuck it," said Robinson.

The Canadian Food Inspection Agency (CFIA) makes it even harder. Its regulations governing poultry production are set out in a publication titled *Bird Health Basics: How to Prevent and Detect Diseases in Backyard Flocks*. Robinson elaborates:

"The rules say 'every exempt [namely non-quota] grower shall produce chickens in accordance with the standards set out by the CFIA.' The very first rule in those regulations is that your poultry cannot be exposed to any wild birds or animals. Which means that you can't have anything free-range or outdoors." Raising free-range chickens is thus expressly outlawed by the federal government, unless of course you are a millionaire quota holder with a minimum of 125,000 birds!

"I've argued with them for hours," said the exasperated Robinson. "Every outbreak around the world [of so-called avian flu] has been occurring in these large corporate farms. One genetic strain, huge numbers of birds all in a confined space, no immunity, no resistance because they're in germ-free barns, and once something gets in there it just spreads like wildfire. So now they want us to do the same thing. They want us to make our birds more susceptible!"

Castro agreed. "At the CFIA seminars on poultry bio-security, they hand out these leaflets. The first thing in the leaflets says you must separate your birds from any wild animals. That means having them in cages. No more free-range birds." And no more humane growing conditions.

She sees the rule as biologically self-defeating. "How do you encourage people to breed for disease resistance when you're making them keep everything locked up and indoors? It's the opposite of what we should be doing."

The situation is akin to that created by the decades-long practice of suppressing all forest fires, to prevent losses by large timber companies. In actuality, wildfires are natural and for centuries have simply burned off dead wood and trash, in limited areas, thus allowing forests overall to flourish. There are even species of pine that cannot reproduce unless there is a fire, which makes their cones pop open and releases their seeds. By suppressing all fire, huge amounts of dead trashwood are allowed to accumulate, thus guaranteeing that when a fire finally does start, it will be of colossal proportions.

Factory poultry operations, by suppressing all possibility of disease—and thus all possibility of birds developing resistance—guarantee that when an outbreak occurs it will be devastating. It's a bit like trying to keep all human children in hermetically sealed, germ-proof bubbles, preventing them from catching even the most fleeting common cold. If they ever try to leave their bubbles, the first bacteria or virus they encounter—chicken pox, for instance, or measles—would lay every single one of them low in a massive pandemic. It's a recipe for disaster.

As for genetic diversity—a mechanism that even the most elementary biology student knows is necessary for the survival of species—officials of some poultry marketing boards appear to consider it of no importance, or even as a thing to be deliberately stamped out.

"Rare breeds are not considered important, essential, or anything else in Ontario," said Robinson. "I'm the only distributor [of such breeds] and they don't want me doing it. Rare Breeds Canada went to the marketing boards a few years ago on my behalf to try to get exemptions for rare breeds. They scoffed, they laughed. They said no deal, no way. They weren't going to do it. Roy Crawford was a professor at Saskatchewan University [University of Saskatchewan]. He had quite a number of rare breeds there, chickens, ducks, geese, and turkeys. When Roy retired he approached me and asked me to take a hundred Ridley Brown poults, and start that breed going. I said it's not legal. Even though I have licenses coming out my ying-yang, I can't have more than ten. So Rare Breeds said they would go to the boards and fight them. They spent a year, and the answer was constantly no, no exemptions. We don't care if they're rare breeds. We don't care. It doesn't matter. And they wouldn't do it.

"The fellah that was running the Chicken Farmers of Ontario then—he's since left—insisted and insisted in every conversation we had that people like me were the problem, because small farms, mixed farms, rare breeds, and varieties were just tantamount to disaster. We were going to break down the industry by destroying the corporate farms, by spreading disease to them because we had no biosecurity. And I said one day, 'When you have only one genetic strain of birds and something happens that you lose that entire strain, you're going to have to come back to people like me to start over again.' And he just laughed."

"There is a federal animal health strategy being developed," noted Castro. "We [Rare Breeds Canada] are not even being consulted. They are not even thinking about livestock genetic diversity."

As with other domesticated livestock, there are—or were—thousands of breeds of poultry, each with its own genetic advantages. Some are resistant to particular poultry diseases, some thrive in drought conditions, others in cold, some produce large eggs, some small, some have more white meat, or grow faster than others, and some are just plain physically beautiful, worth keeping for the simple aesthetic pleasure of looking at them. The Silver-Spangled Hamburg, Silver Gray Dorking, and Redcap are unforgettable sights. But they—and the Barred Rocks, Scots Dumpys, Derbyshire Redcaps, Croad Langshans, Black Australorps, Hungarian Yellows, and so many, many others—are all seen as expendable. And that doesn't even begin to mention the multitude of breeds of ducks, geese, and turkeys.

Ontario's major hatcheries and largest factory farms are gradually moving toward a system that utilizes an extremely narrow genetic band. "They take a strain, and use the females in that strain," said Robinson. "And they take another strain and use the males. And they cross them, and the young they get, they'll take the females from them. And they use the same type of system to get males. Then they take the [resulting] males and females and cross them. It's called a terminal cross."

All the birds are hybrids, "four-way crosses, over two generations." Some farmers refer to them, pejoratively, as "mud birds," or "no-names."

"With chickens, there used to be multitudes of hatcheries all across Ontario, a lot of smaller hatcheries, and it's all gone," said Robinson. "There're only three small, independent hatcheries left, but the marketing boards have been fighting them tooth and nail for quite awhile. As for the big hatcheries, they're gigantic. Four hatcheries in Ontario: Maple Lodge, Maple Leaf, Cargill, and Stratford."

In fact, an increasing amount of control over the Canadian poultry industry—and all of Canadian agriculture—is passing into non-Canadian hands.

"The other scary thing I've been finding out lately is that with chickens, with turkey, with milk, a lot of the quota is held by foreigners, in Germany and elsewhere," said Robinson. "They own the quota. And they rent it back to the farmers because the farmers can't afford to buy their own quota. In western Ontario, a lot of the big chicken and turkey producers no longer own their land or their buildings or anything. Many of the farmers are now tenant farmers. They manage the farms. They don't own the birds.

"And basically now, in the world, there are only two companies that control all of the genetics for the [corporate] egg-laying industry." Both are in Europe.

Agribusiness: The Main Players

The international food industry, from seed to dinner plate, is dominated at all levels by large multinational corporations, most of them headquartered in the United States or the European Union. Many of these corporations have interlocking directorates—that is, the members of the board of one firm also sit on the boards of other companies with different specialities. Although competitors, technically speaking, there is often a high degree of cooperation between the major players, particularly in regard to prices and political policy. In short, they form an economic oligopoly, in which a small number of producer/sellers dominate the market.

Where food is concerned, eight corporate sectors are involved: pharmaceuticals, animal or veterinary pharmaceuticals, biotechnology, seeds, pesticides/herbicides, food retail, food and beverage processing, and nanotechnology. Several firms are leaders in more than one sector, such as the Swiss-based Syngenta, which in 2005 was the world's second-largest pesticide producer and the third-largest seed producer. The U.S.-based Monsanto is the world's leading seed producer, second-largest biotech company, and fifth-largest pesticide maker. Each transnational company may operate subsidiaries in different countries, with a variety of local titles.

A number of leading banks provide financing for the industry, but a few, such as the Netherlands-based Rabobank, specialize in food and agriculture financing.

For a detailed description of the industry's leadership structure, see *Oligopoly, Inc.*, a report published and updated periodically by the activist ETC Group (www.etcgroup.org). The group's most recent survey was completed in 2005.

THE SITUATION IS part of an overall trend toward major-fund investment in agriculture, which increased sharply in 2008 in the wake of the bio-fuels craze and the resulting food price bubble. Not only were institutional and other non-farmer investors attracted to the farm sector, but national governments were as well. Their favored investment vehicle was the so-called "sovereign wealth fund," which permits foreign governments to buy farm land in other countries without revealing their identities.

New York Times senior financial writer Diana Henriques has been following the trend. "You have some sovereign wealth funds," she says. "These are the investment vehicles for some national governments . . . All of the big hedge funds and investment partnerships that I've talked to, who are marketing new farmland investment funds, are marketing them to the word's sovereign wealth funds." An example, she said, was "China investing in African land, Nigeria in particular." [10]

The North American Free Trade Agreement (NAFTA) made things still worse in the Canadian poultry industry.

"When the free trade treaty went through, 10 percent of all Canadian chickens had to come from the U.S.," explained Robinson. "They must. So if you have quota, and you don't bring in 10 percent of those either as eggs or chicks from the States, then next year you only have 90 percent of that quota. And the next year, if you don't bring in the 10 percent, you have another 10 percent less."

Quota's End

The large, factory-farm producers and the marketing boards they increasingly dominate have developed relatively positive relations with both government and the corporate food sector, cooperating in a variety of areas. For example, the website of the non-profit charity Ontario Agri-Food Education, Inc. notes that the charity receives its baseline funding from the Ontario Ministry of Agriculture, Food and Rural Affairs (OMAFRA). It also posts a list of corporate donors, which includes such food industry heavy hitters as: Agribrands Purina Canada Inc., Bayer Crop Science, Campbell Company of Canada Ltd., Dow Agrosciences Canada, Maple Leaf Foods, Pioneer Hi-Bred Limited, Syngenta Crop Protection Canada Inc., Monsanto Canada Inc., Bank of Montreal Agri Business, Canadian Imperial Bank of Commerce, Ontario Mutual Insurance Association, Scotiabank Agri-Business Banking, TD Canada Trust and most of the province's agricultural marketing boards or associations, including those for producers of chickens, cattle, fruit and vegetables, maple syrup, mushrooms, milk, eggs, pork, turkeys, potatoes, soybeans, wheat, and veal.

Despite such cooperation, and what are sometimes mutual short-term political interests, marketing boards and the multinational corporations they sell their products to are fundamentally at odds. By the very nature of things, buyers and sellers always are, with sellers looking to raise prices and buyers hoping to lower them. Whether the sellers are struggling family farmers, or marketing boards dominated by large, industrial-scale producers, is irrelevant. Corporate buyers will naturally seek to undercut them.

And thus it is that, as the global push for free trade has grown in strength, beginning with the earliest negotiating rounds of the General Agreement on Tariffs and Trade (GATT) and culminating in the creation of the World Trade Organization (WTO), a simultaneous push to curb the power of marketing boards, and eventually to eliminate them altogether, has gained strength. The pressure comes chiefly from the largest multinational food mega-corporations, whose most effective instruments for bringing pressure in trade talks have been a bloc of European Union (EU) countries, and the U.S. government.

In the EU, this pressure has already resulted in a series of "reforms" to the EU's Common Agricultural Policy (CAP). Of course, when the corporate sector or right-wing politicians use the word reform, it most often means "eradication" or "elimination." Thus, "welfare reform" means scrapping welfare; "government health insurance reform" means eliminating government-paid health insurance, and "labor reform" means eradicating unemployment benefits and weakening labor unions.

Recounting the gradual and quite complex economic and political process by which the EU's marketing board system has been weakened over the years, especially in the dairy sector, would take more space than is available here. Suffice it to say that the process will come close to culmination in the year 2015, when all dairy quota in the EU is to be "reformed"— that is to say, eliminated. After 2015, there will no longer be a supply-management system that uses quota to influence prices and give milk producers bargaining power in the market place. Producers, whether large or small, will be utterly at the mercy of the market and the multinationals.

"Quotas do not sharpen competitiveness; they stifle it," said EU Agriculture and Rural Development Commissioner Mariann Fischer Boel. "They should go."[11] Those whose competitiveness this will improve, however, won't be small farmers, but the corporate giants.

As reported in *Food Production Daily:*

> Abolishing milk quotas is likely to help larger dairy
> producers and processors to expand, speeding up the
> consolidation trend within the sector, said a report
> by Siemen Van Berkum delivered to the World Dairy
> Forum. The report also speculated that phasing quotas
> out as early as 2009 may help larger firms become more
> competitive, although this would further reduce milk
> prices paid to producers in the short term.[12]

Pressure is building in Canada from right-leaning, busi-
ness-oriented think tanks like the Montreal Economic Institute (MEI) for a similar series of "reforms" here. The MEI, in
various reports overseen by its director of research, Valentin
Petkantchin, stresses that:

> The "supply management" model in agricul-
> ture...was first applied in Australia in the 1920s to pro-
> tect farmers' incomes against economic swings and
> lower prices for their products as well as to increase
> their power in relation to buyers. Supply management,
> which is held out today as an indispensable element of
> Canadian agricultural policy, is in reality a needlessly
> costly system, particularly where dairy production is
> concerned.[13]

Petkantchin insists that "the supply management system
in Canada's dairy industry will have to be reformed in the
longer term," because it "stifles entire industries that have to
pay more for their milk." [14] Pay farmers more, that is.

Similar arguments are made by frequent MEI contributor Sylvain Charlebois, now an associate professor of marketing at the University of Regina. An outspoken critic of supply management, he has attacked "the questionable economic functions"[15] of the Canadian Dairy Commission (CDC).

"Severely criticized by many members of the World Trade Organization, the CDC has demonstrated serious supply management inefficiencies, with its price fixing mechanisms and quota setting powers," he writes, adding that "too many dairy producers tend to protect themselves and to balk at the need for market efficiencies."[16] In fact, small farmers appear to him—much as they do to Gary Blumenthal (mentioned in chapter I)—to be mere sentimental anachronisms:

> We must consider lingering nostalgic attitudes towards dairy farming in Canada. Many stakeholders in the dairy industry believe that farming is more than just a business. This sentiment suggests that if a farmer fails, the soul of the country fades away. Future policy processes related to dairy marketing in Canada would not only need to disengage itself [sic] from that mislead- ing paradigm, it would also need to include the inter- ests of all stakeholders mentioned in the first part of this paper.[17]

Those additional stakeholders, whose interests he defends, are "comprised of the top dairy processors in Canada, such as Kraft, Agropur, Ultima Foods and Danone."[18]

Charlebois and his like-minded colleagues are equally critical of other marketing boards, including the Canadian Wheat Board (CWB). And their message has been taken to heart by Canada's political conservatives, at both provincial and national levels. Many defenders of the family farm saw the 2006 attack by Stephen Harper's Tory government on the CWB as no more than the opening shot in a long-term campaign to take Canada down the road toward complete deregulation of agriculture, leaving small-scale producers with no way to defend their interests. Rather than rehabilitate the existing system—which admittedly badly needs it—the plan appears to be to eliminate it altogether, returning to the free-for-all, merciless, bad old days of the exchange.

When the Tories under Stephen Harper were elected in 2006, they moved to weaken the CWB by removing its single-desk marketing powers over sales of barley—much as Manitoba's Tories had moved earlier to eliminate the single-desk powers of that province's hog board—and to turn the board's control of Canadian malt and feed barley over to the globally dominant grain multinationals. The CWB was likely picked because it is one of the largest, best-known, and powerful of the nation's marketing boards, and because a minority of Western barley producers had been voicing dissatisfaction with it in the wake of price fluctuations for barley on the world market.

As the NFU's *Union Farmer Monthly* warned, the "moves against barley will be quickly followed by similar moves against wheat. The loss of the CWB's wheat and barley marketing advantages will cost a typical prairie grain farm $10,000 to $20,000 per year. And if the CWB goes, supply management becomes much more vulnerable."[19]

When the board's directors publicly defended the single-desk system, they were slapped with a gag order, and when board president Adrian Measner spoke out anyway, he was fired. The firing was followed by an announcement by federal agriculture minister Chuck Strahl that regulations to remove the cwb's authority over barley sales would be imposed through a cabinet order. However, in August 2007 federal court judge Dolores Hansen struck down the regulations on grounds that such rules could only be enacted by a vote of the full federal Parliament. She accepted the cwb's argument that farmers, not the federal Cabinet, were given control of the board when Parliament amended the Canadian Wheat Board Act in 1998.

Board supporters were relieved, but knew it was only a temporary reprieve.

Minister Strahl vowed not to give up, but to continue with efforts to curb the board's authority. "We'll consider everything from appeals to [new] legislation and everything in between," he said. "We're determined to move ahead with this." [20]

Strahl's successor as agriculture minister, Gerry Ritz, continued the same policy, vowing to introduce legislation to curb the cwb's single-desk marketing authority. He called a January 29, 2008 meeting between the cwb directors and representatives of what he called "farmer and industry interests" to urge the directors to endorse the coming legislative proposal. [21] At the closed-door meeting were representatives of the Western Grain Elevator Association, an organization of western Canada's largest grain companies, including industry giant Cargill; the Malting Industry Association of Canada, whose members include Cargill and Archer Daniels Midland, and Grain Vision, another industry organization with ties to Cargill, Pioneer Hi-Bred, and James Richardson

International (the latter apparently shares the same Winnipeg office with Grain Vision).[22]

"It is now clear that some of the world's biggest grain, malt and brewing corporations are behind and beside Gerry Ritz," the NFU editorialized in its newsletter.[23]

A Wider Attack

The see-saw battle over marketing boards and quota, however crucial to Canadian farmers' future, was not the only arena where government made small farmers' lives difficult. Producers who had not fallen afoul of any marketing board were attacked on other fronts. The favorite tool of those doing the assaulting in this wider attack was a near-fanatical application of health, environmental, or building code regulations.

Prescott, Ontario vintners Gene and Marsha Countryman and their son Eli have been dealing with this kind of hostility for years, first while trying to succeed as market gardeners and then as developers of a high-quality line of fruit wines. Marsha Countryman recounts the story of the family's attempts to succeed on their 83.5-acre farm, first with market vegetable gardening:

"[We started] with market gardening, growing fruits and vegetables for local farmers' markets in Brockville and Prescott, and at the farm. At one time we were supplying a substantial nursing home, and we were dealing with the purchasing agent and everything was going on fine. Then he got sick and died and they brought a new person in during the winter. Everything was fine at first and we put everything [crops] in the ground.

"And then they cut us off. We had all this produce and no market for it. We were growing it exactly for them.

"We were preparing the produce for them. It was all cleaned, washed, snapped, cut, the corn was all husked. All they did was pick it up, dump it in their pot and give it to the residents that night. They got it fresh everyday. We were peeling the potatoes for them and everything. We did green and yellow beans, broccoli, cauliflower and sweet corn, tomatoes, cucumbers. And then they didn't want to deal with us anymore, because the government said they [the nursing home] had to have a dietician on staff, or find a food supplier that did have a dietician. And they went to a company in Toronto, called Aramark. They're quite a big outfit."

In fact, Aramark is a U.S.-based multinational corporation with some 240,000 employees, doing business in 18 countries. According to its website, Aramark's fiscal 2007 total sales were $12.4 billion.[24]

The nursing home wasn't the farm's only customer, however, and the family struggled on.

"It was 2004, and we were still growing a fair amount of vegetables, and we got caught in the potato crunch. We had around 10 or 12 acres of potatoes in. The exchange on the dollar, and there was some sort of a blight in New Brunswick, so the Americans stopped [importing] them, so they were shipping them all up here. They [New Brunswick potatoes] flooded the market. We had been selling our potatoes for $15.50 for a 50-pound bag, and they dropped it down to $4.50. So we took 2,000 or 3,000 bags back in the bush and dumped them. We figured we lost about $60,000 in potential income that year. Then in 2005 we had about 7.5 acres in strawberries. Because it turned so hot in June, 30 degrees day and night, we got them all in ten days. So we couldn't market them fast enough to keep them freshly picked. And a lot of them rotted in the fields. We actually had about two acres that never even saw a picker of any kind. We were really quite upset. We said, 'We got to do something. We can't keep on taking this kind of a loss,' because that was about 4,000 baskets of berries that never made it to market.

"Our farm is our only source of income.

"Well, we had some set aside for making strawberry wine for our own use. So we said, 'Maybe we should have harvested those berries and started making wine.' We'd been making jam and all that kind of stuff. So we talked it over, did a little investigating, and found out what we had to have. At that time OMAFRA had come out with a book, *Starting a Winery in Ontario*. So we sent in for their book. For our market research, I went to my contacts at city hall, for the economic development sector for the city and province. They said that fruit wines were the up-and-coming thing. We already had the fruit, raspberries and strawberries and blueberries, and saskatoon."

As for wine-making equipment, "we had to scrounge, because we didn't have a lot of dollars. We started out with five-gallon pails and carboys. But we found that every pail, even though we measured the ingredients all throughout, it came off at a different time, a little different flavor. So we went to 45-gallon barrels, and we blend them in one large volume, so it's all the same.

"You have to have some wine already made to get your manufacturer's permit, and we had to send in a sample to the Liquor Control Board of Ontario (LCBO) lab. If it passes their lab, then there are three or four steps in the permit process, and then you have to apply for an on-site retail outlet permit. We just got our [approval] this past weekend, confirming our first wine with the LCBO for Strawberry Delight.

It took us almost nine months. We have thirteen stores that we can deliver to. We have to supply a minimum of ten to start with. You have to make sure you have enough volume to supply ten stores, year-round. To get your manufacturer's license you have to have a minimum of five acres of fruit year-around. We have 8.5 acres of strawberries right now, for fifteen stores."

The nine-month process was longer than expected, and not all of the LCBO staff were helpful. "It's supposed to take six weeks," said Countryman. "We waited and waited and didn't hear anything. Fortunately for us we have a local store manager that is very interested in carrying our wines. He'd like to get more of our products in. He couldn't even answer the questions [on the application form], and he's used to working with the board. So he went back to his store and he contacted his head office and got the information and helped us fill it out. And he was quite disappointed that we got no response. [Finally] he got us a name and number.

"Whether we contacted them on a bad day, or whatever, they were quite terse and not very helpful. So we went to our MPP [member of Provincial Parliament] about it. And I had been in touch with Jim Warren of Fruit Wines of Ontario, and said what had happened. He called the person I'd been talking to on the phone and gave him shit, gave him a rough time, and after that they were quite pleasant about things.

"They don't come out and tell you all the stuff that you need to do, or what the next step is. But Jim Warren told us, 'Don't give up.'"

It would seem that a branch of the provincial government should be bending over backward to help local producers, but Countryman laments, "They're not. They're only interested in large volumes that they don't have to do a lot with. Fruit Wines of Ontario have come up with what they call a 'QC' program, quality certified, done through the LCBO, through their labs and their tasting panel. You have to pay for it. They insisted that our wine had to go through the QC system. Which we did. Got a very nice score on it. But they still didn't want to recognize it. We applied for approval in April, and got our final letter of approval this weekend, December. The letter added that whatever the retail price of our wine is in their store, they take the first 58 percent and then we get what's left."

After working, fighting bureaucrats, and waiting eight months for approval, more than half the profits were taken by government. But at least Countryman could now sell fruit wine through the LCBO. "Just the one variety though, Strawberry Delight. None of the others. We cannot direct-sell to other licensees, either. There's some varieties we don't intend to put in, because getting the volume is too labor-intensive. Like our melon wines, watermelon, very labor-intensive. We have several high-end restaurants in our area that would really like to carry some of our wines, so they can serve something different. But we can't sell to them because the LCBO won't let us. There are quite a few people who are surprised that we've been able to get [even one wine] into the LCBO as it is. They figured it would take us four or five years."

Getting approval from the LCBO and other liquor authorities, however, turned out to be the least of the hurdles the family would have to jump. A far more implacable foe soon put in an appearance: there was a visit from the local health authorities.

"How that got started, this year we had difficulty getting in the berry crop. So we brought in three offshore workers from Jamaica. We went through the federal government program. It's not cheap. It's around $600 for their air flight, and you have to pay for their housing. You have to pay for, there's quite a few fees. It was about $2,000 to bring up three. They are quick learners and we happened to hit three very good ones. You can get real duds sometimes. But they worked out very well. Their housing comes under the [Leeds, Grenville, and Lanark District] Health Unit's jurisdiction. But we had arranged with a local apple grower to board them at his facility.

"So when they [the health unit] phoned up, we said, 'They are not staying here, they are just working here. They are being boarded at so-and-so's farm.' They wanted to come and look anyway, because we had a winery. The day they showed up, it was with a building inspector. They had been in touch with the LCBO and tore a strip off of them because they had not been notified that there was a winery in their jurisdiction. They had contacted the Alcohol and Gaming Commission and tore a strip off of them. And they had been in touch with the Ministry of the Environment, before they ever even came to the farm."

"So then they started condemning all kinds of stuff. They condemned the floors, they condemned the holding tank."

Of course, this had nothing to do with the Jamaican workers, whose presence had only served to put the Countryman farm on authorities' radar. The vineyard's very existence appeared to be seen by them as some sort of provocation.

"I had some home preserves that we were doing in what we call our cupboard side, because the wine has to be separate from everything else. So they started in on me about my preserves and said I didn't have a health certificate. I said 'I certainly do, signed by your boss!' They kind of looked at me. They had checked everything out, but they hadn't checked their own records! And they couldn't find permits for the holding tank. And my husband said, 'You do not require a permit for a holding tank.' They were just checking on everything. They said they would give us two weeks. They wanted a pumping contract for the holding tank. And they wanted the holding tank dug up so they could make sure it wasn't leaking."

All that was in the tank was "wash water off the fruit, just washing water," which was 100 percent organic and could be used as green fertilizer for crops.

The sheer aggressiveness of the inspectors' visit had made the Countrymans angry. Their backs were up. "When they came back, we had dug our heels in and decided we weren't going to do anything. We'd been to our MP and unfortunately they kind of sided with the health unit. But the day they came we had the Landowners here [the Ontario Landowners Association, the same citizen activist group that had helped the Carmichaels, and which is discussed in detail in chapter 10]. It had gotten out that the Landowners were going to be here. And they [the health unit] phoned and I said no, that I didn't know that they were going to be here. If they were coming I didn't know about it. So they [the Landowners] were all gathered at a neighbor's place up the road. So when they [the health unit] got in here, they just phoned and the Landowners all landed in here with their placards and everything. Our son had been away and he'd just come home from his job and he was here. And he demanded from [the health unit representative] what was going on. She had a paper with the MOE [Ministry of the Environment] address, and she said, 'If you're not going to work with us you're going to work with them.' The Landowners were here and they realized they weren't going to get anywhere, so they were trying, hoping the MOE was going to jump on us.

"So we phoned the MOE up, the number that they had given us, and they said we were breaking the law. We didn't have enough permits. So I said, 'Whoa, wait a minute, what's this fine about?' Come to find out the health unit had told the representative of the MOE that we were cooking and preparing food in this building, we had public washrooms in this building, we were pumping all this stuff, food scraps and grease into the holding tank, taking it out, putting it on the crops and then harvesting them. And we weren't doing any of that.

"They can dream up anything if they want. I don't know what they were up to. So we got it straightened out, that it was strictly wash water off the product and we take it out and we put it on fallow land, that's summer fallow for the year, and work it in. So the guy said, 'We'll have to check back with our agricultural representative to be sure.' He came back and said, 'You're perfectly within your rights. What you're doing is normal farm practice. You do not require any permit.' So my son said to him, 'Will you put this in writing?' And he said yes, and we got it in writing. About two weeks after we got that, we get a letter from the heath unit stating they wanted a septic system, and they wanted the pumping contract and they wanted all this stuff. Same as what they had started out with. A holding tank does not have any piping on it. It's a field tank, and you pump it out and spread it wherever. But they were insisting that we put bells and whistles on it and a pumping contract every two weeks, which is really ridiculous. A lot of times there wouldn't have been enough water in it, during the winter and that, to even try to do that."

The inspectors were treating the tank as if it was even more toxic than a septic tank for a toilet, and insisted that the tank should be emptied every two weeks, even though there may have been nothing in it.

"And they wanted a copy of the contract, so that they could contact the contractor and make sure he was doing the job. And then we had to spend $15,000 to $20,000 to put in a weeping system for this, like a septic tank. And this was just wash water. We were upset enough that I took it to our federal MP (member of Parliament), because the off-shore program is under his jurisdiction. I had found out in the meantime that the health unit had charged all offshore farms in this area and were shutting them down. There was another fruit grower in the area and he had just set up his system, and they were saying his system wasn't sufficient and he couldn't have his offshore help, who were [already] on the plane to come here.

"We didn't know what the reason was. But I know that there is a government union that is trying to get the off-shore help under their contract, which is even worse for the farmers. He [the MP] said he'd called the health unit up and asked them what the problem was at the offshore sites. And they told him, 'Oh no, no, we don't have any problem.' They did phone once afterwards, in strawberry season, and she happened to get my son on the phone. She admitted that he [the MP] had told her to get out of his territory and hung up on her."

"They've been quiet ever since [the MP] had a whack at them. We're just going with the status quo. We've got the MOE letter and we're going on that. We're ignoring the health unit. We have a manufacturer's permit from the Alcohol and Gaming Commission, and we have our retail outlet permit from the LCBO, to sell any of our wines on-site, but only on-site. At the LCBO, the only wine we can sell right now is our Strawberry Delight. [The health unit] tried saying our wines weren't supposed to be any good so we said, 'Do you want to see the certificate we got from the LCBO's million-dollar lab saying it's perfectly legal to sell?' We've just gone back to what we were doing. We're not doing anything to change anything. They haven't been back."

Officially, however, the health unit has not cleared the winery either. So the Countrymans continue to work in a sort of bureaucratic limbo, not knowing when or if there will be another knock at their door by hostile officials.

Government appears to be ready to zealously use laws and regulations against small farmers, but not to do much to actually protect them, as farmer and Landowners Association member Merle Bowes complained.

"Under the new Species at Risk Act, using the loggerhead shrike as an example, if a shrike were to build a nest in one of my vegetable-growing areas, I'd just be out of business. No compensation, nothing. Fines up to $250,000 for interfering in any way with habitat or nest or anything else regarding that bird. Which in my opinion is a backward way of going about it. If I was going about my activities and a loggerhead shrike saw fit to come and nest there, he must not be bothered that much by me. I must be doing something right. If ministries of the government would give you a pat on the shoulder for having a shrike on your property, rather than punishing you for having it, it would be a much more effective program. They are rare in this area anyway, and always will be, because we're on the very northern fringe of their range. What changes that is the MNR [Ministry of Natural Resources] working to breed and release shrikes in this area."

And when a small farmer needs government help, it's slow in coming or doesn't come at all. "For five years or so I'd been growing vegetables with no fences, and deer were around but were never a serious problem," said Bowes. "Then all of a sudden we began getting this population increase and it became impossible. The deer herd numbers were beginning to explode. In the bush on my property there are no young trees left at all. The deer have eaten everything they could reach, to the point where they started, of necessity, eating species of trees they don't normally browse on. I even had the biologist coming from Peterborough taking pictures of the types of trees the deer were browsing in winter time. This was a new activity for them. We were getting trees from the MNR to plant on our property in clearings, white pine and spruce. There was nothing. The deer ate them all.

"I spent over $15,000 on deer fence, but I still couldn't grow my vegetable crops anymore. I just couldn't do it, because of deer. And this is my only source of income. Meanwhile, the Ministry of Natural Resources wasn't dealing with the problem. The Kemptville [MNR] office wasn't interested [in controlling the deer]. They wouldn't even send anyone out. They just weren't interested."

Chilling Effect
The Carmichaels, the Countrymans, Larry Robinson, and Frey's Hatchery are only a few examples of the seeming

vendetta against small-scale agricultural producers. So many attacks, on so many families, can only have a chilling effect, discouraging the entry of industry newcomers— that is to say, newcomers who aren't large corporations, or industrial-scale producers under contract to and sheltered by them. Marketing boards, now dominated by such large producers, and governments, responsive to the financial might of the corporate sector, appear to see smaller family operations as so many economic weeds, to be sprayed out of existence with a variety of bureaucratic poisons.

Such an attitude makes little real sense, either in terms of the much-vaunted economic "efficiency" trotted out so often to defend the "economies of scale" of industrial-sized operations, or of the quality of the food products they offer. As demonstrated by a landmark series of studies by Nobel Prize–winning economist Amartya Sen,[25] and several other enquiries that followed, small farms are actually far more efficient than large ones. Sen found that there is an inverse relationship between the size of farms and the amount of crops they produce per hectare, or per acre. The smaller the farm, the greater the yield. In fact, one study found that farms of less than one hectare are twenty times as productive as large factory farms.

As for food quality, small organic farms are far more likely to produce healthy food than large industrial operations. One recent study found that "organic plant-based foods are, on average, more nutritious in terms of their nutrient density ... The average serving of organic plant-based food contains about 25 percent more of the nutrients encompassed in this study than a comparable-sized serving of the same food produced by conventional farming methods."[26]

One would think every effort would be made to encourage small, organic operations, rather than the opposite.

But farm people aren't the only targets. One need not raise a crop or a herd or a flock to become the quarry.

Because so many of them live in and have traditional claim to rural lands, indigenous or aboriginal people all over the world are also in the legal, bureaucratic, and police crosshairs. So are small rural businesses that support local farmers, and community groups that provide markets for them. In fact, nearly anyone—aboriginal or otherwise— who tries to live in or run a business in a rural area could become a sitting duck.

All are unwanted in the new, corporate/government Eden.

And First Nations people have been unwanted for centuries.

(**6**)

What's Yours Is Mine

Neither man nor beast, neither cattle
nor sheep, shall taste anything, they shall
not eat, nor shall they drink water.

BOOK OF JONAH, 3:7

THROUGHOUT THE 1970s AND into the late '80s, debates raged
in nearly every industrialized country over the safety
and financial viability of nuclear power. Nuclear industry
critics like physicist Dr. Ernest Sternglass (a one-time col-
league of Albert Einstein) and mathematician and health
statistician Dr. Rosalie Bertell, activists like Karen Silkwood,
and popular films like *The China Syndrome* (1979) made the
graphic and devastating case that nuclear power was neither
safe nor financially viable.

The nuclear industry, of course, fought back fiercely,
and its opponents sometimes paid a heavy price for their
public stands. Sternglass's first book, *Low-Level Radiation*,[1]
was temporarily suppressed. Silkwood may have been mur-
dered,[2] and Bertell, who was a Roman Catholic nun as well
as a scientist, suffered an attempt on her life. Sternglass was

savagely attacked in the press and in scientific circles by those determined to discredit his work.

Despite such dangers, the critics had begun to tip the balance.

Then came the 1979 disaster at Three Mile Island in Pennsylvania, followed by *Harrowsmith* magazine's report "The Silent Toll,"[3] and a spate of books ranging from Sternglass's *Secret Fallout*[4] and Harvey Wasserman and Norman Solomon's *Killing Our Own*,[5] to Robert Leppzer's *Voices from Three Mile Island*[6] and Albert Bates's *Shut Down: Nuclear Power on Trial.*[7]

Finally, the scales were knocked totally off balance by the 1986 disaster at Chernobyl, in Ukraine.

As far as the voting public in most countries were concerned, nuclear power was no longer an option. The industry was dead in its own heavy water, and construction of nuclear reactors effectively stopped. For nearly three decades, no new reactors were built in North America.

The uranium mining industry suffered accordingly.

Halfway through the first decade of the new century, however, a fresh threat—global warming—began at last to be taken seriously. So did rising food prices, sparked by sudden investor interest in bio-fuels, such as ethanol, and the resulting competition for crops such as corn, used to produce alcohol fuels. Environmentalists, and a minority of journalists, had been warning about global warming for years,[8] but it was decades before the political classes noticed. When they did, corporate and government supporters of the nuclear option, silent for years, saw sudden opportunity. The bio-fuels/food price controversy added to the sense of emergency. Concluding that the voting public's memory was short and the earlier conflicts over radiation dangers were forgotten (or were simply not on the radar of a new generation), they went to work on a comeback scenario: the resurrection of nuclear power.

Or, as some dubbed it, "Son of Frankenstein."

Government and industry spokesmen in the U.S., Canada, and Great Britain began talking up nuclear power as "the clean option," as if the problems of radioactive contamination caused by nuclear accidents and of the disposal of lethal nuclear wastes (potent for tens of thousands of years) had somehow been magically solved during the long silence that followed Chernobyl. They hadn't, of course, been solved at all.

Nor had the question of so-called "peak uranium," the point where the amount of available high-grade uranium ore (better than 0.01 percent purity) would be exhausted, and the cost—in terms of the fossil fuels used in mining, milling, and processing the remaining lower-grade ore—would be more than the energy gained from the resulting uranium itself. Some estimates gave a mere three years before that point would be reached,[9] others more.

But no matter. Ever-responsive to the corporate agenda of the moment, the politicians went ahead. Britain's Tory government, and the U.S. Republicans under George W. Bush, repeated the mantra "nuclear is clean" and announced plans to start building reactors again. In September 2007, NRG Energy filed an application with regulators to build two new nuclear reactors in Texas, "the first such request in 29 years."[10] The next month, the Tennessee Valley Authority filed an application with the Nuclear Regulatory Commission to build and operate two new reactors in northern Alabama. Behind the scenes, U.S. Vice President Dick Cheney was working to make sure the application process for new nuclear projects would be streamlined and environmental oversight reduced.[11] In all, the NRC expected applications for no fewer than twenty-eight new reactors in two years.[12]

In Ontario, Canada, Dalton McGuinty's Liberal government announced a "balanced plan for Ontario's energy future," in which "nuclear is expected to continue to be the single-largest source for Ontario's electricity in 2025."[13] Use of nuclear power to fuel oil extraction from Alberta's tar sands—a kind of double-barreled pollution nightmare—became a boardroom topic.

Prices for uranium, which had hovered around $8–10 per pound at the turn of the century, leaped to $45.50 per pound by mid-2006,[14] to $90 by September 2007,[15] then to $135—and appeared to be heading higher. The mining industry saw a new El Dorado rising, and long-dormant claims in uranium-rich spots like the Bancroft area in eastern Ontario came alive again with would-be drillers, venture capitalists, and speculators.

One place where the impact of the new policy was felt acutely was the tiny town of Ardoch, Ontario, home of a remarkable band of Algonquin First Nations people, of a smart, courageous old warrior named Harold Perry, and two of his longtime partners in leadership, Bob Lovelace and Randy Cota.

A Rice War Veteran

Harold Perry, then 76, was honorary chief of the fiercely independent Ardoch Algonquin First Nation, while Lovelace was its spokesman and Cota its co-chief, along with Paula Sherman. Perry cut his teeth as an activist—and a remarkably effective advocate for the rights of native peoples—as far back as 1981, when he led his band and their local white neighbors in a successful defense of their rights to harvest the wild rice *(Zizania aquatica)* in the area around Mud Lake.[16] That right had been challenged by a commercial harvester, the Lanark Wild Rice Company (when not working as a rice entrepreneur, one of Lanark's co-owners was—perhaps ironically in light of later developments—an engineer for Atomic Energy of Canada). It would later be brutally challenged by the armed force of government.

Standing on the lake's shore one day in late summer, local resident Howard Hermer was startled by what sounded like a helicopter engine. It was an aluminum airboat, powered by a scaffold-mounted Volkswagen engine and sporting a red plastic pilot's chair, roaring across the lake, harvesting the area's just-ripened rice. Hermer was astounded. All of the land around the lake was privately owned, with no public access, and local people, native and white alike, regarded the rice on the lake as community property, like the commons in a fifteenth-century English village. The outraged Hermer tried to make a citizen's arrest, but the power boat operators showed him a "license" from the Ontario Ministry of Natural Resources (OMNR), turned around, and kept cutting the stand.

The Algonquin had been harvesting rice on the lake, and sharing it with their white neighbors, since Perry's great-grandmother originally planted it, decades before. They also had a legal claim as strong as their neighbors' to the land around the water, which they had occupied for perhaps ten thousand years or more—"since the last Ice Age," as Perry put it. Aside from their physical presence on the land for so many centuries, they could also point to the Royal Proclamation of 1763, in which their proprietorship was recognized by England's King George III.

Finally, along with other First Nations bands across the province, they believed their rice rights had been protected when Ontario Premier William Davis's minority Tory government imposed a five-year moratorium on commercial expansion of the wild rice industry, to give native people time to solidify their own place in it. The moratorium was prompted by a highly publicized report by Ontario Supreme Court Justice Patrick Hartt, describing the terrible social and economic problems of many of the province's native bands. Under it, no new licenses were to be issued to nonnative harvesters.

Unfortunately for the people of Ardoch, neither tradition, nor probable legal rights, nor political promises of a moratorium seemed to offer real protection. Commercial harvesters across the province had been pressuring the government for a long time to open the resource to them, claiming that native people and local landowners were under-utilizing the available rice.[17]

Lanark, whose owners "usually"[18] sold their harvested rice to a processing company owned by a prominent political backer of Ontario's northern affairs minister, Leo Bernier (actually Bernier's election campaign manager),[19] was determined to bring in a mechanical harvester and take away Mud Lake's rice. Although there was a strong likelihood that this could leave the people who lived there, and who had harvested it for decades, with little, the province, moratorium or not, appeared determined to let it go ahead. The prohibition on granting new licenses was gotten around by claiming that Lanark hadn't been given a license, but only "a permit." [20]

As Lanark's Clifford Zarecki explained at the time: "Taking a stand here would have economic repercussions in the Kenora region, where we're talking a million pounds [of wild rice] a year being produced. It's important because it can be used as a legal precedent. Anything that happens in the Ardoch area can be directly applied up north [where other native bands were insisting on their rice rights]." [21] At the time, rice was retailing for around $20 per pound.

The company was given a green light to take off the rice stand and, while Hermer watched, did so.

But the people of Ardoch, both white and native, objected to the "high-handed" way a community resource had been given over to a private firm, and contested the issue through a series of complaints, appeals, and rulings. Lanark was turned away in 1980, but in 1981, benefiting from a later government ruling, came back again to take the rice.

The people decided to fight. In a tribute to racial harmony and cooperation, virtually every resident of Ardoch, Algonquin and white, rallied to Perry's call for resistance.

Like the first President Bush, uniting the allies for the first Gulf War, Perry was a diplomat and pointed out the mutual interests of whites and natives alike. He reminded them that not only did they need to preserve the rice for itself, as a product to sell and to grace their own tables, but to protect what was a key food source for the ducks, geese, and other migratory birds whose presence on the lake acted as a draw for the hunters who provided one of the local area's main sources of tourist dollars. He convinced Ardoch's residents that, if Lanark or any other commercial entrepreneur gained dominance over the rice resource, everyone in town could suffer. Commercial harvesters' mechanical airboats, he explained, take too much rice off the stands, damage the stems, and don't leave enough for the plants to naturally reseed themselves. Compared to traditional harvesting methods, they also leave little grain for wildfowl to glean.

Ardoch responded.

Residents threw a cordon around the lake, to block any attempt to enter. CB radios were broken out, patrols organized, sections of the lakeshore designated for each family to watch, and a round-the-clock sentry shift established. "We were fighting for what we believed in," said Perry,[22] to preserve the community character of the traditional harvest. Signs blossomed on barns and sheds all over the county, most of whose residents supported Ardoch's fight: "Hands off our rice!"

The government was nevertheless determined to squeeze the tiny rural hamlet, official population 100, into line. On Sunday, August 30, its full armed might came down upon Ardoch.

"When they came in, about 9:30 AM, it was like an army," recalled resident Doug Watkins.[23] "They came very fast, with no regard for anybody in the way. One police cruiser came right up and struck the bumper on my half-ton. Later, when I was standing on the shoulder of the road, another one came whipping by and hit me. Its side-view mirror hit me on the elbow, and my fingers were numb all afternoon. They never stopped to see if anybody was hurt."

"It was like an invasion, a war," said Bob Lovelace.[24] "We had no idea of the force they would use. The police cars came in at high speed. Some people on foot got knocked right down."

"The police got pretty brutal, pushing and shoving people and hitting them with cars," said Perry's daughter Mona, then 17. "It made people pretty mad."

Officers of the OMNR, shouting from their boats offshore, taunted the townspeople, urging police to "throw them in the paddy wagons!" [25] In all, twenty-seven Ontario Provincial Police cruisers manned by armed constables, two "Black Maria" paddy wagons, two tow trucks (to haul cars out of the roadway), eight OMNR patrol boats (each with two pistol-packing wardens aboard), and a police helicopter all took part in the strike. With them, protected by the wall of police vehicles, was Lanark's airboat, towed behind a truck.

"I couldn't believe it," recalled a resident. "There were more police and wardens than there are adult men in the whole village."

Right Trumps Might

But despite the massive force marshaled by the province, right, as far as Ardoch's people were concerned, trumped might.

"That Sunday morning we had three cars parked at each end of the road along the lake and had picket lines set up," recalled Lovelace.[26] "The police came in en masse at the end toward [the neighboring town of] Ompah. A meeting of the local conservation association was going on at the community hall there, but the police just stormed in and ordered everybody out. They took over the hall as a sort of forward command post, then went and set up roadblocks of their own there and at the iron bridge nearby. Reporters and newsmen who had got wind of the strike were kept out while the police went to work breaking up the picket lines.

"They got pretty rough, pushing people down in the road. There was lots of shoving at the bridge and two people were arrested for breach of the peace. But once the police broke through the picket line, people just jumped in their boats and formed a blockade on the river. There were boats full of local people and boats full of OMNR wardens everywhere. The police had on their running shoes and expected to be chasing people into the water, and it was then that we first heard the chopper overhead, its motor throbbing. We set up a blockade with two or three motorboats at the narrows around ten AM. I stood offshore in my boat and told them it was private property and they couldn't pass."

On shore, as well as on the water, all was confusion. "It was hard to believe—unreal," said Freda Perry.[27] "But the people had their backs up and were determined to fight back." Parents and children scurried back and forth, messages got garbled, rumors of fights and arrests circulated while Harold Perry, darting here and there on a red Honda motorcycle, strove to maintain order and keep the local demonstration nonviolent. The local people kept in touch via CB radios.

"We had a pretty good CB system worked out," said Lovelace. "The police jammed it for awhile, but we got back on the air later. There must have been about a hundred people out there at any given time, while the others [including supporters from outside the village itself] were being kept away behind the police roadblocks. People who live on the lake weren't allowed to go to their own homes."

Finally, around eleven AM, the turning point came.

The police had forgotten or overlooked the fact that the land around the lake was private property and that Lanark would be trespassing if it tried to enter where there was no access. "When they realized this, it confused things," said Lovelace. "Nobody would let them through. Then an officer there heard that the land 20 feet on either side of public road is legally open to public access, and they looked for a narrow spot where Green Lake Road swings near the shore of Mud Lake.

"The officer walked to a spot near a rock outcrop just west of the bridge and I asked him to measure it. They took a tape measure marked off in meters and paced it off, and it came out around 7.6 meters. 'That's 20 feet,' the officer said. But I took a calculator and insisted on working the conversion. It came to 23 feet—three feet over the limit!"

At 11:30 AM, with sour looks on their faces, the police withdrew. The people of Ardoch, and through them the province's First Nations bands, had won their rice war. "We beat them back with a tape measure," grinned a resident. "Next time they better watch out, or we'll use yardsticks!"

But, once burned, once wary: the local people weren't quite convinced. Doug Watkins, who'd been hit by an OPP cruiser, was still smoldering with anger. He happened to be the roads supervisor for North Frontenac Township, where Ardoch is located.

"I didn't like that kind of treatment at all," he said.[28] "I paid my dollar for a rice-harvesting permit and I'm allowed only 20 pounds. [Lanark] paid the same as me and gets to harvest thousands of pounds and has all this police escort. I thought they were being too darn pushy.

"We heard that they were coming back in with a crane to lower the boat from the bridge, and had an injunction to get them in. I talked to my reeve and we noted that a lady had just complained that she wanted a culvert put in near her house. So I told him we would just get to work and put that culvert in. We tore up the road. Just by coincidence, the reeve in Palmerston Township also had roadwork going on. So they tore up the other end of the road. A remarkable coincidence."

Today, motorists driving through Ardoch can stop to look at a very solid-looking stone monument, erected by the townpeople at their own expense. The white boulder, set on a landscaped patch of garden, holds a bronze plaque that reads:

> In the Mississippi River below Ardoch is a stand of Manomin, "wild rice" that has been cared for and harvested by aboriginal people for many generations. Mary Whiteduck brought the rice here from Rice Lake on the Trent River to provide for the Algonquin families living at Ardoch. In 1979 a conflict began over control of the "wild rice" that resulted in a 27-day stand-off during August and September 1981. Standing strong, aboriginal people and their neighbors in North Frontenac were victorious in re-establishing Algonquin jurisdiction over the land and resources.
>
> "We cannot blame the old people for losing the land, or the language, or cultural ways. They did not have an education, they had no money and the racism was so strong. But if we do not do something about it in our time then we will be the ones to blame." Harold Perry.

This plaque was placed here on 21 August 2004 to commemorate the solidarity between the Ardoch Algonquin First Nation (AAFNA), the community of North Frontenac Township, and the aboriginal people of Ontario.

In the years following the rice war, Perry continued actively defending his people's rights, ably seconded by Lovelace and later by the younger Randy Cota. Harold went to court to defend Algonquin rights to hunt migratory birds, as well as moose, deliberately going out and hunting so as to provide his own test cases, which he won.

In one instance, Harold and his 88-year-old brother Neil went out hunting together and shot a bull moose with a 52-inch rack, field-dressed it and packed it back in a boat, to demonstrate that—as aboriginal people—they had the right to do so without paying the province for a hunting license.

It is entirely possible that the erstwhile uranium miners who appeared on the scene in North Frontenac more than twenty-five years after the rice war didn't know about this history, or exactly who the people were that they would be dealing with. If they did know, they must have been endowed with either a healthy dollop of hubris or an absolute conviction that they really had found El Dorado and the price would be worth it.

Frontenac Ventures

They called themselves Frontenac Ventures Corporation, and when company founder, president, and CEO George White (company secretary and fellow board member Scott White is his son), with company lawyer Jack Kirkland, pulled up in front of the Ompah, Ontario fire hall where the North Frontenac Township Council was to meet, it was in a sporty BMW 333, and both men wore tailored suits. Most of the other meeting attendees arrived in older pickup trucks, wearing jeans.

When Mayor Ron Maguire, his ribbon of office draped over his shoulders, gaveled the meeting to order and invited George White to speak, Kirkland jumped up instead, with an earnest expression on his face, and blurted: "I would indicate that I was born and raised in eastern Ontario by farming people, I know the concerns that people in this area generally would have, and that I have known Mr. White as a friend for forty-five years, and he's very open. And he's a man whose word is his code of honor. Now I'll let George White give his presentation."

Mayor Maguire frowned briefly at the interruption, then turned again to White. It was June 28, 2007, and the venturer whose word was his code of honor was there to explain to a nervous and largely skeptical local populace why Frontenac Ventures had been staking claims, flying airplanes trailing bizarre instruments overhead, cutting down trees, and marking off perimeters on other people's private land in the area.

The local people might have been a lot more nervous if they'd known that Frontenac Ventures' lead lawyer, who would shortly take the spotlight away from Kirkland, was Neal J. Smitheman, of the law firm Fasken Martineau DuMoulin LLP, whose website announces that Smitheman has

> an extensive criminal and quasi-criminal practice. While he has successfully defended numerous individuals charged under the *Criminal Code of Canada*, the

main focus of his practice has been directed towards corporate criminal and quasi-criminal matters. Neal frequently is called upon to represent clients being investigated and charged under the *Competition Act*, *Environmental Protection Act*, the *Ontario Water Resources Act*, the *Fisheries Act*, the *Occupational Health and Safety Act*, the *Electricity Act*, the *Atomic Energy Act*, and other regulatory statutes."[29]

When not "defending individuals and corporations charged under various regulatory statutes," the site added that "as a member of the Aboriginal Law Practice Group, Neal is called upon to advise and represent clients in this burgeoning area of legal specialty."[30]

But now it was George White's turn to speak, and he launched into a detailed description of "what we're doing and how we think we're going to get there,"[31] a phrase he repeated several times. Noting that he'd been "exploring for uranium in this area for forty-five years," and had "staked large blocks of claims in the 1960s [newspaper reports said these included more than 30,000 acres[32]]," he repeatedly stressed that "millions" were involved: "I am thankful to our investors, who in the first couple of years put up the millions of dollars that we spent," "we raised several millions of dollars," "we will be spending multi-millions of dollars." He also repeatedly emphasized that, though Frontenac Ventures was "a small company," they had hired "a highly-renowned consultant," "world-renowned environmental specialists," "world-renowned environmental experts," and were "seeking some world-class advice" from "the world's top scientists" on how to dig six-foot trenches and diamond-drill core samples in "an environmentally friendly way." Among the world-renowned environmental experts, he said, was Victor Emery, who White recalled had "won a gold medal for Canada at the Olympics in '64" as a distance runner.[33]

"Is this some kind of Impress the Rubes Show?" a man sitting in the second row of spectators whispered to his female companion.

Though cautioning that actual mining and processing were "ten years down the road," White predicted that if tests were successful and the dream became a reality, it would mean a bonanza for local people, as well as for the mine investors.

"If there was a viable economic resource confirmed, first thing is the immediate employment in the area of five to six hundred people, who would operate the plant and the mill," White said. "Then there is the multiplier of all the related industries that will come in to support what we're doing. Use five to six times. So you're talking employment, direct employment in the area of three to four thousand jobs. The mining industry in Canada is either the highest paying industry or it's one of the highest paying industries. So these are very, very good, high paying jobs. There'd be management, there'd be trade personnel, truckers, equipment operators, laborers, geological staff, engineers, clerical staff, professionals, scientists, security, welders, you go down the line and these are the kind of jobs that will be available. Children would not have to leave Palmerston or Olden-Oso [former township designations in the area] to find a job. There's good paying jobs available. The subcontractors, such as the electrical, plumbing, etc. will find employment...

"The capital expenditure to build a mining operation is somewhere in the neighborhood of $125 to $150 million Canadian. So immediately, I guess from the council's

perspective, the industrial tax base would increase exponentially. It's just a huge increase in industrial taxes, which
would hopefully form relief to the residents. The residential
rate would go down . . .

"Mining operations such as ours require medical centers, and communities that can't hire a doctor, nurses, etc.,
the mining operation has a medical center which is available to the local applicants. So the health care services
would improve exponentially. Community center activities,
whether you take [the Ontario mining towns of] Timmins
or Porcupine or wherever it might be, the mining company
has built the hockey arenas, the baseball fields, the community centers and so on and so forth, because it's part of their
community and becomes a community kind of operation."

He noted that documentation he'd submitted to council
included a photograph taken by Cameco, "the world's largest
uranium company," of sheep grazing on Cameco's uranium
tailings field in Wyoming. "The sheep, the other livestock,
the deer and the antelope play, are reportedly healthier than
normal," he said. There was laughter from the audience at
White's "deer and the antelope play" slip, and Mayor Maguire had to rap his gavel: "Order, please!"

The only thing standing in the way of this Eden-to-
be, White insisted, were "a number of the people who are
against mining. I call them eco-terrorists [more audience
laughter], who have stated that they're really concerned
about the watershed, the pollution of the watershed."

Permanent Pollution

Indeed, they ought to have been. As Sternglass and many
others pointed out in the 1970s and '80s, nuclear radiation
is capable not only of causing the radiation sickness and

multiple cancers associated with high doses, such as were seen at Hiroshima and Nagasaki, but also of causing "spontaneous abortion, stillbirth, infant death, birth defects, leukemia, respiratory malfunction, infectious disease, thyroid disorders [especially hypothyroidism] and even a drop in the intelligence levels of university applicants,"[34] at very low doses. Most disturbing was the work of Canadian Dr. Abraham Petkau, who in papers published in 1972 and 1974 showed that *the risk of damage to a living cell from radiation, per unit of radiation absorbed, could actually increase, rather than decrease, as the radiation dose rate was lowered to background level.*[35] There was strong statistical evidence that the 1979 Three Mile Island accident caused a sharp spike in infant deaths in the areas downwind of the reactor.[36]

Two speakers who followed White with presentations for the council, particularly local resident John Kittle, made it clear that not only would a mining operation risk causing such pollution, but any such pollution would be permanent. Kittle, who introduced himself as a physicist and mathematician with "a background in nuclear physics, including three years in fundamental research in a high energy physics laboratory, looking at the properties of uranium," noted wryly that he was "not an eco-terrorist."

"If a spill [such as from a leaking mine tailings pond] occurs, then the Mississippi River watershed could be polluted. And this pollution, from my experience, is toxic, radioactive, and permanent, permanent being measured in hundreds of thousands of years... Typically the uranium ore is crushed and leached, leaving very large quantities of water and sludge, to where the tailings from that process, which still contain substantial quantities of radioactive material [some 85 percent of it made up of such non-uranium waste products as thorium, radium, radon, etc.] are dumped into what are called tailing ponds."

He added that the mining industry's record, not only in containing the sludge in tailing ponds, but also in preventing the spread of radioactive dust downwind from mining and processing operations, "is not something to be proud of, on average."

In fact, evidence from earlier spills indicated that the odds could be as high as two to one that over a period of twenty-five years a pond or dam will fail to hold its tailings,[37] and once a leak happens there is a good chance that nearby water bodies will be polluted. "A pond failure or accidental spill could pollute the Mississippi River watershed and its aquifer, where we all get our well water, thereby impacting thousands of people and villages and towns downstream," said Kittle.

He forgot to add that the Mississippi feeds into the larger Ottawa River, which runs through the city of Ottawa, and thus *Canada's capital city could at least theoretically be in danger of having its water supply contaminated with radioactive waste as well*. Waste that could remain toxic for thousands of years.

Considering the possibility that the supply of high-grade uranium ore could be used up in as little as three years, making it uneconomical to continue mining, the sheer magnitude of the risks involved seemed wildly disproportionate.

On a smaller but more acutely personal scale, the risks to individual landowners whose property would be directly impacted by mining activities also appeared disproportionate, as the other speaker on the council agenda—Marilyn Crawford of Bedford Mining Alert—explained.

Noting that the government of Nova Scotia had already enacted and renewed a province-wide ban on uranium mining, she described the legal position of landowners in the face of mining activity. She pointed out that "on many eastern Ontario properties there exist two competing rights," namely the surface rights and the subsurface, or mineral, rights. In some cases, property owners hold both, but in many others they only hold surface rights—that is, the right to control what happens at ground level or above. What happens underground is governed by the Mining Act of Ontario, originally enacted in 1873, when laissez-faire was the economic watchword, and the province's main interest was in rapidly expanding the exploitation of natural resources in the comparatively sparsely settled Ontario of the day. It was also an era when picks and shovels, rather than backhoes and bulldozers, were used for mining exploration, and most mining activity took place on a small scale and in what were then remote areas.

Under the act's liberal terms, anyone over the age of eighteen and willing to pay $25.50 for a five-year provincial license can become a "prospector." No training, diplomas, apprenticeship, degrees, or special expertise is needed. Once licensed, such prospectors have the right to enter, at any time of the day or night, without permission or any previous notice, any land whose legitimate owners do not hold subsurface rights, and there stake claims. This can involve cutting down trees and marking off sections of land. No notification and no landowner consent is required when a claim is staked and registered.

After a claim is staked and registered, exploratory work can start, with only twenty-four hours notice to the landowner—who has little say in the matter. Crawford gave the council documents showing that White had done this with at least one North Frontenac landowner. An owner can file a dispute against the claim, but the dispute mechanism is controlled by the Provincial Mining Recorder and the Mining and Lands Commissioner, and is a very expensive process in which the onus is on the landowner, not the prospector, to prove a case.

Once begun, exploration can involve cutting down still more trees, sometimes clear-cutting whole acreages, stripping away the surface soil, digging six-foot-deep trenches, drilling test boreholes, and bringing in heavy equipment to remove soil and rock. This work can continue for years, providing the prospector keeps renewing his or her license.

There is no requirement in the act that an eighteen-year-old or older prospector engaged in trenching, bulldozing, stripping, or clearing trees from a property should restore the land or repair the damage done. As for compensation for damage, the operative phrase may be "lots of luck," that is, if a 1996 ruling by the Mining and Lands Commissioner is any example. The MLC awarded $875 in compensation to a landowner who had proven damage, and then required her to pay $11,000 in costs to the holder of the mining claim.[38]

If exploration shows a prospector that there are exploitable minerals on the property, he or she has the legislative right to obtain a mining lease—which the government cannot legally refuse to grant. The lease, for a fee of three dollars per hectare (2.47 acres) per year, gives the prospector security of title to mining and surface rights for up to twenty-one years. Regular mining operations can begin with the lease, at which time landowners may be obligated to sell their property. By this point, of course, the property isn't likely to be worth very much, so the sale price is likely to be a lot less than the owner originally paid for it.

By the time of the North Frontenac Council meeting, this nightmare scenario had already begun for Frank and Gloria Morrison, owners of a 100-acre property about ninety minutes west of Ottawa, in the Algonquins' territory.

On June 28, shortly after the council met, Gloria Morrison was standing on the shoulder of Route 509, just south of Mississippi Station, along with twenty or thirty other people, mostly Algonquins, who had just launched a blockade at the dirt road entrance to the main property where Frontenac Ventures wanted to pursue its explorations. Here and there along the highway, and at the intersections nearby, black and white Ontario Provincial Police cruisers kept vigil. Periodically, a cruiser would prowl past, its uniformed occupants eyeing the people suspiciously. A television news crew had just arrived, trailing cameras and microphones.

"Our land is staked [by Frontenac Ventures]," Morrison said. "I think we were the first ones. And so I contacted Randy [Cota], and he was on it right from the beginning."

At the time Morrison contacted him, co-chief Cota and the Algonquins were already embroiled in a land claim controversy centered around the Ardoch band's desire to build a community center at Pine Lake. But when he heard the Morrisons' story, he quickly saw its importance and the band shifted its attention to the new emergency. Asserting their right to decide what went on—both above and below ground—on their territory, the Algonquins made immediate common cause with local white landowners and mounted their blockade of the proposed mine site.

Cota, Sherman, Harold Perry, and Bob Lovelace, working with Ormond Lee of the local, white "settlers committee"
and Chief Doreen Davis of the nearby Shabot Obaadjiwan
Algonquins, would soon need all of the skills they'd honed
in the rice fight and other battles.

One of their greatest strengths was precisely the fact
that they did make common cause with non–First Nations
people. Unlike other native bands, such as the Tyendinaga
Mohawks, whose battle against a quarry operation on their
lands near Deseronto had been turned by the media into an
"us against them," whites versus natives struggle, the Algonquins were seen from the start as the champions of white
and native alike, as well as guardians of the environment.

"I'm so glad to have them here," said Morrison. "They
have my total support." Earlier, she had written out her
story for the activist group Mining Watch Canada, to post
on their website:

Frank and I have both lived in Ottawa for most of
our adult lives. Beginning in 1990 we started looking for the perfect piece of land in the country to use
for recreation now and eventually to retire on. In 1996
we fell in love at first sight with a property that had the
wonderful mixed forest that Frank wanted, as well as a
decent meadow area that would support growing herbs
and vegetables.

It also included what always moves my heart, a wonderful stream and huge rock boulders. It was also within
90 minutes of Ottawa. It did not include any structures
or services but we had found our dream property so we
would manage. That first fall, Frank started building a

tiny cabin to serve as basic shelter, until such time as we could build a proper home. The cabin he built measures 10 by 14 feet, has no amenities except a wood stove, and was completely constructed by hand with no power tools. It served as our retreat until we moved permanently from Ottawa in 2002. It still serves as backup for visitors and although not a thing of beauty to others, it is a constant emblem of Frank's hard work and his love of the land.

The modest log cabin that is now our home was built from a stand of trees on our own land. We decided not to install hydro and instead manage with a solar powered system. We have an open concept, small home and heat entirely with a high efficiency wood stove. Of course this means that we are very conscious of our energy needs and our lifestyle is much more physical than many would care for, but we do not mind.

We share our land with many animals, including bears, wolves, coyotes, partridges and wild turkeys. We love this wild and rugged terrain. Our 80 acres of forest has a registered plan—under the Managed Forest System. It is designated as recreation land for animals and people with the focus on trails and natural growth, with particular attention to the healthy maturing of a mixed variety of trees.

"Frank has spent 10 years clearing and grooming this land... Our hope has always been to pass this little bit of heaven on to our children.[39]

That hope was rudely shattered by Frontenac Ventures:

During the first week of October 2006, Frank was out collecting firewood to top up our winter supply. He came upon an area where several of our trees had been severed, and the four feet of trunk that was still protruding from the ground where the trees once were had been squared into posts, were tagged and had notes made on the newly razed trunks. The steel tags had numbers and the emblem for the Province of Ontario. The pen writing included a date from the previous week and a man's name. Besides the several severed posts there were about 30 trees that had been 'blazed' along approximately a 1,200-foot line of pink marking tape. Frank correctly guessed that our land had been staked for mining. We had not received any notification or warning that this was going to happen...

We are now facing the reality that not only have our dreams disintegrated but we are left with a property for which—although it took a lifetime of effort to pay for—the market value is most uncertain. Who would buy land expecting that trenches and huge holes can be dug, vast amounts of soil removed, trees cut, terrain disturbed in any number of ways, and large equipment coming and going at the mining company's will?

Do we continue to care and groom and put our remaining time and energy into a property we love, knowing that on any given day, with a mere 24 hours notice, the mining company can walk right in and start work?

Standing by the road, she elaborated on her writeup.

"Whoever did [the staking] didn't know how to blaze. So many of our smaller trees were effectively girdled, and they'll die, definitely. We have yellow birch, maple, pine, ironwood, black cherry." She paused, a brief expression of sadness crossing her face. "The thing is, our modest little 100 acres is nothing, but those trees we see as an environmental filter for communities around us, and for the animals and for the cities around us, you know?

"Most of what's been staked in this area is Crown [provincially owned] land. We're one of two private pieces that have been staked. But we have three creek systems on the staked part, and those creek systems flow directly into the Mississippi, the Little Antoine, and the Big Antoine. That land, to me, ought to be privileged because we have fish in there. And that flows into the Ottawa [River]."

Actually, if the Algonquin claims are valid, the land in question belongs neither to the Crown nor to any local, private owners. Harold Perry and Randy Cota explained:

"We're part of the overall Algonquin Nation," said Harold. "The Algonquin Nation is the watershed heading to the Ottawa River, both north and south. That's the territory of the Algonquins. There have been Algonquin people here for at least eight thousand years. And this point we're on here was a recognized settlement since way before [European] contact. We [the Ardoch band] are part of that overall nation. And we have no treaty, no deals of any kind. We never surrendered ourselves or the land to the government. We're one of the few bands, if not the only band in Canada that hasn't surrendered their rights."

"The Royal Proclamation of 1763 is only a two-page document, but it says very clearly all lands are Indian lands *unless taken by an act of war or by treaty,"* [40] added Cota. "We've never had a war, and we don't have a treaty." As a result, under the proclamation, the whole watershed, including Canada's capital city, is still Algonquin land. What's more, when the Canadian constitution was repatriated from England by the Trudeau government, the proclamation was integrated in the new constitution.

Technically, not only are the Morrisons squatters on Indian land, but so are the inhabitants of Ottawa, including the House of Commons and the senate on Parliament Hill!

And for this, Gloria Morrison is grateful. If her "perfect" home was on anything but Algonquin land she and her husband would have little legal chance of avoiding the death of their dream. The law and the system that administers it would be stacked against them.

"The irony here is, you know this expression, 'what goes around comes around'? Here I'm a descendant of those who actually took the land, I would say unethically, certainly, away from the natives. And now we turn to them to protect us when we're the ones that robbed them. And now they're our only hope to be treated equitably. So this is the irony here. I'm just grateful they haven't signed a treaty. The laws of this land do not protect people like me, and there's nobody for us to go to.

"Thank goodness our Algonquins are not status and haven't signed any treaties. They're a small group. They're taking tremendous risks. We know there are a number of native groups who have fought against mining companies. They win, and then they're sued by the mining companies for the loss of income. All I can say is hurray for the courage of our Algonquin First Nations people. They have a lot of courage, courage that many of us on my side of things don't have."

And then Gloria Morrison said something unexpected, something that showed she had risen above any merely personal stake in the battle.

"You want to know the truth of it?" she asked, her eyes now fiery. "I will gladly sign it back, according to our present laws, to the natives so that they can protect it." The Old Testament story of the two women who come before Solomon to contest the maternity of a child came to mind. Gloria Morrison and Frontenac Ventures both claimed the land, but like a true mother, rather than see it destroyed, Gloria Morrison would have given it up.

If the Algonquins had anything to say about it, however, she wouldn't have to. Despite years of injustice and economic losses, their goals remain astonishingly open and generous.

"Every day we see tractor trailer loads go by with our logs on them [taken from so-called Crown land], and we get zero revenue from it," Randy Cota points out. "Last year $5.1 million of logging royalties came out of Algonquin Park alone, $5.1 million, and the Algonquins get nothing. That's not, doesn't include, gravel quarry extracts, that's not mining, that's not hunting and fishing licenses—and we can go on forever with revenues the province of Ontario is getting from our land, and we don't get a penny."

The Algonquins would like to negotiate a fair deal with the province to share in the revenues from Crown/Algonquin land, to be sure the uses to which the land is put are not noxious to the environment, and to guarantee protection for traditional Algonquin land uses, such as hunting and fishing.

But when it comes to private landowners and householders, they are happy to let the status quo remain.

"We're not there to fight against our neighbors," Cota explains. "We aren't there to negotiate or go against the private lands that people have deeds for, because they're our neighbors."

Perhaps more important to the Algonquins than economic justice, however, was the overall good of the environment itself.

"The trouble with the European systems is they deal with me, I, and now," said Cota. "We involve the teachings of the seven grandfathers, which say that we're responsible for seven generations past and seven generations in the future. Meaning the seven generations past we're to respect as father and as grandfather and a great-grandfather by seven generations in our families. It means if there's going to be a development over there in that area, and that's where they were buried, we'll do whatever we have to, to defend that area. We have to. We are obligated. In the same breath, we are obligated to keep for seven generations in the future.

"It's a way of life. It's respect for the earth, respect for the animals."

Unfortunately for Frontenac Ventures, the Algonquins did not perceive the company or its principals as likely to respect the earth, or the interests of seven generations to come. Nor did they see them as good neighbors.

Gandhi, Suits and Counter-suits

Unlike many native bands across the nation, whose straits in 2006 and 2007 were desperate enough to tempt them to violence, the Ardoch Algonquins and their leaders were firmly committed to the nonviolent principles of Gandhi and Martin Luther King. In Harold's own case, this flowed not only from his Algonquin cultural background, which has traditionally stressed negotiation and consensus, but from his years in martial arts—he is a black belt in judo. The Buddhist philosophy on which both judo and aikido are based comes down firmly on the side of non-aggression and approves the use of martial arts techniques only in defensive situations.

Throughout the 1981 rice war, Harold had successfully strived to keep all tactics nonviolent, repeatedly intervening in tense situations to cool tempers and restore order. The heart attack that eventually sidelined him and forced him to reduce his role to honorary and advisory, rather than active day-to-day, leadership, was partly a result of the constant strain required to keep a lid on things.

Harold and the Algonquins had a lot of nonviolent techniques to fall back on, including those to use in public relations campaigns and those to unleash in the suit/counter-suit paper-and-verbal bloodletting that we euphemistically call the North American court system.

Their immediate task was to rally and unify support, and after that to get the story out to the media.

The white settlers in Ardoch proper were already predisposed—after their experience in the rice wars—to support the Algonquins. But the Algonquins themselves had unity problems. In the 1930s, one branch of the nation living around Golden Lake had accepted government jurisdiction and become the Golden Lake Reserve. Ever since, though they represented only those Algonquin who lived within the reserve's geographical boundaries, this group was frequently

approached by government officials during land claim negotiations and treated as if they represented all Algonquins.
In addition, in 1996, a small group of Algonquins in the
Ardoch area who preferred to be governed through the electoral process rather than traditional consensus mechanisms
split from the Ardoch Algonquin First Nation and became
the Shabot Obaadjiwan Algonquins.

The Golden Lake Algonquins had no part in the uranium
controversy, which did not impact their reserve. As for the
Shabot group, their chief, Doreen Davis, quickly rallied to
the cause and sided with Harold and the local white settlers.
It was time to open the public relations campaign.

The Ardoch allies began with a guaranteed attention-
getter: they got together as a group on that June 28 and
physically blocked the mine exploration site. Picket signs
and placards went up, volunteers were organized into
round-the-clock shifts, coolers full of food were brought
to the site, along with juice and soft drinks (no alcohol was
allowed), lanterns and flashlights, and folding lawn chairs to
sit on. Whole families joined in, as they had during the rice
war, mothers and children (the latter toting soccer balls and
softballs to play with), grandparents—what Zorba the Greek
would have called "the full catastrophe"—and they all contributed to what soon became almost a carnival atmosphere.

At first nervous, fearing the blockade could turn violent, the provincial police arrived on the scene ready for
trouble. But the presence of Ardoch Algonquin co-chief
Randy Cota—who happened to be 'a detective sergeant in
the Ontario Provincial Police (his blockade appearance was
strictly on his off-duty time)—proved reassuring. Cota kept
in regular contact with his fellow officers from the proposed

mine site, via cell phone, emphasizing that the demonstrators were peaceful and even included children.

The media picked the story up fast, with reports appearing in weeklies like the *Frontenac News* and the *Community Press*, in dailies like *The Kingston Whig-Standard*, and on local radio and television stations. Blockaders took advantage of the Internet, posting their story to discussion groups and on activist websites. Letters to the editor flooded the mail. The Morrisons were particularly active, with Gloria giving interviews, including one on the nationally broadcast CBC radio program *As It Happens*. The national press, including *The Globe and Mail*, the Toronto *Star*, and other dailies, picked the story up too. Before long, everyone in the country knew about the newest battle in Frontenac County.

Allies appeared from everywhere, including Mining Watch Canada, Greenpeace, Canadian Coalition for Nuclear Responsibility, Christian Peace Workers, and others—in all some eighty-one groups. New groups, like Community Coalition Against Mining Uranium, started up. In Ottawa, whose water supply was potentially under threat, groups like ACT City swung into action, organizing meetings and presentations. Soon, the local blockaders were joined by sympathizers from all around eastern Ontario. Motorists driving past along Route 509 pulled over to talk.

On July 8, after being contacted by word of mouth, e-mail, Facebook, and telephone, several hundred people turned up at the junction of Route 509 and Highway 7 (one of the two principal roads between Toronto and Ottawa), near the popular summer resort town of Sharbot Lake, to protest the mining plans. The crowd, which grew as it marched, paraded along Highway 7, led by two Algonquins carrying the Ardoch Algonquin First Nation Unity Flag, and followed by mothers with children in strollers, Harold Perry and Doreen Davis, and what the *Frontenac News* later called "a sea of aboriginal and non-aboriginal supporters,"[41] blocking all traffic on the major highway.

None of this sat very well with the folks at Frontenac Ventures. Lawyer Smitheman went to court on July 24 and filed a suit for no less than $77 million against the Algonquins and their leaders, including Harold Perry, band spokesman Bob Lovelace, Ardoch co-chiefs Randy Cota and Paula Sherman, and Shabot Obaadjiwan chief Doreen Davis. Initially, no non-natives were named in the suit, despite their prominent involvement in the anti-mine battle.

Launching a high-ticket suit was a technique Smitheman had used in the past, on an even-grander-than-$77-million scale, to overcome the resistance of another First Nations band struggling against a mining company. Roughly a year earlier, acting on behalf of a firm named Platinex Inc., he'd filed a suit for $10 billion against the Kitchenuhmaykoosib Inninuwug (Big Trout Lake) First Nation, who had opposed Platinex's staking and drilling of land that it was believed held large deposits of platinum.[42]

At the time, David Peerla, mining coordinator for an allied native group, said "the number ten billion is designed to intimidate, silence and harass."[43] Said Smitheman: "The life of a platinum mine could be thirty years, so the value could be $10 billion."

The tiny Big Trout Lake band, many of whose members still supported themselves with such traditional activities as hunting, fishing, trapping, and plant gathering, could no more come up with $10 billion—more than the gross national product of some United Nations member countries—than they could build and send a rocket to Mars. Nor could the Ardoch Algonquins and their neighbors, in all perhaps seven or eight hundred people, be expected to cobble together $77 million. Asking for such ridiculously large sums from small rural communities obviously unable ever to pay them may not have been the wisest public relations move the company could have made. "It's a David versus Goliath fight," said Cota, and by now many people in the area agreed.

The company claimed that time was of the essence, and that its investors stood to lose substantially if work on the site was held up. This prompted interest in the company's financial status and its connections with its backers.

At the time of the June North Frontenac Council meeting, Frontenac Ventures was no longer alone, but was already planning to merge with Sylvio Ventures Inc., of British Columbia. According to a May 30, 2007 announcement by Sylvio, the B.C. company had "signed a binding letter agreement" to "acquire all of the issued and outstanding shares of FVC" and then to "incorporate a wholly-owned subsidiary, which will amalgamate with FVC to form a new company Amalco, which will become a wholly-owned operating subsidiary of Sylvio." [44]

Sylvio itself hadn't been around very long, at least not under that name. The company was previously called Pangeo Pharma Inc., and described itself in 2002 as "a specialty pharmaceutical company with core competencies in pharmaceutical manufacturing." [45] In June 2003, the company was issued a cease-trading order by both the British Columbia Securities Commission and the Manitoba

Securities Commission "for failure to file its annual financial statements for the year ended January 31, 2003."[46] In July 2003, in Quebec Superior Court, it obtained protection from creditors pending a restructuring, and began selling assets.[47] On October 21, 2003, its creditors approved a Plan of Arrangement "whereby all of the assets of the applicant would be liquidated and the proceeds distributed to creditors."[48] On November 12, 2004, the Toronto Stock Exchange (TSX) suspended trading of the company's stocks.[49]

On June 24, 2005, the Ontario Securities Commission issued a cease-trade order against the firm, preventing it from trading its shares due to "failure to file its annual financial statements for the year ended January 31, 2003," and failing to file "audited financial statements" for the years ending in January 2004 and 2005, as well as "all interim financial statements since January 31, 2003."[50]

On September 29, 2005, Pangeo shareholders held an extraordinary meeting to approve the election of a new director, and to change the company name to Silvio Ventures Inc. On November 28, 2005, its shares were moved to the NEX venture exchange, which "allows 'inactive' companies to maintain a listing while they complete their reorganizations."[51] On December 21, 2005, the osc allowed a variance of its earlier cease-trade order, to permit a proposed stock consolidation and private placement of three million post-consolidated common shares at five cents per share, "to raise proceeds of $150,000," and approved the change of name to Silvio Ventures Inc.[52] Silvio subsequently filed its required financial statements, and on October 27, 2006, the osc revoked its earlier cease-trade order altogether.[53] Silvio was now able to trade its stock.

And that stock attracted interest from investors, several of whom discussed it in online fora such as Stockhouse's Bullboards. None of the discussion participants knew much about either Silvio or Frontenac Ventures, and their sometimes hasty, informal opinions could be very judgemental and wide of the mark. But their comments give an idea of what investors—some might call them speculators—were thinking at the time:

Early in May 2007, an investor calling himself *Bushed* noted: ""I have to say I was pleased to look on the NEX and see SIV [Silvio] trading, as I got stuck with a few Pil [Pangeo] shares as well...I see they have brought a medical technology person onto the board of directors and I suspect this is the direction they will go with the company. I think we old Pil holders should be grateful to the director who just resigned and the president for bringing the stock back from the dead." [54]

Next day, however, he was less enthusiastic: "It is a shell," [55] and then "Kurt Lahey resigned and a fellow with a history in medical devices has stepped in. Check Sedar. I would have thought it would have become a mineral exploration company as well. Now I don't know." [56] Share prices rose, and he asked: "somebody needs to be buying it to make it rise. Why and who?" [57] Then, on May 10, "This isn't a pharma company, it is a shell. Chances are the only reason the stock is rising is because someone is trying to consolidate the shares before they do something with the stock. The stock would have to hit between $8 and $10 for me to break even on what I lost on Pangeo." [58]

By this time, investors were getting wind of Silvio's interest in Frontenac Ventures. Wrote *Ktritt* on May 26: "Uranium property coming on board? You bet!" [59]

Shiningstar complained: "It's pretty disrespectful how they keep shareholders in the dark for this long...what's going on? I haven't been able to find any old news on this company let alone any recent news. What kind of company that tries to keep in touch with shareholders doesn't even have a website? Does anyone have any info on Silvio I can access? Besides the Pil connection." [60]

On May 30, Silvio publicly announced its plans to merge with Frontenac Ventures, and reaction was swift. "Wow...if we get a 12 bagger here I can break even," wrote *Windigo69*. "Don't see any of those PIL snakes on the bod. Let's get trading and hope they can put a good spin on the story." [61]

"The difference between a fox and a dog is about eight beers. lol," wrote *Xlong*.[62]

"My Pangeo stake has already been written off, so anything gained here is a bonus," said *fanman*. "A coincidence for myself is that our family cottage is right in the middle of the area described in the press release. Questions: will it still trade under the same symbol??? Anyone have an idea of when the deal closes??? Any idea when trading will resume, ie. Is there some industry requirement that they have to meet?

"We are an hour north of there. Beautiful country in that whole region of Ontario. We drive through the Bancroft mining area frequently. I think of it as 'the past,' not as the future...but now having inherited a few siv shares I hope that there is a future." [63]

Bullboarders' reaction to the June 28 Algonquin blockade of the mine site was somewhat slow in coming, but on July 17 *algrove* wrote to the list:

Globe says Silvio target Frontenac battling Indians.
Silvio Ventures Inc (C:SIV)

Shares Issued 8,556,438

Last Close SIV.H 5/23/2007 $1.16

Monday July 16 2007 - in the news

The Globe & Mal reports in its Saturday, July 14 edition that prospectors hoping to make the case for a multi-million-dollar uranium mine north of Kingston have access to the site denied by eastern Ontario Algonquins. The Globe's Bill Curry writes the Algonquins appear to be winning the battle for local public opinion..." [64]

"This may still workout someday," wrote *Shiningstar*. "I sold my shares about 2 weeks before the alt. At first I wasn't too happy about my timing but now I'm glad I did. Maybe I'll be sorry someday but for now I'm moving on." [65]

A provincial election was looming, to choose members of the Ontario Legislature in Queen's Park, and the local candidates weren't slow in sensing which way the winds of public opinion were blowing. At an all-candidates meeting on July 21, the Liberal, Conservative, New Democratic Party, and Green Party candidates all came out in favor of a moratorium on uranium exploration, while the NDP and Green candidates said they actually supported the protesters' occupation of the mine site.

Only a few days earlier, Frontenac Ventures CEO White had told *The Globe and Mail* that police efforts to avert confrontations by keeping him away from the property and the protesters meant that "it's similar now to Niger, where you have to bring in [private] armed guards to protect your rights." [66]

The comment reminded the Algonquins of the conflict at Big Trout Lake, where lawyer Neal Smitheman had represented Platinex. At one point, Platinex brought in an ex–British Army officer to mediate, which local band members interpreted as a scare tactic. Said David Peerla, a consultant for the native group: "There are no checks and balances on private security firms entering into disputes with First Nations. They're not accountable to anyone. They're common in Africa, where they send an army to take over valuable mining deposits and protect them or to overthrow governments. The strange and worrying thing is to see them come to Canada." [67]

Smitheman riposted: "It's not because he was a former British Army officer that he was sent there...I was in the Boy Scouts one time, but I wouldn't be referred to as a Boy Scout." [68]

During that earlier dispute, Smitheman had sought an injunction to allow Platinex to continue its work, claiming that "if we don't get onto the property to do exploratory work, it'll cause irreparable harm to the company financially." [69]

He sought a similar injunction against the Algonquins, for similar reasons, telling the court "if we [Frontenac Ventures] don't have access to the property, even limited access, we're out of business." [70] On August 27, the Ontario Supreme Court ordered the mine protesters to leave the site, and the police to arrest anyone who didn't.

But the Algonquins and their allies remained defiant, staying in place at the mine, and the OPP, remembering only too well the 1995 Ipperwash crisis, in which police shot and killed an unarmed native protester, hesitated to do anything that might provoke violence.

The conservative *Kingston Whig-Standard* railed against the blockaders (and like Frontenac Ventures' initial $77 million lawsuit, ignored the white protesters' role): "If the aboriginals succeed in flouting the court, they may never pay directly. Instead, they will damage democracy...The ultimate end of such scenarios can only be anarchy."[71]

Locally, however, several municipal councils had voted to side with mine opponents, including the North Frontenac Council, which despite George White's earlier appearance and submitted documents had passed a resolution on September 13 asking the province to imitate Nova Scotia and declare a moratorium on uranium exploration and mining.[72] Altogether, seven municipal councils and one county council voted to express solidarity with the protesters.

It's possible that North Frontenac's decision was partially influenced by a budding tax-revolt movement, launched by Mr. and Mrs. Earl Recoskie, property owners on Route 509, who wrote to council to warn that: "We, along with other residents of North Frontenac Township, are withholding our tax payment submissions until Your Honor and each council member takes a stand on whether you support uranium exploration and mining in our area."[73] The letter included a photo of the 30-foot-high Stanrock Tailings Wall of radioactive mill waste in the Elliot Lake area, and the dead trees close to it.

Meanwhile, Smitheman's $77 million suit appeared not to faze the Algonquins, who on September 18 upped the ante by countering it with one of their own, a cross-claim asking $10 million from Frontenac Ventures and $1 billion from the Ontario government. The same day, a Superior Court judge in Kingston cited the six leaders of the Algonquin protesters for contempt of court. Later, Frank Morrison's name was added to the list.

On September 22, the anti-mining groups launched a "canoe protest" against the proposed mine, to feature a long-distance paddle from Ardoch all the way to Ottawa, highlighting the Mississippi/Ottawa River watershed and the danger it faced from future uranium pollution. Hundreds of people joined the event, in kayaks and canoes on the water and in motorcades following the paddlers from shore. The event concluded on September 28 with a rally on Parliament Hill, a protest at Dow's Lake, and a visit by protesters to Premier Dalton McGuinty's Ottawa riding office.

Even before the paddlers had launched their boats, however, Silvio Ventures Inc. had apparently decided enough was enough. On September 18, it announced that it had "terminated the proposed acquisition of Frontenac." [74] By way of explanation, the news release added vaguely: "Since entering into the agreement in principal [sic] on May 23, 2007, the company and Frontenac have been unable to settle certain terms of the definitive agreement for the proposed acquisition." [75]

On October 2, the Algonquins wrote to Premier McGuinty, asking for mediation in the dispute, and proposed that during mediation they would suspend their occupation of the mine site. "Big deal—we lose," grumbled Bullboards participant *moe4*.[76] As the dispute dragged on, an even more disgruntled *Windigo69* lashed out: "Gawd that's annoying...seems the natives do little more than keep an eye on any land they feel they have a claim to...not like they would ever develope [sic] the property or even plant a fs#%ing garden." [77]

Like the *Whig-Standard* editorial writer, he or she had nothing to say about the mine's white opponents, such as

protestor Donna Dillman, who had carried on a highly publicized hunger strike against the proposed mining of uranium, which she called "the most dangerous substance on
earth."[78] After a 51-day fast at the mine site itself, she moved
her protest to the provincial legislature at Queen's Park.
Premier McGuinty said he would halt the use of uranium
in a perfect world, but that half the province's power comes
from nuclear plants.

The anti-mine groups got a major boost on November 21,
when the Kingston City Council became the latest municipal
government to call—this time unanimously—for a province-
wide moratorium on uranium mining. Except for Ottawa,
the nation's capital, Kingston was the largest city in the
region, and getting its council on-side was a political plum.[79]

The protesters' reaction was tempered, however, by
an ominous rumor that had started to make the rounds,
namely that an advertisement had been posted with the
Job Bank by a security company named Knights on Guard,
saying it needed a large number of recruits to work near
Sharbot Lake. The Knights on Guard website featured an
oddly misspelled motto, "Secure, Detere and Protect," and
photos of uniformed guards in flack vests, carrying night-
sticks and working with vicious-looking Rottweiler attack
dogs.[80] Mine foes wondered if the guards might be intended
to work at the Frontenac Ventures site, but up till then there
had been no indication of such a move.

The battle, evidently, was far from over. As one mine
opponent remarked: "This could turn out to be a long
winter."

His comment proved accurate, before the winter was
over. On February 15, 2008, bowing to the wishes of

Frontenac Ventures lawyer Smitheman that "incarceration" be used against mine protesters, Superior Court Justice Douglas Cunningham sentenced Algonquin protest leaders Bob Lovelace and Paula Sherman to the highest possible punishment permitted for the offense of contempt. Lovelace was given six months in the penitentiary, plus a $25,000 initial fine and $2,000 per day in additional fines for each day Lovelace refused to guarantee he would not continue opposing the mine if released (this, effectively, amounted to an *infinite* sentence, one without any possible end, which would obviously bankrupt not only Lovelace but his eventual estate, unless he publicly agreed to renounce his most cherished personal beliefs and what he regarded as the good of his community). Sherman was fined an initial $15,000, plus the same "infinite" $2,000 per day ongoing fine as Lovelace. She was spared hard jail time only when it became known that she was the mother of and sole support for three children, and would "lose them if she goes to jail."

The Ardoch Algonquin First Nation was fined $10,000, thus collectively punishing every member of the band, including those who may not have joined the protest.

The harsh sentence, which punished the innocent along with the "guilty," was deplored by both the human rights watchdog group Amnesty International and by legislative representatives in the area:

"Indigenous leaders and their supporters are facing stiff punishments for doing what they feel is necessary to protect rights that may one day be upheld in court or in the land claims process," an Amnesty release said. "Meanwhile the provincial government is ignoring its own legal obligations without any accountability."[81]

Federal MP Scott Reid and member of the Ontario legislature Randy Hillier published a joint statement of con-
demnation of the sentences, calling Cunningham's decision
"a grave injustice." They said the combination of fines and
imprisonment given Lovelace, in particular, were "grossly
disproportionate" to his "act of civil disobedience." [82]

Similar outrage had followed the jailing of six members
of the northern Ontario native community of Kitchenuhmaykoosib Inninuwug First Nation (KIFN), for opposing
the plans of lawyer Neal Smitheman's other mining client,
Platinex, mentioned earlier. Canada's Anglican primate,
Archbishop Fred Hiltz, labeled the jailings a throwback to
colonialism. [83]

If, as some critics of the heavy sentences claimed, their
effect would be to frighten opponents of the mining interests into silence or to curtail anti-mining political action, it
didn't work that way. On February 27, the list of municipal
councils demanding an immediate moratorium on uranium
mining and exploration in the province gained its most
importand new adherent.

The city council of Ottawa—Canada's national capital—
voted in favor of the moratorium, and also called for an
immediate review of the Mining Act. [84]

Months later, the injustice of the harsh sentences meted
out to the Algonquin leaders by Justice Cunningham were
reviewed by a higher authority. A panel of three Ontario
Court of Appeal judges freed Bob Lovelace on May 28,
and on July 2 they went further, ruling that the sentences
of Lovelace, as well as those of the six KIFN leaders in the
Platinex case, were "too harsh." [85] In what amounted in
legal circles to an official rebuke to the lower court judges,

the appeal court reduced the protesters' sentences to time served, and also dismissed all fines faced by them. The "infinite" financial punishment of Lovelace for opposing mining interests was thus curtailed.

"I did do three and a half months in jail," said Lovelace. "That's three and a half months lost out of my life, but I guess if it brings some clarification to aboriginal rights, that was time well spent."

Neither Lovelace, nor many of the other scrappers who took part in the mine resistance movement said much about the personal toll the battle had taken on their lives. Not long after his release from jail, Lovelace had to go into hospital for open heart surgery. His family life has suffered, as has that of several other leaders of the Ardoch group. Couples have divorced, friends have become enemies.

The miners, seeking riches and willing to go to any legal lengths to claim them, seem not to have similar problems. A waitress in a town near the center of the battle recalls one of the pro-mining luminaries coming in to her restaurant. "He ordered and I just looked at him," she recalls. "I didn't say anything, just looked at him. I did nothing to get his order. After a while, he realized that I wasn't going to serve him. He just laughed, got up and left. I don't think he gives a damn."

Whether the miners' plans to develop the Ardoch site would go forward, with all their possible dire environmental consequences, was unfortunately not yet resolved.

Since Time Immemorial

*...it is expressly provided that the Indians
shall not, under any pretense whatever, be
deprived of the lands claimed by them...*
JOHN JOHNSON, British Superintendent of Indian Affairs, November 5, 1824[1]

THE ARDOCH ALGONQUINS' STRUGGLE to protect their and their white neighbors' land from pollution by uranium miners was not the only battle they were forced to fight in 2006–08. Nor were the Algonquins' multiple confrontations the only ones going on in the area. Barely more than an hour's drive away from Ardoch (if you knew the shortcuts and went a bit over the speed limit) was the Tyendinaga Mohawk Reserve, where the descendants of the famed Joseph Brant were engaged in another fight, also in part with would-be miners.

Headlines in the local weeklies and the daily *Kingston Whig-Standard* ping-ponged between the two battles, recording the most recent moves, first of the Algonquins, then the Mohawks. The tactics in each fight were different, but the stakes in both were the same, and both were of national importance—physically, geographically, politically, financially, socially, and especially morally.

In fact, if one looks at the picture in many countries elsewhere in the world, they were no more than the local examples of a worldwide battle being fought by once forcibly colonized indigenous peoples, from Australia's Aboriginals and the Ainu of northern Japan, to the Hmung of Vietnam and the decimated tribes of the Amazon, to regain the rights and human dignity their one-time conquerors had taken from them at the point of a gun or sword, or by simple swindling, by insisting on equitable treatment today.

In Australia, the Wangkumarra people have engaged in battle with mining giant Santos over oil exploration and mining activity on their traditional Outback lands.[2] In the U.S., the Dineh-Navajo of Arizona have struggled against forced relocation of their people to make room for coal mining operations,[3] while in Canada, British Columbia's Coast Salish people have had to struggle against gold mine expansion on their lands that would have damaged local lakes.[4] Other First Nations peoples are still fighting against loggers, recreational land developers, and others who encroach on their lands.

Rights, and A Priceless Gift

The Ardoch Algonquins' other big fights, before the uranium controversy began, were to maintain their traditional hunting and fishing rights, and to give the region in which they lived a priceless gift, which too few seemed to want to accept: a cultural center at Pine Lake, called the Manomin Center after the rice which had been a staple of the traditional Algonquin diet. Open to all, the center would tell the

story of the area's aboriginal people and foster the preservation of the Algonquin language, way of life, and traditions.

Hunting and fishing rights had been crucial to the Algonquins for decades. Even after the initial onslaught of white
invasion and land-taking, they still depended on such activity to survive. As the authors of the Canadian Algonquin
history *Since Time Immemorial: Our Story* recall, the Great
Depression of the "Dirty Thirties" was a time of particular hardship for those Algonquins living near Maniwaki, in
Quebec:

> On the reserve, times were always tough for the
> Algonquins, which was why many families kept gardens
> and root cellars. Also, men hunted to supplement their
> seasonal wages [as guides or lumberjacks] and their ice
> houses were always stocked with an adequate supply of
> dried and smoked meats. The River Desert Algonquins,
> by the very hunter-gatherer tradition that they always
> maintained were able to get through the severe hard-
> ships of the Depression.[5]

As noted briefly in chapter 2, Harold Perry's boyhood in
Ontario was very similar.

"Those were hard times," he recalled. "I was born in '30,
you know. There was no power, electrical power. The roads
were poor. It was all horses. Later on, when I got a little bit
older, you'd hear maybe one car a week come up to you. You
could hear them coming maybe two miles, and you'd go out
and watch them. We all lived off the land, everybody. I mean
ours [the Algonquins'] was more hunting and trapping and
fishing. But the [white] homesteaders raised all their own
stuff too. That is one of the better ways of survival, to have

a garden and to raise some chickens and have a cow and whatever. They raised their own stuff. So even though they had no money they survived all right. The old people here made maple syrup, up the river less than a mile. Then when they surveyed the roads they gave all the adjacent land to the settlers. And so my great-grandfather, for example, after him doing the sugar bush and getting it ready and all that, they [the provincial government] gave it away on him, and he had no place to go."

Since the Algonquins had never been conquered in war, nor negotiated a treaty regarding land rights, under the Royal Proclamation of 1763 it was actually illegal to give their sugar bush away. It was also illegal to insist that Algonquin subsistence hunters or fishermen pay for a license from the province before they could hunt or fish on their own traditional territory.

At the time of European settlement and for decades thereafter, Perry's family and others like them felt too vulnerable to resist. But after the 1980s rice war, the Ardoch band knew the time had come to take some of their own back. So did other Ontario Algonquin bands, both those that had previously made treaties with the government, which assigned them specific geographic "reserves" (so-called "status" bands), and those who had not ("non-status" bands).

In 1991, the Ontario provincial government, which under Canada's federal system has jurisdiction over natural resources, agreed that the Algonquins had the right to hunt big game for food. The agreement, however, was not sufficiently specific on other aspects of fishing and hunting rights, and often local enforcement officers were confused as to the details. Hence Perry's hunting and fishing expeditions. He went to court to assert his right to hunt migratory birds, the license "stamps" for which are issued by the federal, rather than provincial, government (migratory birds, by definition, cross provincial boundaries and are thus a federal matter), and won his case. The moose hunt with his elderly brother, mentioned in chapter 4, and Randy Cota's hunts, were designed to reinforce and publicly assert the Algonquins' traditional rights, and provincial authorities didn't dispute them. When Harold and his brother shot their moose, authorities left them alone.

Sadly, this didn't sit well with many local people. Even some long-time, year-round residents—including people who had witnessed the rice war and at the time gave at least lip-service support to Perry—turned on the native hunters when their photo with the dead moose appeared in the local papers. And their feelings spilled over into the Pine Lake Manomin Heritage Center issue as well, to the deep disappointment of both Perry and Cota.

"What upsets me is a man who owns [a local business] and is a [relative] of Harold and Neil Perry," Cota recounted. "I went to [his business] and sat down and said, 'Boy, it's a good thing you know, back there at Pine Lake. It's going to be great. We're going to get a modern facility there and the community will be able to use it for dances, and it'll be high-tech and have everything there, cost the people of North Frontenac absolutely nothing, thanks to people like Neil and Harold Perry.'

"I've known Harold and Neil Perry all my life. Neil's a Christian man that wouldn't say boo if he had to. Soft-spoken, easygoing, meek, mild man. If there was a picture in the dictionary of a gentleman it would be Neil Perry.

"And that man [the business owner] said to me: 'This Indian stuff is bullshit.'

"I started to step backwards there, and I said: 'No. You got Harold and Neil Perry, good men, they deserve to see this in their lifetime, the fruits of all their hard labor.' And he says, 'I've known Neil Perry all my life and I lost all my respect when I saw a picture of him and Harold holding a bull moose rack. I have no respect at all for Neil Perry.'

"In other words, as long as he is a good little Indian and plays by your rules, you love him. But when he stands up for what he believes in and what he was taught as a kid, [he's] no longer a good person. I told that man, 'If you lose all respect for him over a newspaper article, you never did respect him, because of the color of his skin.'"

Detective Sergeant Randy Cota is a hard-boiled, tough provincial police officer, with years of trouble under his belt. He is no emotional creampuff. But you could see in his eyes, without his saying anything more, how deeply that conversation had cut.

And the "bullshit" heritage center which had lost the businessman's support?

It would not only be an excellent community-building and educational resource for the Algonquins themselves and for local school districts (whose students would find there the story of at least eight thousand years of human settlement), but also an obvious tourist draw, bringing visitors from across the province. As posted on the the Ardoch Algonquin website,

> According to the AAFN, the community center will provide "a space for community members to come together in a culturally significant space for community gatherings, cultural and linguistic programs, education and training, as well as social and health services." As

well, the center will "offer programs to non-members who want to learn about Algonquin people, culture and history." In addition, the center hopes to attract one or more health professionals who can provide health services to community members and also regional residents.

AAFN ensures that the project will benefit the municipality of North Frontenac and bring welcome revenue to its communities, as well as providing opportunities for locals to learn about the history of the place in which they live. Members are certain that the Manomin Heritage Center will become something the whole community can be proud of.[6]

"You tell me why you would not want a possibly half-million-dollar development, that's going to be good for everybody, shared with everybody, in your backyard, that's not going to cost you a penny?" asked Cota. "Give me one good reason why you wouldn't."

His interlocutors couldn't think of one. After all, the center would be built on what is almost certainly Algonquin land, and would blend with and respect the natural environment around it. Kingston architect Alexander Wilson's project drawings show a rustic, two-story log building, with a landscape around it of cedars and maples, fully in keeping with its natural setting. The Algonquins would be paying for it, and it would bring tourists' cash to the coffers of every small business in the area, white and native alike. It would also give Algonquin youngsters a stronger sense of identity with the past, more personal pride, and greater strength to fill their roles as Canadian citizens in the future. As the AAFN website said, it would be a meeting point for native and non-native students, and their families, fostering mutual respect and understanding.

Unfortunately, neither Cota's local businessman, nor the provincial government, nor a substantial percentage of the non-native population around Pine Lake appeared to see it that way. Opposition to the center seemed strongest among the purely seasonal non-native residents, members of the Pine Lake Cottagers Association.

"Everybody's just bucking us every way they could," said Perry. "They want an environmental assessment, and bring up this kind of regulation and that kind." It looked to him as if people were being hyper-vigilant with anything the Algonquins wanted to put in, but not with non-native projects.

"A lot of those cottages are down close to the water," he said. "They've probably only got drums for a septic system. And they have boat launches where they put in gravel, and where these ramps are, everything just washes into the lake, oil and grease and gasoline and silt. And they don't worry about that. It washes straight down into the lake. But if we want to level off a spot for parking and a pow-wow ground, they complain it will create silt. The cottagers are putting pressure on the township and the [provincial] Ministry of Natural Resources (MNR).

"When we first moved in there, the MNR said they would give us the land. But we said no, it's not yours to give. The same with the township, for the building permit and the health permit and all of that. We told them we'd abide by the building code and even make it better than the code. We'll follow all the rules as close as we can, but we can't accept a permit because they don't have jurisdiction over the land to issue one to us. It's our land. Legally, we can't take anything from the Crown because that would be ceding our rights."

Essentially, the Algonquins saw many of the complaints as nit-picking. They also suspected racism might be an issue with some their opponents, but not with all of them.

They believed the biggest problems lay elsewhere, and that at the level of individual residents one of them was fear.

A spokesman for the Pine Lake Cottagers Association, Toronto lawyer David S. Rose, may have expressed it in a letter to the editor of a local newspaper. After first complaining about a list of comparatively minor problems, centering on building codes, septic tank regulations, and the design details of the planned center's boat launch space, Rose added:

> AAFNA [Ardoch Algonquin First Nation and Allies] will not publicly denounce [sic] any intention to take the rest of the undeveloped shore of Pine Lake. This shoreline is over several thousand feet of pristine forest and is currently titled to the Crown. When will AAFNA publicly denounce any intention to take the rest of Pine Lake...?[7]

A Bigger Puzzle

As Rose's letter strongly hinted, the Ardoch band's fights over rice, hunting, and uranium, despite their media prominence, were actually relatively small pieces in a much bigger puzzle.

After decades of native pressure and government stalling, a framework for negotiations for an overall Algonquin land claim settlement was signed in 1994, to include all of the region's Algonquins and both the provincial and federal governments. Negotiations—involving the Algonquin

Negotiation Representatives (ANRs) of some eight thousand Algonquins in a number of separate bands located in the Ottawa River watershed—began not long afterward.

They proved fraught with difficulty, born of what the Algonquin saw as government attempts to delay, divide, and conquer, as well as with divisions within the Algonquins' own ranks. The longer the talks dragged on, the more the Algonquins' losses continued to pile up—and the more anxiety was provoked among non-native residents of the region.

"We're hearing they're claiming Parliament Hill," one worried Ottawa resident told a reporter.[8]

The timber royalties, gravel quarry extracts, income from the sale of hunting and fishing licenses and other government earnings from Algonquin lands, mentioned by Randy Cota in chapter 4, were only part of native losses. To them one could add property taxes, sales taxes, and a myriad other sums. And that was only what government was gaining, and had been gaining for decades, from the use of the land—never mind private "owners."

Harold Perry cited Pine Lake, to show the mechanisms at work.

"For the most part, it's lined up with cottages," he explained. "Anything you can get a road to is lined up with cottages. Three subdivisions went in there, through the years. It was Algonquin land, but they [the provincial government] called it Crown land and just went ahead and developed it. Small little lots, and sold the lots off. The Ministry of Natural Resources [MNR] did it, and made a good buck out of it. And they've got a tent and trailer park there."

"We call them [cottagers] squatters," added Randy Cota. "But we're not here to fight against our neighbors. We weren't there [at the bargaining table] to negotiate or go against the private lands that people have deeds for, because they're our neighbors.

"You see, when the land claim process started fifteen years ago, Harold and I were there, with Kirby White Duck and a couple of other individuals from different communities. We made an agreement that there'd be no more sale of Crown land. The MNR said, 'Well, we only sell 100-acre parcels.' We said, OK, no more sales of 100-acre parcels.

"So now they sell 99-acre parcels of land. That's what we deal with constantly. It's just, you can't trust them.

"The secret is to keep us poor, keep us in the dark, tell us nothing and hope we'll go away. And they separate us. They say, well there's Métis [mixed blood], and then they say well hold on, you have your status and you have your non-status, then you have your spouses that are non-status—they make all these divisions. Divide and conquer."

The Ardoch Algonquin First Nation is a prime example. Because its members never negotiated a treaty with either federal or provincial governments, and never agreed to take money from government or retreat to the confines of an assigned geographical reserve, the band is considered "non-status." Their fellow Algonquins at nearby Golden Lake, who did sign a treaty and retreat to a reserve, are examples of a "status" band.

In the past, government tried to exploit this kind of thing, insisting that only status bands had the right to make agreements, or trying to use a status band to take away the rights of non-status Algonquins living elsewhere in the area. The practice goes back to the nineteenth century.

"Down in early history, and we have archive papers and stuff to document it, Algonquins were living down near

Bedford," said Perry. "The Algonquins and the Mississaugas were living together there, the Bedford Band. So Kingston was expanding out north. They wanted more land. So they went to these Algonquins and Mississaugas and said well, you know, we want to buy it. And they wouldn't sell it. So they [Kingston's representatives] went down to the Bay of Quinte and they got somebody down there to sell it to them. Came back up and said, 'Somebody's got to go over and tell these guys that we've bought the land.' The Algonquins [eventually] moved from there up to Bob's Lake, and they were supposed to give them a reserve there. And they promised them and they [the government] didn't follow through. Finally, they just denied even promising them a reserve. So this was in one way good for us. They [the Ardoch band's ancestors] never took anything or surrendered anything.

"So we're one of the few bands in Canada, maybe only the last one or two, that haven't surrendered their rights."

When disputes over Algonquin land have arisen in the region, the government has sought out native groups they see as more cooperative, even when the groups have no geographical or legal connection with the area in question.

"Up at Mazinaw Lake, they want to put in a great big time share development there," said Perry. "Hotels and golf, whatever it takes. This was way up along Highway 41, north of Cloyne. And they want aboriginal consent to go and do this. So they went to Golden Lake [southwest of Pembroke, on the far eastern side of Algonquin Park—and about four times as distant from Mazinaw Lake as Ardoch]. They never came near us. But they go to Golden Lake because Golden Lake is a status reserve."

"They're trying to get one group to sign away the rights of others in the area?"

"Absolutely."

However, thanks in large part to Perry's efforts, the Ardoch band had forced government to recognize its legitimacy as a community. Even if its members were not located within the boundaries of a designated reserve and hence were not "status Indians," they were a legal entity: the Ardoch Algonquin First Nation.

"When I was fighting the duck-hunting case, awhile back, we established that we were a community," Perry said. "I paid a lot of money to a researcher out of Ottawa, for genealogy. We went through the courts, at my expense, and we established ourselves as a bona fide community. We have archive papers that document that."

Technically, since the Ardoch band had been recognized legally, and was far closer to the planned development than the Golden Lake Reserve, the government should have come to Perry's group. Unfortunately, having established its bona fides as a band wasn't enough. Not long after they were recognized, the Ardoch group watched as a rival entity, with the government's apparent blessing, appeared to them to simply take over their name.

Randy Malcolm, an Algonquin living in Eganville [near the Golden Lake Reserve] who had been listed as the Ardoch band's Algonquin Negotiation Representative (ANR) at the overall land claim talks, ran into trouble with the band. "We kicked him out of the position of negotiator," said Cota. As the *Frontenac News* reported:

> One of the reasons the Algonquin Negotiation Representative process was undertaken was to deal with the competing claims to the name of Ardoch Algonquin by

two groups. This precipitated a dispute over membership lists...

In the end, the Ardoch Algonquin First Nation and Allies (AAFNA), under honorary Chief Harold Perry, the original Algonquin First Nation in Frontenac County and one of three off-reserve groups that were involved in the land claims process when it started back in 1992 (*sic*), decided to opt out of the Algonquin Negotiation Representative process.

Their decision was explained in an ad that ran in this newspaper...In that ad they charge that "The group known as the Algonquin National Tribal Council is the only non-status group to have political access to the Algonquin Negotiation Representation process. Through their lawyer, they have constructed a process that ensures their leaders will be the elected representatives..."

The boycott of the Algonquin Negotiation Representative process by the Harold Perry group left Randy Malcolm, the Chief of the Ardoch Algonquin First Nation that is recognized by the Algonquin National Tribal Council, as the sole candidate for Negotiation Representative from Ardoch, and he was acclaimed to the position.[9]

According to Perry and Cota, Malcolm's membership lists are not accurate, and even include Perry himself as a member, when clearly he is not. They regard Malcolm, who doesn't even live in the Ardoch area, as an interloper trying to claim the band's name. Malcolm insists that he is the duly elected chief of "what was originally the Ardoch Algonquins, and now we've in the last year changed our names to *Snimi-koea* Algonquins."

Making matters worse, in the eyes of the Harold Perry band, was the fact that the "chief negotiator" for the Algonquins in the overall land claim bargaining was a Toronto lawyer named Roberts Potts, a partner in the law firm Blaney McMurtry LLP, which, as Perry noted, "Came against us during the rice wars in the 1980s." The firm's best-known member was Roy McMurtry, former Ontario attorney general and solicitor general, who was in office at the time of the rice fight. Perry and his group saw a fundamental conflict of interest in appointing someone from a firm with a history of opposing the Ardoch band as chief negotiator for the Algonquins. They also found it suspicious that Potts should be receiving money from the government during the negotiations, when he was supposed to be representing Ardoch against the same government. They saw it as stacking the cards against them.

Potts saw no conflict of interest in the arrangement. "I'm not being paid by the province," he said. "I'm being paid by a trust which receives funding from the [federal and provincial] governments like in any other land claim. The governments have a process that they fund negotiations to enable them to continue and for people to hire professionals and pay certain stipends and out-of-pocket expenses. You can't hire experts and get things done without money."

As if matters at the overall negotiations weren't complicated enough, another equally vexing difficulty arose. The Ottawa Algonquin First Nation, another of the groups taking part in the land claim bargaining, also withdrew from negotiations. As announced on its website:

In April 2007 the Ottawa Algonquin First Nation, representative of the Ottawa area Algonquins, withdrew from the negotiations due to several unresolved issues. Unresolved issues include the exclusion [from negotiations] of several communities, the lack of consultation, the total lack of transparency, the abuse of inherent rights and the misrepresentation of the negotiator. Rather than address these issues, the principal negotiator, Bob Potts, as well as the negotiators for Ontario and Canada, chose to ignore the facts and proceed with an election to put in place a new ANR for the Ottawa community. It is interesting to note that the individual who was elected was not even on the Ottawa electors list at the time the election was called, and yet this individual was elected as ANR for the Ottawa Algonquins.

The Ottawa Algonquin First Nation has not returned to the negotiation table and does not recognize the ANR elected by Mr. Bob Potts.[10]

Potts completely rejected all of these claims, insisting that the negotiations are "very transparent" and that "we have impeccable records to substantiate the people we represent." Noting that he has been involved in several previous land claims negotiations, he insisted "I'm not the kind of person whose integrity is in any way questioned."

Nevertheless, the Ottawa Algonquin First Nation joined several other Algonquin groups in the region—including Perry's—in a class-action lawsuit over what they saw as a skewed and unfair negotiation process designed to steamroller local bands into an unjust settlement.

Another favored government tactic, as Perry, Cota, and

others in the Ardoch band saw it, was delay. They believed the government had little interest in clearing up land claims as long as government (and the majority white voting population) were making money from Algonquin land. Not until land claims became a hot national political issue, with native bands everywhere in Canada demonstrating and provoking highly publicized clashes, did the government's tune change. Then, it appeared to the Algonquin, the goal became to rush through a quick settlement that would essentially buy off native groups, as Cota put it, "for a pittance."

Rightly or wrongly, they believed that local groups and leaders who saw through this tactic were unwanted at the bargaining table, and complications were being deliberately introduced to enable other, more tractable bargainers to take over the process.

"They say 'Hurry up, the claim's going to be over," said Cota. "How many times have we heard this one, Harold? 'You've only got six months more and we're shutting down the claim. You guys are taking too long. You're not getting your act together. By March of next year we're shutting it down.' March comes and March goes and it's still going on. The claim [can] always continue, because underneath the bargaining table, they [the government] are pulling in millions and millions of dollars."

Given the long years of victimization that the Algonquin had already suffered, such suspicions were at least understandable from a human, emotional standpoint. Whatever else government negotiators were doing, they seemed not to be taking this into account. The Ardoch band's interest was not in taking a quick "golden handshake" that would enable the province to continue taking in millions, but in retaining a measured, reasonably negotiated control over

their land and its fruits, a control that would be viable—at
the very least—for the next seven generations.

The Mohawk Fight

Meanwhile, to the southwest, the Tyendinaga Mohawks had
their own battle going. Unlike the Ardoch Algonquin, they
were a "status" band, living on a defined reserve, but even
on their reserve they were not masters of their own house.
Some 900 acres of their land, referred to as the Culbertson
Tract, was occupied by others—including up to 60 percent
of the Ontario town of Deseronto,[11] and a gravel quarry
operated by a company called Thurlow Aggregates.

In 2006, a Kingston land developer named Tim Letch,
of Interface Finance AG, announced his intention to launch
a 15-acre, $30-million housing subdivision in Deseronto,
located in the Culbertson Tract, with waterfront access to
the Bay of Quinte. Letch was aware that land claim negotiations between the Mohawks and government were ongoing,
but said he planned to break ground for his development
on January 10, 2007 regardless of whether a settlement had
been reached.[12]

For many Mohawks, especially the 50 percent of the
reserve population under the age of 22,[13] this was the straw
that broke the camel's back. Already frustrated by the slow
pace of the land claim talks (even Deseronto mayor Norm
Clark thought the talks were too slow, and if not speeded up
the town would "surely die."[14]), they were highly irritated by
the sight of some eight hundred dump trucks of gravel per
month being taken away from the Thurlow quarry,[15] with
no economic benefit to the Mohawks, who badly needed
money. As one resident told a reporter: "Fifty percent of our
wells are contaminated. We're talking about people's day-

to-day existence. But the only thing we get when government opens its purse is money for a police station." [16] The Mohawks decided to act. Believing Thurlow Aggregates would be supplying gravel for the proposed Letch development, they targeted the quarry.

On March 22, 2007, led by Shawn Brant (a descendant of the historical figure Joseph Brant, whose eighteenth-century loyalty to Britain had earned the thanks of England's king), a group of younger Mohawks seized the quarry, which soon became a campground for a revolving, semipermanent population of thirty to one hundred aboriginals, in tents and trailers. Quarry operations and the parade of gravel trucks ceased.

Little did the protesters imagine that their tactics, though non-violent, would divide their own people, and lead to the threat of draconian punishment for their main spokesman.

The land settlement talks dragged on, and the protest ended up continuing for weeks. The young Mohawks claimed they had discovered evidence at the quarry of possible dumping of toxic wastes, which, if true, would constitute a violation of environmental laws. In April, Brant took reporters on a tour of the quarry, pointing out industrial garbage—used batteries, gas canisters, oil bins, building materials, burnt shingles, chunks of old asphalt paving, and used pesticide containers.[17] Protesters invited officials to come to inspect the waste. A Ministry of the Environment district manager scheduled an April 5 visit to the site, then canceled it, claiming concern for her personal safety.[18]

The Mohawks' frustration continued to grow, and their tactics escalated. On April 27, a group of about 150 protesters gathered at the CN Railway line just north of the quarry, for what Brant said would be a forty-eight-hour blockade of rail traffic. Rail movement on the busy track, which normally sees as many as twenty trains passing per day, abruptly halted, gaining the protesters instant national headlines.

At this point, generational cracks began to show in the Mohawk ranks. The original quarry occupation had never been approved by the official leaders of the Mohawks of the Bay of Quinte. "They [the protesters] just took it upon themselves to do it," said band researcher Lisa Maracle.

In a news release, Tyendinaga chief R. Donald Maracle distanced his band from the protesters and their actions. "I know that people involved may think they are helping to advance our cause with regard to the land claim, however they are misguided," he said. "There was no reason to take this action while diplomatic processes are in place and under way." [19]

Official band council spokesman Brant Bardy echoed that view. "We seriously hope that any action taken doesn't jeopardize the negotiation that's under way and that is a concern that the council has," he said. "It just seems pointless to take action that may jeopardize the diplomatic process that's ongoing." [20]

Shawn Brant riposted: "We're talking about a quarry license and we're talking about land that the government acknowledges is Mohawk land. We respect the processes involved in resolving these issues, but we can't sit by and allow the land to be trucked away at the same time." [21] He also pointed out that the protests were having a positive effect on the morale of native young people, who according to Health Canada would normally be seven times more likely to commit suicide than non-native youths. "Today, suicide, despair, is the farthest thing from their minds," Brant said of his community's youth. "They're focused socially around the Longhouse, politically around the land" for which they were fighting.[22]

The rail blockade lasted for nearly thirty hours before protesters let the line reopen.

In May, CN Rail filed a suit against Shawn Brant, several protesters, and the Mohawk band council for damages caused by the blockade. A court injunction was granted, prohibiting further blocking of the rail line, and criminal charges were filed against Brant. CN later amended its suit, dropping the band council as a defendant, after seeing evidence the council had not authorized or approved the protest.

But the quarry occupation continued.

On May 4, Brant was arrested for mischief, disobeying a court order, and breach of recognizance, then released on bail. Then, in late May, as part of a nationwide aboriginal Day of Action, the protesters mounted a new blockade, this time of the nearby County Road 2. Brant was re-arrested, and this time denied bail. The prosecuting Crown attorney said he would demand that Brant, who faced a total of six charges, be given two years per charge, for a total of twelve years in prison.

Brant's supporters pointed out that convicted murderers had been given lighter sentences. They saw the threat as a government vendetta.

By October, Brant—who was under strict pretrial conditions—was replaced as official protest spokesman by nineteen-year-old Dustin Brant. The young Mohawks continued to occupy the quarry site, and the land claim talks continued to drag on, with no end in sight, into another year.

Brant, seen by police as a prime mover in the protests, and thus evidently a prime target, was repeatedly arrested and charged, acquitted, then re-arrested on new charges. On April 14, 2008, he was cleared of three charges of uttering threats during a demonstration against a planned housing project on Mohawk-claimed land. But on April 25, he was arrested again, during a traffic stop on the highway—an arrest that saw demonstrators who protested the arrest faced with drawn police guns.

By now, along with his Ardoch Algonquin neighbors to the northeast, he was becoming a cause célèbre. He was invited to speak in Toronto, and benefit concerts were being given for both Brant and the Ardoch Algonquin, to finance their legal battles.

Ironically, as the arrests and trials continued, the man whose actions had originally helped spark the quarry dispute, developer Tim Letch, was himself convicted on earlier drinking and driving charges, pleading guilty to driving while disqualified and to refusing to provide a breath sample.

Brant's legal troubles eventually saw him spending sixty-two days in prison, only a month less than Bob Lovelace, before he was released as part of a plea bargain in July 2008.

Circumstances surrounding the release became sensational when it was revealed in trial evidence that had at first been suppressed, then later made public, that Brant had been threatened by Ontario Provincial Police commissioner Julian Fantino during the National Day of Action blockades. According to wiretap transcripts, Fantino threatened Brant that he would "do everything I can within your community and everywhere else to destroy your reputation." He told Brant, "your world's going to come crashing down" and he would "suffer grave consequences" if the blockade didn't end.[23]

There were calls for Fantino's suspension.

Meanwhile, like their Algonquin brothers, Brant's supporters were determined not to give in. The fight continued.

None of Your Business(es)

You can't just swat mosquitos; you have to drain the swamp.
ANONYMOUS[1]

AMONG THOSE SUPPORTING THE Ardoch Algonquin in their fight against the uranium miners were the area's small-town business people, who depended for a sizeable chunk of their sales on the tourist trade. They knew that, if their watershed became polluted with radioactive waste, the fishermen, cottagers, and hunters who kept their cash registers ringing through the summer and fall would disappear. Much as they had in the earlier rice war, they realized that their own survival depended on an Algonquin victory.

In small towns across Ontario, Canada, and North America, small business people also realize that their existence depends in large part on the very family farmers, subsistence farmers, hobby farmers, and rural-by-choice residents targeted for elimination by the corporate/government sector. Without these customers, they couldn't stay in business, and without their businesses, rural people wouldn't remain either.

Nor would rural families be able to stay on if their children couldn't attend local schools, if slow financial starvation forces yet more consolidation of small town elementary and secondary schools into larger and larger, and more and more distant, mega-schools.

As they multiply, attacks on smaller family farms and on small-town businesses, on schools and even on local church or fraternal organizations, slash like so many knives through the skein of symbiotic social and business relationships, draining the countryside of anything that might sustain its life. It is death by a thousand cuts.

Of course, not every assault on rural institutions is consciously intended as such, nor are the authors of all of the myriad onslaughts necessarily conspiring with each other. But deliberately intended or not, their combined effect is to "drain the swamp" and clear the territory for corporate dominance.

Banned Butchers, Prohibited Potlucks

Small-town butcher shops and abattoirs seem to have become particular targets because they provide services to local, small-scale livestock producers—as well as to hunters in season—and constitute competition, however minor, for the large-scale, centralized plants of corporate meat packers.

Alphons Vaneyndthoven, owner of the Windmill Sausage Co. Ltd., in Trenton, Ontario, has been making quality sausage for twenty years, with as much as possible of the meat for his sausage sourced locally, from organic growers. Recently, he became an Ontario government target.

"They want to close me down," he said, adding that the excuse for doing so, as in the shutdowns of many farmers, is "new regulations. All of a sudden they've got different inspectors here, and my shop is no good. My countertops are no good, my ceilings are no good, my walls are no good. I have high-gloss, washable paint on them and all of a sudden it's no good. Before, it was all good. Now it's not good anymore. My counter has to be separate, has to be a separate room. My serving counter has to go in a separate room. My spice has to go in a separate room. I need a women's washroom and a men's washroom."

He notes that he has no lunch counter and does not serve any food to eat on-premises. "It's just a small butcher shop. But they go way overboard. My wooden back door is no good anymore. I'm supposed to have a steel one. My smoke house has to come inside, but then I can't get insurance for it. I'd have to spend between $200,000 and $300,000 on this place to get it up to par the way they want it. My floors, my draining system is no good anymore. I have to put new drains in my shop. It's just one thing after another. To wash my hands, I'm supposed to get three sinks in here. One to cool my sausage down, one for the casings and one for washing my hands. It goes on and on and on."

He is convinced government is doing this "to get small business out of business. They want to make sure every small business is gone out of business. I've been here nineteen years. It was good till lately. They started two years ago, and then backed down, and now it's starting all over again. I'm probably going to close up here. I've had customers all the way from the east coast to the west coast, who tell me it's the best sausage they've ever had. I get some meat from local farmers. I try to get organic. But some comes from packing houses. What comes from the farmers is better, on the average."

The new rules, he said, are both federal and provincial.

"They say, 'We do it for the good of the people.' That's bullshit as far as I'm concerned. They want to give it all to big business. That's what it's all about. They want to look after big business. They want me to change over, but there's too many changeovers. I just can't afford it. To heck with them. It's just a hassle they make you go through, for no rhyme or reason. The government, whatever is their agenda, they're going to go through with it regardless. They [protesters such as the Landowners group] can stop it for a certain length of time, for two years. But now they come back in higher force. They come against us. The government is supposed to work for the people, but they want it so you work for the government.

"People in the cities don't know what's going on outside the cities. They don't want to know."

Vaneyndthoven's problems stemmed from meat inspection, but other shops have been targeted over a lack of inspection, proving the old saying, you're damned if you do and damned if you don't.

For example, the Sunrise Meat and Sausage butcher shop in Barwick, Ontario, was targeted over the long-standing rural practice of having uninspected meat—meant for farmers' own consumption and not for sale to the public—processed in local butcher shops. In October 2006, provincial officials raided the shop and condemned $40,000 worth of meat, the owners' entire inventory, including meat that had been inspected and wild game owned by the Rainy River First Nation. Officials said all of the meat was to be destroyed.

The Rainy River band pointed out that in Ontario it is an offense to destroy wild game meat. It also became apparent that the band's property was under federal, not provincial jurisdiction. Subsequently, the inspected meat and game meat were exempted from the destruction order, but the province insisted the rest had to go. A van full of meat inspectors, clad in bulletproof vests, pulled up to the shop, ready to take the meat away in a dump truck.

But they hadn't counted on the independence and sense of solidarity of local people. As the media reported it afterward:

> The inspectors tried one entrance to the meat store, only to discover that it was blocked by a broken down farm tractor. As locals explained to irritated officials, it can be very difficult to find a mechanic in Barwick on a Friday afternoon. The inspectors, now escorted by Ontario Provincial Police officers, then tried the other entrance. It was blocked by an ailing pickup.
>
> Official: "Sir, do you own this pickup?"
>
> Local nods.
>
> Official: "We need the entrance cleared so that the truck can get in. Will you please move your truck?"
>
> Local: "Gosh, I really wish I could move it, but you see a wheel fell off and I had some lug nuts but someone came along and stole them."
>
> Clearly, it was a bad day for breakdowns in Barwick.[2]

Eventually, the inspectors and police gave up and left. But everyone knew they'd be back again another day.

Such attacks on small local butcher shops are far from merely anecdotal, one-off incidents, as the National Farmers Union has testified in formal briefs presented to the

Saskatchewan and Ontario provincial governments, and the Canadian federal government. In a brief to the Ontario government's 2004 Meat Inspection Review, the NFU pointed out that:

> Since 1991 the number of provincially inspected [meat-processing] plants in Ontario has decreased by 40 percent. Each time an abattoir closes, local farmers are forced to either travel further to get animals killed or to stop slaughtering their own meat for personal consumption or sale to customers.[3]

In a 2005 brief to the Saskatchewan Meat Inspection Review, the NFU reminded prairie legislators that:

> A number of studies have shown that high levels of corporate concentration in the marketplace are a major factor contributing to depressed commodity prices at the farm gate. Nowhere has this been more evident than in the livestock sector, where three large companies, Cargill, Tyson and XL Foods, control over 80 percent of the processing market. Cargill alone controls 50 percent of the Canadian market...
>
> Meat inspection standards should not be used as a vehicle to facilitate further corporate concentration of processing and slaughter facilities in fewer and larger hands.[4]

Preventing such concentration made sense not only in terms of keeping small producers viable, but in terms of food safety as well, the brief added:

As the farm income crisis deepens, one solution for farmers is to capture an increased share of the food dollar by selling food directly to consumers at a retail price. To sell meat directly to consumers, however, farmers must have access to abattoirs in their community which are able to work with a variety of animals and to return the exact animal to the farmer...

Small, local, inspected abattoirs are an essential part of a diverse farm culture and local food system. Farm families, consumers and rural economies all benefit when farmers sell directly to the public in their home communities. Farmers selling meat direct to consumers, or to small butcher shops, make more per animal than through regular [i.e. corporate] livestock market channels...Ontario farmers who produce and sell certified organic lamb, killed at local abattoirs, through wholesalers in Toronto receive a premium of between $30 and $40 per lamb.[5]

Small local processors ensure a safer meat supply, the NFU explained, precisely because they *are* small and local:

A safe meat supply involves the whole chain from farm to consumer—from healthy animals to correct storage and preparation. The shortest and most direct chain reduces risk with fewer handlers, less transportation and less mixing of meat from several animals.

For farmers, a major advantage of small, local abattoirs is the opportunity to talk face-to-face with the butcher to get feedback on the care that was taken in preparing the meat. Feedback to farmers of any disease

or abnormalities found during inspection is readily possible and benefits the farmer, the inspection service and
the public. Individual service and feedback cannot be
offered by large packing plants. It should also be noted
that the inspection time per carcass in small abattoirs
is much higher than it is in large, federally inspected
plants.[6]

Indeed, this was borne out graphically—and tragically—
in 2008 when an outbreak of food poisoning due to the
deadly bacterium *Listeria monocytogenes,* was traced to the
Toronto meat-packing plant of industry giant Maple Leaf
Foods.[7] As of September 11, 2008, at least fifteen people had
died due to the outbreak,[8] while many others had been sick-
ened. Officials feared more deaths would occur.

In the scrutiny that followed, it was revealed that at the
Maple Leaf plant in question, "a single federal inspector [who
should have been trying to inspect meat] was relegated to
auditing company paperwork and had to deal with several
other plants... contradicting the impression that officials
had left last week that full-time watchdogs were on-site.

"Under the new system [adopted on March 31], federal
inspectors do random product tests only three or four times
a year at any given plant. And [corporate] meat packers are
required to test each type of product only once a month."[9]

Compared to this relaxed inspection environment for
major corporate plants, the regulations being applied to
small, local butchers appeared almost hyper-stringent.
Small operators saw it as a double standard. As one put it: "If
you're big, you get off ridiculously easy. If you're small, they
[the inspectors] are all over you."

In the Western provinces, a similar script is being played out. The British Columbia Ministry of Health recently imposed more stringent inspection regulations that force small-scale sellers of red meat, poultry, or eggs to submit to inspection in centralized, provincially approved facilities. This adds such a large shipping and inspection cost to their expenses—officially approved inspection sites may be hundreds of miles away—that many are being forced out of business.

Meanwhile, on the prairies, farmer, social anthropologist, and National Farmers Union member Birgit Muller, of Colonsay, Saskatchewan, explains that a much more important feature of the rural economy has been all but wiped out: the grain elevator.

"For the butchers, it's true, some of them were shut down," she said. "Though now they are having a sort of small renaissance because people living in the countryside will go and buy half a buffalo, store it, and eat it over the year. And these are butchered by small shops. But what is really the main thing that is destroying business in the rural communities here is the destruction of the grain elevators, the systematic destruction that has been going on, especially over the last six years, of all the small, wooden grain elevators in the communities, which were the places where farmers would go to deliver their grain, and go shopping after. They were also points of input distribution, seeds and fertilizer and so on.

"Western Canada used to have the Wheat Pool, a cooperative of farmers that owned these elevators. But the cooperative became a private enterprise in 1995, and completely changed its policy. They began investing like madmen in huge inland grain terminals, building them and at the same time pulling down these local elevators. Big, central- ized, concrete elevators had never been profitable previously because people preferred to haul their grain five miles and not seventy-five."

However, with the local elevators closed, farmers now have no choice but to ship to the distant, concentrated facil- ities, incurring "enormous freight costs." And the much larger loads of grain must now be transported in large, heavy trucks "that destroy the provincial roads, as they transport the grain seventy, eighty or a hundred miles."

The change has been more than economic. There has also been an aesthetic price paid. The once-typical vista of the West's wide, flat fields of grain, dotted with the ubiq- uitous wooden elevators and topped by the broad expanse of the "Land of Living Skies" (the motto on Saskatchewan automobile plates) is vanishing. "The whole landscape has changed," lamented Muller.

All-vegetarian

Lest anti-hunters or non–meat eaters should take heart from the troubles of butchers, there is also the example of Iilah and Tawlia Chickalo, of Marlbank, Ontario, whose success- ful all-vegetarian restaurant on a beautiful, lakeside rural property was shut down by provincial authorities because, among other things, it had oaken countertops rather than stainless steel ones. Before provincial bureaucrats shut them down, the energetic couple had built the imposing, four- dining-room structure themselves, by hand, imbued it with rustic ambiance, and were attracting patrons from across the province and the country.

"It took us twenty years to build that up," said Iilah. "It was four and a half stories high and about 8,000 square feet, had four dining rooms in it, a yoga hall, big banquet facilities. We were employing thirty-five local people at times. In '94 we were getting about thirty thousand people a year here without advertising. I had four dining rooms in there. We would feed 285 people in one sitting. We had bus tours, busloads of people coming up. We were making beef bourguignon, veal fettucine, shish kebab, steak au poivre flambé, hamburgers, pizzas—all these things without meat. Tastier than any meat.

"In the late eighties, early nineties, a new government regime came into the area, young bucks out of Toronto, and they were amalgamating all the different communities into the bigger ones. We weren't zoned commercial, so they put in a stop-work order. They were just like Gestapo. We were faced with all sorts of regulations, one of which was to get rid of our oak counters and put in stainless steel."

The latter requirement was aimed at restaurants serving meat, which of course the strictly vegetarian Chickalos were not. The oak countertops, together with the hand-carved wall panels and other wood materials, were part of a deliberately rustic decor.

"We had two wood-fired brick ovens, which would also heat the whole place. Every weekend we'd do music, live music, different themes. We'd be Latin one weekend and we'd be jazz another weekend, and our food went along with it. People loved it. Every time they came up it was a whole different thing. We'd put on different clothes, and it was absolutely wonderful. Everything was hand-carved. We took down barns. We used all these big beams, elmwood beams.

"If we tore out our oak counters and put in stainless steel, and changed everything to suit their criteria, it wouldn't have had the same ambiance," said Iilah. "We weren't putting meat [in any food], but the inspector said, 'Well, one day you might.' And I said, 'Well, at that point we'll put stainless steel down on top of the oak.' We were very respectful of their unknowingness, and treated them with the respect due their position."

To no apparent avail. The shut-down order stuck.

"We were dealing with these new people from Toronto. They had no sense whatsoever as to who we were. They were pretty ignorant. They were asking: 'What are you guys? Are you a cult?' And we realized that we were dealing with some pretty uneducated people. We said, 'No, we're a family, with some friends.'

"It cost me $56,000. They wanted me to re-survey my land, which had to be a winter and summer survey for the extent of the land and because of the wetland and everything else, and the water frontage. And then we had to get all the papers made for this building, engineer's papers. And we had to get septic approvals. And they started treating us like we were some Ramada Inn hotel. And we're not. We were back-to-the-land."

On top of the bureaucratic Gestapo, there was also a disastrous fire that destroyed most of the restaurant building. Finally, the Chickalos gave it up and quit the restaurant business. Fire and the government, equally destructive, had succeeded in destroying another rural enterprise and throwing a lot of people from the tiny hamlet of Marlbank out of work.

The Chickalos' restaurant was a fair-sized entity. But no enterprise, it seems, is too diverse, too small, or too harmless to escape notice, even those formed for purely charitable, non-profit ends, like church suppers, potlucks, ballpark beef or chicken roasts, backyard fish fries, and other fund-raising events. For decades, small town Canadian legion branches all over the country, like the Delta Legion in Lynd-hurst, Ontario, have held bullhead (catfish) suppers to raise money for community activities. The Delta branch usu-ally raised $4,500 that way. The Athens, Ontario, Snowmo-bilers Club earned around $2,000. Both got their fish from Wilson's Tent and Trailer Park, whose fish-processing facil-ity in Lyndhurst was built fifteen years ago, to the standards of the Ministry of Fisheries and Oceans, and sourced from local lakes. Recently the standards changed, and owner Bob Jaquith was told he had to make $25,000 worth of altera-tions to comply with the new, book-length set of rules. One new requirement was to increase from one sink to four and install a "footwash" at the entrance to his building. The facility only processes about 5,000 pounds of fish per year, and can't afford such an expenditure.

Jaquith will likely be forced to close.

Jack MacLaren, president of the Ontario Landowners Association, complains that overly strict interpretations of the rules mean "we can't have church suppers because the water doesn't meet the standards of the Clean Water Act, or the ladies who make the sandwiches haven't got stainless steel countertops at home in their kitchens, therefore the food's not safe. It's going just a little too far."

Added fellow OLA member Merle Bowes: "Governments are suggesting you do the value-added thing with your prod-uct, make strawberry jam as well as grow strawberries. But as soon as you do, they come and clamp down on you. The regulations are so strict there's no affordable way to comply. Those who have tried to follow the route of compliance have found that they can never be in compliance. There's always something else that costs you more and more money. And eventually, you just say well, I can't afford to run this business anymore."

Such, in fact, was the complaint of eastern Ontario cheese factory operators when new waste disposal regulations under the Nutrient Management Act were announced in 2008. Under the new rules, factory owners would be forbidden to continue their long-standing practice of disposing of organic "gray water" waste from their plants by spreading it as fertilizer on farm fields approved by the provincial Ministry of the Environment. The new rules prohibited spreading between December 1 and January 31 every year, when the ground is normally frozen, and some of the water might not be readily absorbed in the fields.

Spokesmen for the industry said they had no quarrel with government wanting to prevent runoff, but that they needed time to come up with affordable ways to meet the regulations. Jim Atchison, general manager of the Black River Cheese Company, south of Picton, said he was exploring possibilities, including building "our own sewage disposal system. But the system is expensive and we're busy exploring areas where we can raise the capital." [10] He said the cost of building a new sewage plant would be around $200,000.

Other operators painted a darker picture, as *The Kingston Whig-Standard* reported:

> Forfar Dairy and Cheese Factory near Elgin, north of Kingston, recently announced that it will stop making its own cheese at the end of this month because

of the new regulations. The factory will also cease making cheese deliveries to retailers in Kingston and the Ottawa area.

Forfar President Murray Campbell has said the high cost of fuel and the new waste disposal regulations contributed to the decision. Three of the company's 15 workers will lose their jobs ...

Jack Oliver, general manager of Empire Cheese and Butter Cooperative in Campbellford, said that the new regulations pose "a real problem" for his company. The company was started in the 1970s and has been a cooperative, owned by 10 area farmers ... The farmers have about 320 to 360 hectares of ministry-approved land on which the grey water is spread. Oliver said there are about six cheese factories in eastern Ontario that employ about 200 people, all of whom stand to lose their jobs if the companies can't find a solution to the waste disposal issue.[11]

The government's deadlines for compliance were not very sympathetic to small operators, complained Norm Brooks, manager of the Wilton Cheese Factory in Wilton. "The new environmental laws don't look at an individual's conditions," he said. "They apply to the good, the bad and the ugly, regardless of your history."[12]

As chapter 2 recounted, small, local cheese factories were once one of the main outlets for local, family-owned dairy farms. Their gradual demise over the decades, now likely to become precipitous if provincial governments are not willing to compromise on deadlines, or to help finance the required improvements, has been a major factor in killing the Canadian family farm.

Farmers' markets, another traditional market outlet for family farm operators, have also faced attack. Already hampered by marketing board rules that prevent sales of some farm products at their market stalls, small-town vendors, until recently, were being harassed and charged as lawbreakers over the labels on jars of jam, jelly, or preserves sold in the markets. Farmers' Markets of Ontario (FMO) executive director Robert Chorney explains:

"The market in Gananoque had [only] three or four vendors. But a lady and a man got into difficulty last fall with the health unit out of Brockville, and called us in alarm relative to a charge that had been laid against them on labeling. They said that their preserves weren't properly labeled."

What was missing?

"Name, address, that stuff. I jumped in and got very upset with the health unit. It's still indelible on my mind. I said that I would go to court with them, and the Crown withdrew the charge two weeks out. I took the position that the health unit should have educated prior to charging. I said you have a duty to educate prior to zapping people. I said that would make the health unit look very bad in court, and the Crown withdrew the charge.

"And farmers' markets were declared exempt from premises regulations a year ago May. There was a huge hue and cry that health standards, the health rules were not being applied consistently and uniformly across the province. So George Smitherman, the minister, exempted farmers' markets. Now the health unit has a formula to determine that the market is indeed a farmers' market. If more than 51 percent of the vendors are producers, then that market is exempt. The only time the health unit will step in is if there is a complaint, or they will deal of course with hazardous foods. Hazardous foods are cream pies, cabbage rolls, things that can spoil. But non-hazardous stuff, like baking and jams and so on, is exempt. The health units have backed off considerably."

The fact that the province's farmers' markets are now well organized, and carry a lot of economic clout, no doubt decided this outcome. Prior to 1990, there were about sixty farmers' markets in the province. But over the years since, Farmers' Markets of Ontario has been busy organizing and promoting. As of 2007, there were 135 farmers' and public markets, most of them FMO members, with annual sales of about $700 million. They attract close to a million regular shoppers yearly. Even the most hostile bureaucrat, or jealous corporate CEO, must tread lightly with such a force.

There is strength in numbers.

Unfortunately, the less numerous have no such protection.

Schools Closed, Water Metered, Archery Outlawed

Rural school districts, slowly being depopulated by the combined onslaught of the cost-price squeeze and government regulatory attacks on family farms and small businesses, are seeing a renewed effort to shut down local schools.

Each such effort strikes at the very heart of rural community, as this author knows from personal experience. In the 1980s, while working as an editor at *Harrowsmith* magazine and a part-time farmer, my own children attended local schools, first the Harrowsmith elementary school, and then Sydenham High School, where one of my good friends was a teacher.

To this day, I vividly recall the weekend when Harrow-smith parents converged on their kids' grade school to build an outdoor playground, complete with swings, monkey bars, climbing platforms, and merry-go-round. It was a pot-luck event, with food prepared by participating families. Everyone pitched in on the building, with saws, hammers, drills. Beams for the big playhouse were lifted in tandem by the fathers, slid into place and hammered home. It took an entire Saturday, but when we were done, the playground was at least the equal of the best Toronto could offer—and we'd done it ourselves, just like an Amish barn-raising bee. There was a tangible sense of community, of cooperation, rarely found in urban neighborhoods.

The sense of community, and of parental pride and affection, was expressed still more strongly at the high school in Sydenham, particularly in two events, one a student play and the other the school band's participation in an international competition.

The play, appropriately, was *The Farm Show,* a Canadian theater classic created by the Theatre Passe Muraille and first staged professionally in 1972. The play's original cast held meetings and interviews and later worked with farm families near Clinton, Ontario, to gather material and then create a show that mirrored the lives, hardships, and joys of rural people. One warm spring evening, the students of Sydenham High School produced the play, to an audience of parents, many of them working farmers. My two daughters were involved, the youngest as one of the directors and the oldest as one of the actors. By the time the show was over, there wasn't a dry eye in the crowd, students or parents. They, we, had seen ourselves. Our children had held the mirror.

Emotions ran still higher when the Sydenham High School band, in which my daughter played clarinet, was invited to attend an international band competition in Cuba, to be judged by, among others, all-time jazz great Dave Brubeck (one of my personal musical heroes). The band was privileged to even be selected for the competition. I don't, at this remove, recall whether they won any prizes, but the night they returned from Cuba, everyone in Sydenham, Harrowsmith, and perhaps all of Frontenac County was at the high school, gathered in the parking lot to welcome them home. As they got off the bus, people cheered, sang, laughed, cried, hugged their kids. It was one of the most moving and beautiful events I'd ever witnessed.

Rural schools are like that. They matter.

Kill one, and you kill a community.

These were the stakes in play when eastern Ontario's Upper Canada District School Board attempted in 2008 to implement its Boundary 2020 plan, which called for a realignment of local school boundaries, the permanent closure of several rural schools and a reduction in the availability of French language instruction for rural students.[13] The plan was vigorously opposed by parents, by the Elementary Teachers' Federation of Ontario (ETFO), and by elected officials like Augusta Township councillor Lisa Swan, who branded the consultative process leading to the closure decision "flawed, basically, from the beginning."[14]

The board, nevertheless, forged ahead, rejecting no fewer than three appeals.

At one public meeting on the closures, parents who objected to the decisions were admonished by Cornwall trustee David McDonald: "Rural people should all move into the urban centers, close to where they work."

"Closing elementary schools unilaterally and transferring grade seven and eight students to high schools, in effect treating students as if they are simply numbers on a financial balance sheet, is not in the best interests of either students or communities," said ETFO President David Clegg.

His sentiments were echoed in *The Landowner Magazine*, which thundered:

> Upper Canada School Board plows ahead with Boundary 2020 against the wishes of:
>
> · four of its elected trustees;
>
> · 25 groups that had objections;
>
> · the parents of the children;
>
> · elementary teachers union;
>
> · Upper Canada District School Coalition." [15]

Kingston Whig-Standard editorialists also sided with parents, noting that "The social reality is that 12 and 13 year olds are better served and safer at the top of the elementary heap than at the bottom of the secondary one." [16]

All, at least at that writing, to no avail. Nothing and no one would be allowed to block the ongoing agenda of school closures. School plays, playground building bees, community solidarity meant nothing to the bureaucrats and officials whose minds were already made up. As in the corporate world, economic "efficiency" was the only consideration. Money, in that kind of mindset, trumps community.

That attitude is also one of the root causes of a sharp increase in violent crime in small-town Ontario, as a 2008 analysis by the the Canadian Press found:

"Violent crime charges—everything from criminal harassment and assault to robbery and murder—have largely stagnated in Ontario's major cities, but the opposite appears to be the case in the less-populated centres, where the number of serious charges laid between 2000 and 2007 rose last year by nearly 25 percent," said the report.[17] Blamed for the rise were "rising [rural] unemployment and the dissolution of community togetherness."

The report quoted Brock University criminology professor Voula Marinos: "Young people who are idle and don't see much hope for the future are more likely to become disconnected from their community and be more tempted by criminal behaviour." Cornwall, Ontario, police chief Dan Parkinson agreed, pointing out that "young people in small communities need jobs and free basketball courts as much as their peers in big cities—healthy options to keep them from temptation."[18] When schools close, so do their ball courts, and so does a large part of what keeps communities glued together.

"We're fighting to keep schools open in communities," said the OLA's Jack MacLaren. "The school boards are turning to consolidation. They'll close three little schools and build one big one. The minister of education has policies and formulas that they have to conform to. That's the way government works. These formulas are based on urban populations and urban schools. They don't recognize or acknowledge the difference between urban and rural communities."

As for the continuing vendetta against rural small businesses, it has spread far beyond those involved in the production, sale, or processing of food. In fact, it may be spreading beyond businesses to target individual homes, and a wide variety of essential rural services.

An example of the non-food-related businesses targeted is the archery range and school operated by Bob Mackie in Beamsville, Ontario.

I recall, as a grade-school youngster, watching Errol Flynn play Robin Hood and a lesser imitator do the same in a derivative serial on TV. They inspired me to get an inexpensive beginner's bow and go down to an archery range not far from my parents' house in Detroit, where classes were offered. I spent a glorious summer in the early 1950s, shooting my bow, making my own arrows (gluing the feathers on the shafts properly took great skill), and rereading *The Adventures of Robin Hood*. Sometimes, I even hit the bull's-eye on my handmade backyard target.

The idea that this could somehow be construed as an antisocial, noxious activity would have been utterly incomprehensible to my boyhood self, and remains puzzling to me as an adult. Archery, for crying out loud, is an Olympic sport! Mackie has pointed out that his range has introduced more than two hundred new archers to the sport, some of whom have become provincial and national champions. His facility also provides training and recreational opportunities for youth, handicapped persons, Scouts, and schools.

And he is hardly a noisy neighbor. Arrows shot from a bow certainly don't make loud sounds before they hit the straw target. Nor does his facility impact in any way upon local air, water, or other environmental systems.

Yet, the members of the Niagara Escarpment Commission (NEC) saw Mackie's archery range as something that needed stamping out. Mackie's Mountain Archery, which comprised an outdoor range, a pro shop, and a portable classroom converted into an indoor range, was deemed "not permitted" under the Niagara Escarpment Plan. Why it should not be has never been made very clear, but a hint of the problem may be found in the fact that the Escarpment region is a zone where hunting with guns is prohibited. Farmers who want to cull local deer that damage their property or crops are limited to bow-and-arrow hunting. To qualify for such activity, some of them may have attended Mackie's school.

This, of course, was not Mackie's goal in operating his business. But never mind.

The NEC ordered his range—which was his only source of income—shut down. Appeals, public demonstrations in his support by everyone from local mayors to hundreds of members of the Ontario Landowners Association, appeared to have no impact.

The single-minded goal of shutting down rural businesses remained, unswerving.

This is not to discount the overall policy of protecting the Niagara Escarpment, an ecological treasure threatened in the past by mining interests. Many have heard popular singer Sarah Harmer's song "Escarpment Blues," and seen her documentary on the fight to preserve the region's ecological integrity. I have myself hiked the Bruce Trail that runs through it, and support efforts to protect it.

But Bob Mackie's little archery business is no threat to anything. Going after him only brings the NEC into disrepute.

As do many other initiatives, some of which appear staggeringly petty or intrusive.

Recently, word began to circulate that the provincial government intends to force rural residents to put meters on their water wells, and to demand a water tax.[19] When the Ontario government introduced legislation to require rural wells to be "registered,"[20] suspicions increased. Why should a government want to keep a roster of homeowners' wells, unless it intended either to tax them, or to impose onerous "upgrade" requirements?

Rural wells often cost their owners thousands of dollars to drill, with an outlay of hundreds more to buy and install a pump. No provincial or municipal government pays for or maintains these wells, as urban governments pay for, install, and maintain city water systems. The landowners themselves pay for it all. To tax their own, self-installed systems appeared outrageous, an act of harassment designed to make life yet more difficult for people in the country.

Provincial authorities denied any such plan, but the original leakers of the story (unfortunately, still forced to remain anonymous) stuck by their guns.

Rural mail delivery services are also constantly being cut back, with routes becoming steadily fewer, while Internet access is limited to dial-up services, not high speed.[21] This too stokes residents' fears.

Eventually, if these trends continue, some think the only "rural residents" left, other than workers on factory farms or in mines, could be like the neighbors of the industrial-model chicken farm described in chapter 2, whose chemically maintained fields were laid out in a spotless perfection worthy of Disneyland. Just across the road from that farm was a housing development—not a small town, but a typically suburban tract development, with houses and streets laid out as neatly as those of the original prototype for post–Second World War suburbia in Levittown, New York. Looking at it, the lyrics to the Malvina Reynolds song "Little Boxes" came to mind.

Ontario's provincial government is currently studying a ninety-five-page, $1.8 million report commissioned in 2002 by the Panel on the Role of Government. The report, written by academics and public policy specialists, none of whom live in rural areas or have ever been working farmers, is titled "Investing in People: Creating a Human Capital Society for Ontario." Some of its findings were reported in *The Landowner Magazine:*

> If rural Ontarians ask where they fit into this big picture, they'll be disappointed to learn they don't. Support for "economically unsustainable rural and remote communities threatens to crowd out many other areas of needed government expenditure," the report says. One of the most important of those expenditures, it says, is "revitalizing cities" which are the "main drivers of Ontario's economic growth." The report suggests rural Ontario must accept that it may be on the losing end of "difficult trade-offs" the province will have to make...
>
> The panel deems only rural communities that house urban commuters to have the potential for economic growth. The cutoff line is rural areas "where more than 30 percent of residents commute to urban centers." Most other rural areas fall into the "at-risk" category. The panel seems to suggest that the government encourage a quick, natural death of these rural areas by phasing out "regional economic development programs" and

providing "appropriate transitional arrangements" for young people to leave...

The authors of one research paper commissioned by the panel...recommend the government start "planning for decline" in rural areas and begin "restricting further settlement expansion."[22]

In short, drain the swamp.

(**9**)

A Missing of Minds

Nothing can live unless something dies.

CLARK GABLE, as "Gaylord," in *The Misfits*

I N THE WAKE OF so many threats, a kind of siege mentality is growing in rural North America, a feeling that something has to be done, and done quickly, to meet the emergency. But whenever rural people step up to the plate in the game of politics and public policy—before they even take a swing—they have two strikes against them.

First, they are thin on the ground, too thin for the majority of elected politicians to care what they think or how they might vote. As noted in chapter 1, farm populations have been falling dramatically in every province since at least the 1930s, and the fall has accelerated every decade. In the five years from 2001 to 2006 alone, the number of farms Canada-wide dropped by 7.1 percent.[1] In Hastings County, fairly typical of most of eastern Ontario, the Census of Agriculture shows the number of farmers has plummeted by a whopping 75 percent since 1931.

Professional farmers are an endangered species, but unlike the spotted owl or other forms of wildlife, they have few city defenders. Urban-based environmental pressure groups flock to save the threatened habitats of birds, bears, frogs, and even molluscs, like the Gatineau tadpole snail. But there are precious few groups, other than those organized by rural people themselves, rushing to save the habitats of Canada's small growers. Most city-based voters have had no personal or family contact with a working farm or farmer for two generations or more. Even those who have, or had, a grandparent in the profession are increasingly in the minority.

And on those few occasions when farm people's shouts of alarm or pleas for help make it past such distractions as *Canadian Idol* or *Hockey Night in Canada,* the second strike is called: whatever they are saying is perceived as coming from a bunch of mere yobs, hicks, or "dumb farmers." As Brent Cameron put it in an article in *The Landowner:*

> It has been an enduring fact of this human condition that hostility and prejudice are borne of ignorance—of peoples and their condition. When indulged, it transforms into an ungrounded anger, leading to an indifference that denigrates and dehumanizes...[In urban/ rural terms] it has evolved into an arrogance that places a moral superiority of "urban modernism" over a culture perceived as backward and degenerate.
>
> To vocally defend the old compact, and assert one's inalienable rights and interests as rural citizens is to be mocked and ridiculed as a "hick" or a "redneck..." The debate shifts away from the legitimate grievances of the

rural people, and rests on whether those people pos-
sess the mental acuity to understand either the world or
their true welfare." [2]

U.S. Democratic presidential candidate Barack Obama
reinforced the stereotype in his now-infamous comment
that "some of these small towns...it's not surprising when
they get bitter, they cling to guns or religion or antipathy to
people who aren't like them or anti-immigrant sentiment or
anti-trade sentiment as a way to explain their frustrations." [3]
His remarks may have influenced the outcome when 53 percent of rural voters in the nomination run-up favored Hil-
lary Clinton, as against 41 percent for him. [4]

As Obama's words indicated, however, nothing reinforces
the caricature of rural people more strongly, in the urban
mind, than their attitudes toward guns and hunting, as well
as toward livestock. Farmers, hunters, and fishers are lumped
together as so many "redneck...mouth-breathing tools who
just like to kill things," [5] unworthy of a hearing on any subject since what they have to say would likely be no more than
a series of guttural grunts.

But stereotypes, by their nature, tend to oversimplify,
and this one is no exception.

Through a Clear Lens

"Come and see my baby," my beaming neighbor called to me,
waving from his ATV pulled up in my driveway. My neighbor (to protect him from attacks by animal rights groups,
he shall remain anonymous[6]) is my contemporary—we're
both in our sixties. His place is on the next concession road
over from mine, where he raises grass-fed, shaggy-haired

Scottish Highland cattle, descendants of the earliest breeds brought to Britain in the second millennium BC by Neolithic farming peoples. The Highlands produce very lean meat, for which there is a niche market among cardiac patients and the elderly.

He also breeds and raises dogs, and is currently one of the top—if not *the* top—breeder of a particular hunting breed in North America. His walls and shelves are filled with ribbons and trophies, most of them reading "best in show."

I piled into his ATV and went to see the new arrival, a Highland calf born the afternoon before and now carefully guarded by its mother in a grassy pasture. Cows that have just calved can be dangerously aggressive, especially long-horned Highlands, and I'd have been foolish to approach the pair. But my neighbor's cattle are almost like pets to him. When he walked up to the cedar rail fence, they ambled over and licked his outstretched hand.

As he stood there, his cell phone rang, and he took the call. It was a fellow dog breeder, offering condolences on the recent death of his favorite female dam. He didn't talk long on the phone. It was hard for him to talk about an animal about which he had cared so deeply.

My neighbor really does love animals, although he breeds his cattle for meat and raises his dogs for hunting. His view of this is both individual and typically rural.

His father, a leader of the Dutch Resistance against the invading troops of Adolf Hitler during the Second World War, immigrated to Canada after the war, settling on a farm near Guelph, Ontario, where he grew up. Quite early on, my neighbor was forced to enter the School of Hard Knocks. His father had an accident and broke his back, forcing the son to drop out of school in seventh grade and take over running the farm. He has seen his share of tough times since those days, and long ago learned to look at life through the clear lens of realism.

We talked one day about hunting:

"What most people don't understand about hunting is, if it wasn't for hunting and game our ancestors wouldn't have made it," he said. "We wouldn't be alive today. The majority of people don't have to hunt for food anymore. It's all put there in the grocery store for them. But they don't understand how it got there. Something has to die for them to get it. For humans to live, something's got to die."

A good comparison, he said, is with raccoons, which are omnivorous. "People are exactly the same way. They can eat anything. If you're used to it, you can eat anything. People eat almost anything, all over the world. There's stuff that they eat in Europe, stuff they eat in Asia, that we wouldn't eat over here. That doesn't make them barbaric. That's their culture, the way they were brought up. Down in Texas they eat rattlesnakes. A lot of people eat turtles.

"I do think that animals were put here to feed humans. But unfortunately what's happened is some of the people that live in the cities have gone away from reality, have lost track of the reality that something has to die for them to eat."

Often, something also has to die to protect domestic animals, such as cattle and horses, from injury or death. Woodchucks—groundhogs like Ontario's famed Wiarton Willie—are the bane of farmers' pastures, which, when not controlled, they soon fill with tunnels and holes, into which horses and cattle step, breaking their legs. Every spring, farmers used to pay young boys with .22 rifles to go out into the fields and cull the woodchuck population. Cruel? Perhaps yes. But so is it cruel to let a horse break its leg stepping into a hole, when you could prevent it.

In the old days, before factory farms, most rural families kept backyard flocks of laying hens, and sometimes geese or ducks as well. A fox or raccoon that got into the coop could wipe out the entire flock in one night. That's why farmers keep shotguns. Or used to keep them, when there were still family farms and backyard flocks. Today's factory farms, with their hundreds of thousands of tightly caged birds imprisoned inside vast, germ-proof barns, don't have such worries. With the trees along fencerows cleared away to make room for monoculture crops, there's precious little habitat for wild animals near these industrial plants, in any case.

In the farmhouse, barn, and granary, rodents are a constant source of potential trouble. Mice and rats not only eat grain, but also soil it with their feces. Not a few house fires in the country are started by wiring through whose insulation rodents have gnawed, exposing the bare copper wire to wooden joists. That's why most farm people keep cats. Go to any feed store and you'll find sacks of "barn cat" food, for farmers to feed their feline allies. Farmyard dogs are there to keep marauding coyotes, now experiencing a population boom in Ontario, at a distance from livestock—as well as from the cats in the barn, which to a coyote are so many gourmet snacks.

"I train dogs and I hunt," said my neighbor. "Years ago, I lived in Milton. A lady and her husband moved in next door to me, and she had five cats. She'd come from downtown Toronto. And when she found out what I was doing, she was definitely against me. I hunt, I fish, I train dogs to pick up dead birds, I shoot. And she combed me out like you wouldn't believe. I was the worst scum of the earth, according to her.

"The months went by, and I guess it was just shortly after Christmas when she came over to the house again and she wanted to know if I'd seen any of her cats. She only had one left out of five. I said, 'You know those nice coyotes that you hear?' She said yes. And I said, 'They're the ones that are eating your cats. They kill cats. They love to kill cats. That's where your cats are going.' She says, 'Are you sure?' I said 'Yes, ma'am. You hear them every night. You hear the coyotes howling.' And I asked, 'Your cats were outside?' She said, 'Yeah.' So I said, 'They get them and they eat them.' So, it was about three weeks later, she lost her other cat. Not having the fortitude to keep the cat inside. She let the cat outside again. She came over and she said, 'Is there any chance of you shooting these coyotes?' All of a sudden it changed her mind because she lost her cats. To me that just doesn't make sense. Because it affected her, now it was OK to kill coyotes.

"Had she, instead of coming over and ripping a strip off me because I'm training dogs and I'm shooting guns, if she had come over and introduced herself and been nice about it, I would have probably told her, 'Keep your cats inside because the coyotes will get them.' And she might still have her cats. But you see what happens. They're living in their own little world."

Another neighbor, call her Donna, who raises free-range, grass-fed hogs on her farm not far from Napanee, has a similarly practical attitude, in this case toward livestock. Now in her fifties, she's been raising pigs for eight years, and farming is the true heart of her life. She works a day job as activity director for a retirement home, "sitting behind a computer screen, no sunlight, so that I can raise pigs."

In contrast to factory farm–produced hogs, hers live a healthy, natural life. They run free in pasture, grazing on plants and rooting for tubers, just as their wild ancestors did in prehistoric Europe. While she works in her indoor cubicle, "here they are out in the pasture, lounging by the pond. It's a total vacation for them, a totally nice life. The pigs are happy. They're definitely happy."

She has affection for her pigs, and admits that is one reason why her family went into the business.

"We got into it by accident, with a pig named Beaulah," she recalled. "Beaulah was somebody's pet. We saw the ad in the paper around Christmas, and Beaulah arrived shortly after New Year's, and she was pregnant. She had eleven [piglets] and we kept two of those, and it just grew. We didn't set out to have pigs, but those little babies are so cute, and they grow on you. You think, 'We've got to keep this one and we've got to keep that one,' and the next thing you know you've got a whole bunch."

But raising livestock is a business, and eventually the pigs that aren't being kept for breeding must be sold for meat. On a factory farm, pigs whose lives have been completely artificial and unnatural, often filled with acute suffering, are driven in huge numbers onto large trucks, jammed together inside with barely room to stand, shipped over long distances, often without access to water, and slaughtered with great brutality on assembly lines. Donna's pigs, after a natural, happy life, are—when the day comes—coaxed a few at a time onto a trailer and shipped off to a local slaughterhouse nearby where they are dispatched quickly and humanely.

She admitted it's easy to become attached to a pig. "That's a problem," she said. "You just keep a distance. Getting them on the truck is sometimes a challenge. They're smart. They know it's not in their best interest. We usually put hay down [on the floor of the truck] so it looks more like what they're used to, and walk along with a feed bucket to entice them up the ramp, and try to have apples and stuff in the truck. Some of them walk right on, no problem. Usually, the one you don't want on the truck is the one that walks on just like nothing. And the one you want on there won't have anything to do with it."

It's a sad time, for the farmer. No one who raises livestock on a small scale looks forward to it. But, as another neighbor, who raises beef cattle, put it, "It's one of those hard things in life that just have to be done. So you do it." Probably ninety-nine out of one hundred farm people in eastern Ontario would see things the same way as my other neighbors do.

Which is not, of course, to say that they are 100 percent right, and those who oppose guns and hunting, or raising livestock for meat, are necessarily wrong. The fascinating thing about the country is that it has all sorts of people in it, and when they take a position on something controversial involving nature, their approach, at the very least, tends to be far better informed than that of city people who are not in daily, personal contact with the natural world. This may be because they base much of what they say on direct experience.

Iilah Chickalo, mentioned in the preceding chapter, is an example. Iilah, who is also my neighbor, is a vegetarian who formerly operated not only a nationally known vegetarian restaurant, but also an internationally known animal rehabilitation center, which at one time housed 167 animals, including mammals, birds, and reptiles. Iilah and his wife, Tawlia, seem to have a "way" with animals, and not very long after their arrival in eastern Ontario in the mid-seventies they started taking in injured or homeless creatures. Some were injured local wildlife species, while others were formerly captive or mistreated domestic animals. Many were exotic species that came from zoos and circuses, or—like the green monkeys—from experimental laboratories.

"We got here in September of '75, with $200," said Iilah. "We needed money, so we went to work as painters. We painted the town of Napanee. We painted six hundred houses and businesses. And then we started doing animals and before you know it, we had our professional animal haven. And we [eventually] had to get Canadian zoo status because we were getting tigers and cougars, 18-foot boa constrictors and pythons, donkeys with the mange that we healed, and all kinds of different things. And then the government people started bringing us bears. Before you know it we were getting the movie industry, like Goldie Hawn insisted that the tiger that did the movie *Bird on a Wire,* which was filmed in Vancouver, she insisted that tiger, called Cordiana she fell in love with her, went to a good home. Because they have to drug them every time they do a shoot, for insurance purposes. She had no claws. She was raised for the movie industry. They had to give the tiger a drug, which destroyed the tiger's brain after awhile. All of a sudden, before you know it, we've got a tiger here. We never had to look for anything. If it comes up the driveway it's meant to be and if it doesn't it's not meant to be. So we don't go and look for much. We understand how it all works, including work and animals. And all of a sudden we're getting lions, we're getting wolves that were being abused...We had to have three of Canada's zoos back us up. We had the Bowmanville Zoo, the Toronto Zoo and the Fredericton [New Brunswick] Zoo. We had five species of monkeys that were all used for experiments. We had green monkeys, a family of them who were used in lab experiments. They were all very schizoid. It took us over a year to get them to calm...We had an Alaskan brown bear, the size of a grizzly, that was used in a circus. He was abandoned in an illegal zoo north of Sudbury, in a cage on a cement floor. He was over three weeks without food and water. It took us three months, with foot massage and infusements, to get his muscles working. He had his front teeth removed and some of his chewing teeth and he was declawed. After three months we put him into a cage back here. It had ground, it had trees and grapevines, and a good-sized pool for him to get into. He had never been standing on real ground. He'd always been on a synthetic floor or cement. And when he came to put his feet on the ground here, on the grass, he lifted up his feet. He wouldn't step on the living grass. And then he started touching the trees, the leaves, and started jumping up and down, this 700–800 pound bear, jumping and hitting the leaves and lowing. It just put tears in your eyes. We saved his life. It was like that with every animal we had.

"Our cougar had belonged to a bikers' group that used her for rituals. And the OPP [Ontario Provincial Police] asked if we wanted to take it. That was one scary cougar. It took us a year and a half to get her into a calm. She did all of the Labatt's Wildcat commercials for television and for all the big billboards. And here was Amber, our cougar, doing this and she didn't need drugs or anything."

Chickalo, as might be expected, is opposed to hunting, as well as to raising animals for meat. "As soon as man starts to eat meat, he wants to kill," he said. And given his direct, personal experiences and the human-animal relationships that arose from them, this view might appear perfectly reasonable. But those experiences were with tame or semi-tame creatures, accustomed to human company, which he and his family had rehabilitated and taught over a period of months to eat a special diet. His understanding contrasts sharply with that of people like my hunting neighbor, who bases his views on experience with wild animals.

"People are sheltered from real life," my neighbor said. "The only animals they see are on TV and in Walt Disney, and that's what they think animals are like. But [in the wild] little Bambi is not little Bambi, and the little wolf is not the nice little cartoon wolf they think it is. And the nice little bear that they see is not the nice little bear. Because that nice little bear will kill you.

"I was in Algonquin Park fishing. I had my garbage and I had to take it to the dump. They have a dump there for your garbage so you don't leave it in the bush. I drove down to the dump and there was a gentleman and a lady there from Europe. They were looking at four bears that were down eating in the dump. This lady says to me, 'If my husband and I walk down there and pet that bear, would you take my picture?' I said, 'That picture would definitely make the front page of the newspaper!' She said, 'Why?' and I said, 'Because you'd both be laying there dead. She'd give you one swat, with those cubs down there, and that would be the end of you.' 'Oh no,' she said. 'We've seen bears on television lots of times and people pet them and everything else.' I said, 'Not wild bears, honey. You got a female bear there with two cubs. As soon as you come near those cubs that female will kill you right there on the spot.' And she didn't believe me. She proceeded, her and her husband, to walk down towards the bears. I said to them one more time, 'Please, come back.' And all of a sudden this old female stood up and she let one roar out of her. At this time the woman was about, I would say, 25, 30 yards from this bear, and she come running back. She said, 'That didn't sound friendly.' These people were thirty years old; they wouldn't listen to me. They could have been killed there, because they don't know."

In fact, only about a year before this conversation, a woman in a nearby township was attacked by a wild black bear when she walked out into a pasture where she kept goats. She nearly died from the mauling and loss of blood. The bear, later killed by police, was found to be rabid. More recently, in British Columbia, a fisherman standing in a boat tied up at the Port Renfrew wharf was suddenly attacked by a black bear. Six men came to the fisherman's rescue, one of them hitting it on the head with a hammer and the other stabbing it with a knife, but the man was severely mauled before they managed to pry him free.[7]

Philosophical Questions

The difference between domestic, or semi-tame, animals and wild ones actually constitutes a yawning gap, one which leads to a variety of often-profound philosophical, scientific, and even religious questions centered around the idea of predation.

For example, very few, if any, vegetarians will venture the opinion that lions are "bad" or "evil" because they kill and eat zebras. Nor would they attempt to judge foxes, wolves, hawks, underwater predators like the northern pike, or other meat-eaters on such an anthropomorphic ethical basis. Non-human predators are seen as simply "doing what comes naturally."

Only *Homo sapiens sapiens* is viewed as doing wrong when he or she kills and eats prey.

Logically, this position requires that humans be regarded as somehow *not* natural, not part of the natural world to which all other species belong, but rather detached from it, apart or above it—a kind of foreign, ecological interloper. Scientifically, of course, there is no basis for this. Taxonomically, the human species is part of the grand classification scheme memorized by every beginning biology student: "kingdom, phylum, class, order, family, genus, species, and subspecies." In our case, that would be Animalia, Chordata, Mammalia, Primates, Hominidae, *Homo, H. sapiens,* and *H. sapiens sapiens.*

DNA and fossil evidence indicates that our species is roughly 200,000 years old, and just about every example we have from paleontology, anthropology, and archeology suggests that throughout most of our history, we—like many of our fellow Hominidae (chimpanzees, for instance)—have been omnivores. That is, we eat just about anything that we can get our prehensile hands, with their opposable thumbs, on. This, as my hunting neighbor suggested, is likely the main reason why humans have survived to become the most "successful," or dominant, species on Earth (many so-called "deep ecologists" would not consider our dominance, which now threatens the planet with environmental catastrophe, exactly successful).

And our species is unquestionably part of the world of nature, inextricably bound to it. We may sometimes act like African driver ants (genus Dorylini; sixty species), swarming across the forests and fields and devouring everything in our path. But who would say that driver ants, because they are sometimes destructive, aren't part of nature? If ants, amoebas, foxes, and polar bears can kill and eat things, why can't we? At the level of theoretical science, at least, there appears to be no reason why not.

Which is where empiricism, philosophy, ethics, and religion come in. Any decision by a human as to whether or not to hunt or eat meat must necessarily fall under one of those headings.

For Chickalo, it appears to be both a practical/empirical question and a philosophical one. For instance, his personal observations, and those of his family, have convinced him that eating meat is medically bad for people.

"Consider your stomach a barrel in the sun at 98 degrees," he said. "If you throw in sugar, coffee, tea, bread, yeast, meat, and bacon, and lift that lid up in the sun eight hours later, it's really foul. And these gases that are created from the meats and from everything turn to acidity. When people eat meat, or dead decaying flesh or toxic foods, their aura has a greenish gas around it. This greenish gas prevents you from functioning with both sides of your brain working."

He points to a number of examples of people he has known personally whose health, both physical and mental, appears to have been markedly improved by switching from a meat and processed food diet to a vegetarian, whole foods regime. Listening to him, one must admit there could be room here for at least a debate between different schools of nutritionists.

Where Chickalo's arguments seem to fall down, or at least depart from empirical observation, is where the subject of wild animal behavior comes in. To deal with this question, he posits a past world in which not only humans, but all animals, once lived under a regime much different than today's.

"Originally, the first Adam and Eve, not the last ones, were put into a garden where all animals were friendly to each other. The lamb and the lion feasted together, not on each other. The lion would eat the pollens and nuts, the berries, like the bear, the same foods that are now eaten by the bear and by grazing animals, it would eat. We're living in a dualistic world. When things were created out of consciousness, with the original code of ethics and matrix, everybody born to the original planet, to the original Eden, were basically pollen eaters, vegetarians, who ate fruit, seeds, nuts, and which the animals would eat."

This description sounds, at first, like a religious position. Jehovah's Witnesses, who are a religious group, believe something similar, and their brochures and pamphlets often feature illustrations of lions lying down with lambs. But Chickalo's view is at least in part extrapolated, as suggested earlier, from his personal, empirical observation.

"One of our baby tigers was raised vegetarian and grew to be 600 pounds, and he wouldn't hurt a fly. We'd put a piece of meat or of chicken there and he'd look, he wouldn't have anything to do with that. If you raise a baby fox with the second generation, on grains and berries, a fox would eat like a bear. A fox will not eat meat, or kill. I had seven cats that were raised, third generation, they would go into the garden and take the green beans off the plant and sit down like a monkey and eat the beans. These cats that we have, like that, we would put them in, like, a giant aquarium, with hamsters, and they'd play for hours with the hamsters, back and forth. They would rub noses with squirrels in the trees, these cats. They would pick mushrooms off the trees and eat them. They would pick fruit out of the garden and eat them. We fed them on millet, brown rice and different grains, and garlic and vegetables. And we would put fish down there for them to taste. They'd smell the fish, and they'd go eat their almond nuts and their broccoli. They wouldn't want the fish."

The reason why wild animals aren't like that now, he believes, is that the earlier, gentler earth "sustained later in time a cosmic interference, an asteroid hit. The grain fields were gone, the flowers and the pollens were gone, and the nuts and the berries and everything was gone."

He sees the natural world of the moment as an impoverished ecosystem where predators can no longer find what they might have in an earlier era, and so are forced to eat meat, "because they don't have the grains and the pollens and they're living in an environment which lacks natural food. So all they have to eat, like the Eskimo now, stuck there in the ice, they have to eat the whole animal. The animals who are having to eat animals. If they had no other food to eat, then [even his vegetarian cats] would become carnivorous again. They would eat animals again.

"[Predation] comes from evolvement, evolving animals, evolving people. Originally you could walk, as we could walk with our tiger. You could walk with an elephant today if you bring him up [used] to it. And he's not going to, even when he's in musk, he's not going to hurt you."

Elaine Fritz, a 1986 transplant from the Toronto suburb of Markham to a country district near Bobcaygeon, Ontario, agrees with much of what Chickalo said, particularly about the effects on people of killing and eating meat. Her views reflect a viewpoint similar to what may have been the real reason why Mackie's Mountain Archery shop, mentioned in the previous chapter, was deemed "inappropriate" for the Niagara Escarpment.

"I had a deer here who was wandering around with an arrow in her," she said. "I can never forget that. I'm trying to get bow hunting banned in my area. A person who can go and hunt, instead of just going to the IGA grocery, has a whole mindset, and to me they're unable to feel compassion. I don't want that kind of a character wandering around, dealing with people in the area who can inflict pain and suffering. I think that's a lot to do with the video games. You just don't want to be with people who have that kind of a mindset. I think it keeps us from evolving into higher human beings. It keeps us down.

"It's all chemistry," she said. "All emotion is chemistry, brought on by how the brain processes what it sees. There are chemicals of self and chemicals of community. If you're only thinking of yourself, your own self-gratification, someone who could watch torture or violence and play those video games, you're not producing any chemicals of compassion. But if you're wanting to work with the community and in cooperation, you feel for other people, you produce chemicals of compassion.

"I'm not opposed to eating meat," she said. "But I'll always check up on how the animal was dispatched. I think domestic livestock were intended [for more use,] that we use their manure to fertilize the land, and to distill alcohol and produce methane to make our stuff go. Then you eat an animal when it dies of old age, just basically drops of old age."

For her, the main issue is whether or not we inflict pain: "If the victim didn't feel pain, where's the issue?"

Asked about non-human species that inflict pain—lions that eat zebras, foxes that eat cottontail rabbits—she responds: "If a predator felt compassion, it would starve. The way nature—well, who likes to see that anyway? That's what I think debases a human being, if they can act like a predator and not have compassion. A compassionate person would think ahead as to how an animal would be dispatched.

"How can you stop it [hunting by wild predators]? You have to accept it and hope that we don't become like them. We're evolving to an enlightened species. That's where I see us going. I do think people who are vegetarians have a calmness about them. You don't see vegetarians blowing up villages."

It is pointed out that in India the Hindu religion mandates vegetarianism, yet Hindus have massacred Muslims and Sikhs, setting bombs, and Hindu soldiers blew up the Golden Temple in Amritsar.

"Well," she replied, "the Indians at least have not been empire-seeking."

Of course, there is no way to prove that Iilah Chickalo's beliefs about an earlier world, or Fritz's beliefs about a future one toward which we are heading, are either true or false. Chickalo doesn't tie them to God or the supernatural, and so his view is not, strictly speaking, religious. Nor is that of Elaine Fritz. But it is a view that has to be taken entirely on faith, just as Fritz's predictions for the future must be.

Science, of course, is based on rigorous proofs and observations that can be duplicated or observed by other investigators. Purely subjective beliefs have no place in it. And the biological sciences overwhelmingly demonstrate that creatures have been killing and eating each other for as long as we know life has existed on the planet. The physical anatomy of predators, from their teeth to their eyes, to their legs and feet, is adapted for stalking, chasing, and biting. Their digestive systems and body chemistry—unlike those of the herbivores—are adapted for processing meat. (Indeed, veterinarians suggest—contrary to Chickalo's experience— that a purely vegetarian diet, if not balanced with extreme care, may harm carnivorous pets, such as cats.[8])

The dinosaurs killed and ate each other. There is evidence that asteroids have, indeed, struck the earth, and that such a collision may actually have wreaked havoc on the dinosaurs, bringing their one-time dominance as the planet's chief life form to an end. But before that cataclysmic event, the dinosaurs' amphibious predecessors, such as Eogyrinus (300 million years ago) and Eryops (290 million years ago), were killing and eating each other,[9] and before them the earliest microorganisms in the earth's primordial seas ate each other as well, just as an amoeba today absorbs and digests it microscopic prey. No "original sin" by an Adam or Eve could have been responsible. The first humans hadn't yet appeared. Death, killing, and eating were there from the get-go, long before people arrived on the scene.

And that death and eating included plants.

What Plants Feel

Many vegetarians oppose eating meat on the ethical grounds that it causes pain to the animals who are killed, and that humans—alone among all species—ought always to avoid inflicting pain. No such ethical requirement is exacted of any other carnivorous or omnivorous creature, only of humans. Singling out people this way seems logically arbitrary, but at least it appears possible to achieve the

goal. Juvenile humans may, as some nutritional studies indicate, suffer from a purely vegetarian diet at times during
their growth and development, but adult humans can physically survive, at least for a long time, without meat.

Surviving without vegetables as well would be another
matter.

Yet, if the goal is not to inflict pain, ethical people ought
to try to see things from the plants' standpoint. There is a
growing body of evidence that plants, too, have feelings
and may be able to experience something akin to pain. The
authors of *The Secret Life of Plants*[10] cite numerous cases,
beginning with a series of experiments performed by an
American named Cleve Backster. Backster worked with an
instrument called the galvanometer, which measures electrical potential, or basic charge, and can be connected to a
needle and ink, which express these electrical charges on a
paper graph. Its most common use is as a polygraph, or lie
detector, used by police to detect and record minute electrical responses in humans to various emotional stimuli.

Backster connected a galvanometer to a plant (at first to
a house plant called *Dracaena massangeana*),[11] and later to
many plants in a wide variety of situations. He found, to
his astonishment, that plants, just like humans, exhibited
measurable electrical changes—which showed up on the
graph—in response to both pleasant (such as being watered)
and unpleasant (such as being uprooted or having leaves
pulled off) stimuli. Still more remarkable, plants seemed to
be able to communicate with one another. Research chem-
ist Marcel Vogel found that plants apparently can communicate their reactions to stimuli with each other, and maybe
even to or from humans:

Vogel wired two plants to the same recording machine and snipped a leaf from the first plant. The second plant responded to the hurt being inflicted on its neighbor, but only when Vogel was paying attention to it![12]

Other experiments cited in *The Secret Life* yielded still more astonishing results, indicating that not only may plants be "sentient," in that they react with apparent emotional responses to pain and pleasure, but that they may be able to communicate with each other, with humans, and with animals in a wide variety of ways and employing a spectrum of electrical, chemical, and other pathways.

In other words, when we kill and eat plants, they may suffer. If the goal is to avoid inflicting pain, should humans not eschew eating plants? Adherents of the Jain religion in India have looked at this question, and reacted to it. Jain devotees are noted for walking carefully, so as to avoid stepping on insects, and for wearing surgical masks, to prevent breathing in and killing microorganisms. They are, of course, vegetarian. Some go further:

> Some Jains revere a special practice, where a person who is aware that he or she may die soon, and feels he has completed all his duties, ceases to eat or drink until death. This form of dying is called santhara. It is considered to be extremely spiritual and creditable.[13]

Whatever one may think of Jain practices, they at least deserve high marks for consistency.

Asked about the ethics of killing and eating plants, Chickalo noted: "Macrobiotics teaches that when you remove a plant from the ground you should do so gently, and you treat it with reverence. And you use the sharpest of knives, and there's no pain felt because they don't have all that wiring job that we have."

Or so macrobioticists, who may not have read *The Secret Life*, think. Actually, some researchers cited in the book seem to have found evidence that one's attitude toward plants may influence their reaction to being eaten. In fact, the attitude of the eater—or of the hunter or slaughterer in the case of animals—may be central to the entire experience:

> Experience helped to bring Backster to the realization that plants could intentionally be put into a faint, or mesmerized, by humans, that something similar could be involved in the ritual of the slaughterer before an animal is killed in the kosher manner. Communicating with the victim, the killer may tranquilize it into a quiet death, also preventing its flesh from having a residue of "chemical fear," disagreeable to the palate and perhaps noxious to the consumer. This brought up the possibility that plants and succulent fruits might wish to be eaten, but only in a sort of loving ritual, with a real communication between the eater and the eaten— somehow akin to the Christian rite of Communion— instead of the usual heartless carnage.[14]

This approach may be at the origin of the Algonquin hunting rite described by Randy Cota: "In traditional teachings, when we kill an animal we put tobacco down, because tobacco is the sacred gift of a plant that only came on Turtle Island, which is North America. We offer it to the Creator— you can call him God or Jehovah or whatever you like—to give the Creator thanks for giving up that life for us." It is "important that we respect each other," both men and animals, he said. The Cree people have a similar tradition, described in detail by anthropologist Robert Brightman.[15]

First Nations people, if they live traditionally, do not kill lightly. But they do kill.

Which brings us to the ultimate philosophical/religious question at the heart of the whole matter: Are violence, pain, and killing part of the established order of the universe, and thus, regardless of our immediate emotions, acceptable? Is God himself, or whatever force unifies and underpins reality, inherently violent?

It would certainly appear so. Not only have pain and death been part of our planet almost since the beginning, but violence seems part of everything in the universe: stars implode upon themselves, becoming black holes and sucking everything near them into a vacuum. Planets and asteroids collide, as do in fact whole galaxies, in immense displays of spectacular destruction. Who are we to say this is wrong, or even to begin to comprehend it? Is there a way to look at it that makes sense, without being cruel?

"I don't know," admits Fritz. "That's deep. I just know what I have to deal with today, and I don't like the idea that hunters can turn off compassion." Her approach, like not only that of Chickalo but of most of my meat-eating neighbors, is in the end practical.

But even on a strictly practical level, there are arguments in favor of killing and eating other creatures. Hunters are quick to point out that humans have become a necessary part of the balance of nature, originally disrupted when large predators like wolves and cougars were wiped out to

protect livestock. With no natural enemies, deer have multiplied to the point where they are often pests, overrun-
ning farm cornfields and suburban gardens, posing a nightly
traffic hazard on busy highways, and even carrying the
ticks that spread Lyme disease. In winter, there is often not
enough browse to feed the deer, who may starve to death
slowly and painfully. Hunting keeps deer numbers from spi-
raling out of control. In comparison, the quick death from a
bullet is more humane than the slow death of starvation, or
the fear, shock, and pain of a deer being brought down by a
pack of coyotes.

Hunters like my dog-breeding neighbor also see what
they do as a way to understand and appreciate nature in a
way no mere passer-through can. Our hunter-gatherer ancestors were immersed in and dependent upon the natural world
for survival, which made them acute observers. Their senses
were sharpened and their minds attuned to their environment in a way no mere back-country tourist can imitate.

"There's nothing better than getting into a duck blind
early in the morning, before daylight, and watching the sun
and the mist come off the water. You sit there, it's quiet, it's
beautiful, just unreal. You're right with nature. Sitting in a
tree stand, bow hunting, for six or seven hours, you're with
yourself. A lot of people can't live with themselves. You can
take a long, hard look at yourself. You look at yourself in a
whole different way.

"Hunting deer, it doesn't matter what it is, you're sitting
there, waiting, or you're running through the bush chasing,
it's altogether different. It relieves every tension and stress
that man has put on you, in work and everywhere else."
Living as our remote, hunter-gatherer ancestors did.

"It's you and nature. Remember, you're in their living room. You're not in your living room. You hear a blue jay squawk, you know there's something out there. The blue jay comes flying overtop of you and starts squawking at you. Everybody else in the bush knows you're there. This is their living room, their home, their environment."

And for a few hours the hunter's, or the fisher's. My neighbor is also a fisherman, and sees fishing as a way to connect with his grandchildren.

"There's nothing more relaxing, nothing better than taking your boy or your daughter fishing. It's the greatest thing men and ladies can do with their children. People today don't want to play with their kids. They're so busy doing their own things they don't want to play with their kids anymore. They don't take their kids anywhere. It all has to be organized, regimented sports.

"I'll never forget my own grandkids. I took them fishing. They still talk about it today. They're eleven and twelve years old and they still talk about it today. 'Grandma and Grandpa took us fishing.' They actually caught a sunfish and a little rock bass. They were never so excited in all their life. It's the greatest pleasure that a man or woman could have. That's what's missing today. That's really what's missing. Go camping with your kids. Show them nature, show them what nature's all about."

Of all the outdoor activities practiced by modern people, only wildlife photography, which would include underwater photography, can duplicate the experience of hunting or fishing. That's because the photographer, like our ancestors thousands of years ago, is also after prey, and must learn the same alertness and awareness of surroundings as the hunter. Only the result is a picture, not a meal.

Certainly, there are brutal, careless yobs out there, who
think hunting and fishing are simply excuses to get drunk
and make noise. But not many of them are country people,
born and raised in the rural world. The example of the city-
bred, wealthy U.S. Vice President Cheney, "hunting" on a
game farm where the birds were tame and trapped like so
many fish in a barrel, then managing to shoot one of his
own companions, was greeted with universal disgust by the
rural people of eastern Ontario. They regarded him as a *true*
"mouth-breathing tool."

The fact that rural people face these kinds of questions
as a matter of day-to-day routine, and sometimes draw different conclusions than urban people, or each other, doesn't
make them subhuman. Perhaps the best approach, for those
who find country ways harsh, is to agree to disagree, and
move on to other questions.

A Wider Alliance

You can't scare me; I'm sticking with the union.

WOODY GUTHRIE, "Union Maid"

T HE PRECEDING CHAPTERS SHOULD have made it clear that the laws and administrative structures currently governing rural life and enterprise in Canada—and thus *directly* governing the quality and stability of urban Canada's food supply, water supply, and environmental safety—are sorely in need of reform.[1]

As *The End of Food* demonstrated, the nutritional content of everything we eat is in drastic decline, while the amount of toxic substances contaminating our food is rising sharply. Our health, and the health of our children, are gravely threatened. The traditional family farm, once the best guarantor of the quality of our food, has been driven to the point of extinction. In the next decade, we may see the last few remnants of this way of life disappear. Young people trying to enter farming are generally barred by the impossibly high entry expenses, especially the purchase of quota.

At the same time, due to the advent of the factory farm system, as well as the failure to adequately restrain the power of mining, logging, and other extraction-industry interests, our rural environment is in deadly danger. It is, to put it bluntly, being trashed, and through it, the water supply of our great cities—including Canada's capital—could be trashed, along with the quality of the air we breathe, the integrity of the forests that mitigate global warming, and the life in our freshwater lakes and rivers.

This is not something affecting "a few farmers," or the odd cottager sitting by a lake out there in the boondocks, or a small band of First Nations people living in the back of beyond. This menaces everybody. It is fully as serious a threat as that of global warming, and in fact is bound up with and exacerbates the greenhouse effect. Nor, as noted in chapter 1, is Canada the only country in crisis. All of North America, and in fact most of the world, is facing the same kind of danger.

What's Needed Now

What is needed now, urgently, is physical, direct action at the local level and widespread social and political action at every other echelon. So many things need doing that only thousands of people, mobilized, inspired, and working together, can accomplish them fast enough to save the situation.

A "for starters" to-do list in Ontario, for example (a similar list could be drawn up for nearly every other Canadian province or U.S. state), might include:

1) CURBING THE EXCESSIVE political influence of the corporate, industrial farm and mining sector by amending campaign finance rules and shaking up the senior provincial and federal bureaucracies. This, of course, is a political task, requiring both organized, targeted political action

and the kind of incentive that only powerful pressure from the voters can prompt. The corporations and their lobbyists have been there before us, and will not cede an inch of their turf without a fight;

2) ENDING THE SECRECY rules that help to cover up environmental, labor, and other abuses by the corporate farm sector. These would include, for example, the regulations under Ontario's Nutrient Management Act, mandating secrecy in connection with the amounts of manure being spread by intensive livestock operations (discussed in chapter 4);

3) RESTORING SOME OF the powers removed in recent decades from local municipal governments, and devolving over-centralized federal/provincial controls. This would require, for example, repeal or revision of both the Ontario Nutrient Management Act and the Ontario Agricultural Operations Practices Act sections, mentioned in chapter 4, that effectively froze municipal government out of the process of regulating factory farms;

4) REHABILITATING THE AGRICULTURAL marketing board structure and regulations so as to end current abuses (example, gradually ending the sale of quota), while retaining the basic small-farm protections provided by the boards, especially their market leverage. Obviously, those who currently have heavy investments in quota should not lose that investment. That would be comparable to confiscating land without compensation. But neither should entrants to a quota industry have to pay, like Shawn Carmichael (see chapter 5), $2 million or more for the privilege. Either the sale of quota

should be ended, or special arrangements should be made to make it easier for young people to obtain it. Single-desk marketing powers, such as those stripped away from the Manitoba hog board, should also be restored.

Both national and provincial boards, all across Canada, are in need of such repair;

5) INSTITUTING AND PROMOTING training programs to encourage and enable young people to enter farming, especially those interested in pursuing the organic farming route. The National Farmers Union has an active program working toward this goal (see below), but must struggle with limited funds and insufficient government support;

6) AMENDING THE INCOME and property tax structure, as well as subsidy and insurance terms, to remove penalties for small farms and small businesses in rural areas (cheese factories, local butcher shops, local dairies). Subsistence farmers, who produce the majority of what they need to live on-farm, should not be taxed—as they are today—as if they were wealthy cottagers in the trendy recreational Muskokas, just north of Toronto. Nor should large industrial operations receive tax breaks or indirect subsidies denied smaller business operators. Taxes and subsidies should be amended to actively *encourage* small farms and small businesses, and to foster economic diversity;

7) AMENDING ZONING, ENVIRONMENTAL, and health rules so as to protect small farms and small businesses from excessive or unreasonable regulation. Small, local butcher shops like that of Alphons Vaneyndthoven (chapter 8) ought not

to be treated as if they were the same as the major, multinational corporate meat-packing giants, nor should small town church suppers, or local farmers' markets, be saddled with impossibly expensive, often unnecessary, health or environmental restrictions;

8) ENCOURAGING THE DEVELOPMENT and growth of support structures (such as farmers' markets or community-supported agriculture groups) that provide markets for small farms. Municipal governments ought to be at least as generous in providing zoning options, utility services, and market space to farmers' markets as they are to, say, the newest Walmart branch;

9) ENCOURAGING THE INCREASE of organic farming operations, and of opportunities for smaller organic growers to find local markets for their crops and livestock. The recent study, mentioned in chapter 5, that established that organic plant-based foods are more nutritious, often containing as much as 25 percent more nutrients than factory farm products, ought to prompt us—literally—to put our money where our mouths are;

10) FORCING A MORATORIUM on uranium or other highly radioactive mineral exploration and mining, particularly in areas upstream from major water sources. The nuclear industry has yet to solve the problems of nuclear waste disposal or to adequately insure against accidental waste spills or leakages. Given the horrendous—and permanent—damage such accidents could cause and have caused, to expand the industry would be reckless. To expand it in areas that

are sources for the drinking water of large populations is little short of criminal;

11) AMENDING THE MINING Act of Ontario and similar acts across Canada to give property owners control of the sub-surface mineral rights on their properties. People like the Morrisons (chapter 6) should not have their retirement dream homes snatched from them without compensation, or their property trespassed upon and ruined, by provincially empowered prospectors or mining speculators;

12) IMPLEMENTING A FAIR and just settlement of all outstanding First Nations land claims, in a manner that respects native customs and laws, as well as provincial law. First Nations bands across the continent have been waiting not only decades, but in some cases for centuries, to be accorded basic justice. Their lands, already a mere fraction of their original extent, should not be considered open territory for any corporate speculator who comes along. Nor should they be forced to resort to extreme civil disobedience to speed redress via negotiations that proceed at a snail's pace. Like the Ardoch Algonquins, many of these bands have been doing our work for us, protecting rural areas from forms of exploitation that would harm all of society. We ought to be more grateful;

13) RENEGOTIATING THE NORTH American Free Trade Agreement (NAFTA) to remove provisions that threaten or damage small farms and small rural business. U.S. presidential candidates in 2008 continually railed against NAFTA, which they claimed unfairly penalized the U.S. None of them seemed

to have noticed that under NAFTA Canada's quota industry farmers, such as the poultry growers described by Larry Robinson in chapter 5, are forced to buy an increasing percentage of their birds from U.S. producers;

14) DEVELOPING ORGANIZATIONS THAT unite urban and rural voters and provide a mechanism of political influence where the interests of both populations coincide. Rural populations are simply too small to create the critical political clout needed to effect change. Only if urban voters join them in the fight can they hope to win. Both the long-established NFU and the newcomers of the Landowners Association (see below) have the potential to draw urban supporters in, but it is an uphill battle;

15) EDUCATING URBAN VOTERS and consumers regarding the importance to their own food and water supply, and environment, of maintaining a healthy, diverse rural sector.

The last item—educating urban people about what is really going on in the country, and their personal stake in the outcome—is probably the most crucial task. Without the support of a critical mass of voters—and, as noted in chapter 9, rural people aren't numerous enough to provide it—nothing will change.

The destruction of our rural world has proceeded unabated for decades, in both Canada and the U.S., under all four of the major national political parties—both Republicans and Democrats in the U.S., and both Liberals and Conservatives in Canada. The Republicans (as exemplified by the infamous Earl Butz) and the Tories (currently attacking the Canadian Wheat Board) have tended to be more aggressive, but neither the Democrats nor the Grits have much to brag about.

Both countries held national elections in 2008, but in neither national campaign was the rural crisis addressed as a priority. The American candidates never even mentioned it, while in Canada, it almost never appeared on the campaign circuit radar. Despite the national and local media attention given to both the Ardoch Algonquins' struggle and the Mohawks' fight, aboriginal issues were also largely ignored. So much so, in fact, that it prompted a public complaint by Assembly of First Nations national chief Phil Fontaine. "The current campaign [has] what seems to be a serious absence of any discussion on aboriginal issues," he said.[2] "We want [the parties] to take notice as they do with the ethnic vote and the very serious attention that's placed to the ethnic vote." There was little reaction.

As for party platforms, the Tories, already on record as attacking marketing boards, and with a long history of pro–big business bias, had by mid-campaign in September published no platform at all.[3] The Liberals published one, which gave some attention to rural matters. It vowed to reverse the Tory attack on the Wheat Board, to revisit freight rates for agricultural products, as well as to support initiatives to deal with issues such as climate change that impact farmers.[4] But the rural crisis went unmentioned in most of its major candidates' stump speeches, being seen as more or less a peripheral issue.

Canada's New Democratic Party platform, in contrast to its public statements in the previous election in 2006, when ex–NFU president Nette Wiebe was running as a New Democrat for a seat in the Saskatchewan legislature, made little

mention at all of the rural crisis,[5] nor did the NDP leader
emphasize the issue in any reported campaign addresses.
The party website's "plan" for the future made no mention
at all of rural affairs.

Like the Liberals, the Green Party of Canada, smallest of
the national parties and least likely to gain seats in the election, referred to the rural crisis in its platform, which vowed
to "support the family farm" and "encourage production
and consumption of Canadian agricultural products, especially organically grown."[6] However, in national campaign
speeches and debates, the party followed the lead of its rivals,
relegating rural matters to the periphery.

At the provincial level, the Ontario Liberal government
has a rural Economic Development Program, launched in
2003, but the program is aimed primarily at revitalizing the
urban portions of rural regions, rather than the farm population. The disappearance of family farms, once the bulwark and chief support of every small-town, has been the
prime cause of the decline of small-town businesses. How
the latter are to be revitalized without revitalizing the farm
population is something of a mystery. Oddly, the program
also seems to contradict the party's own background study,
quoted in chapter 8, and its recommendations to start "planning for decline" and "restricting further settlement expansion" in rural areas.

Absent the interest of political parties, who else is out
there, able to bring these crucial issues before the voting
public? What would it take to attract the interest of the parties, and get them on side?

Past experience has shown that only determined, well-
organized, and widespread citizen pressure can capture the

attention of North America's major political parties and put any issue on the front burner of the national, state, or provincial agendas. The Vietnam War would have dragged on for another twenty years, slaughtering millions more than it did, if Americans had not taken to the streets and forced a halt. Publicly funded medical care would never have been adopted in Canada if Tommy Douglas and the CCF, buoyed by strong public support, had not forced the issue before the national voting public. Major national parties never lead, they only follow, and most often—without the expression of overwhelming citizen outrage—they follow the money, namely the cash and influence, direct or indirect, provided by the ubiquitous donors of the corporate world.

Unfortunately, there are not many non-partisan organized groups in existence to do the work of educating and mobilizing ordinary people on the issue of rural survival, and its importance to the future of the urban world. And those that do exist too often have, or are perceived by urban people as having, a relatively narrow focus. The Ontario Small Farm Producers Association and the Ecological Farmers Association of Ontario, local groups like Bedford Mining Alert and even national ones like Mining Watch Canada, all share this "one-issue" or "too local" handicap.

Who's left to articulate the grievances of ordinary rural folk, including those who are not themselves active farmers, and bring their issues before a national audience?

The Ontario Federation of Agriculture (OFA), and its national counterpart, the Canadian Federation of Agriculture (CFA), are, as the CFA's website states, a "national umbrella organization representing provincial general farm organizations and national commodity groups." Its board is mostly comprised of representatives of the major marketing boards, dominated, as already described in chapter 5, by large producers, and it is widely seen as overly sympathetic to the policies of corporate agribusiness.

As the NFU recounts, the OFA at its founding in 1935 was "composed mainly of commercial organizations," and the "commercial groups gradually usurped the educational field...The OFA became ever more conservative and it appeared to many that militancy among farmers was a phenomenon of the past."[7]

Not until the efforts of the NFU, and even more so the high-profile public confrontations mounted by the Ontario Landowners Association mentioned in earlier chapters, brought to public attention the harsh effects of overly strict government regulation on small farmers and businesses did the OFA's officers begin talking—in 2008—about the problem. And when they did, the tone struck by OFA spokesmen was almost fawning.

In a newspaper column published in September 2008,[8] OFA president Geri Kamenz was effusive toward Liberal provincial premier Dalton McGuinty, who had just spoken at an annual plowing match. The speech, he said "provided the OFA the opportunity to thank Premier McGuinty for his support." "We are thankful to the McGuinty government's leadership," he added. "We know the premier is intent on ensuring fairness and equity for our province..."

Only after spending several paragraphs on praise for the premier did Kamenz sheepishly, almost apologetically, broach the daring statement that "we have yet to create legislation...that can avoid unintended and unforseen consequences," that is to say "the unintended and unforseen

consequences of legislation and regulations that are causing grief to so many in the agricultural community." Without stating what these actually were, he gently asked the
premier to "come to the table with stakeholders to mitigate those [still undescribed] unintended and unforseen
consequences."

As one local farmer friend said to me, tongue firmly in
cheek: "With strong, fiery leadership like that, how can we
help but prevail?"

In the final analysis, at least as of this writing, only the
National Farmers Union, already nationwide (and international, with its counterpart in the U.S.), and the Landowners
Association—which has begun to attract interest in other
provinces, notably from rural groups in New Brunswick,
which recently invited the Ontario Landowners leadership
to come and speak on how to organize a similar group—
hold the potential in Canada for making the battle a general
one, with widespread urban and rural voter adhesion.

The NFU has been around for decades and has done—
in the literal meaning of the term—yeoman service in the
cause of saving the rural environment and the family farm.
Its roots are in the long tradition of Canadian and North
American farmers' movements, from the Farmers' Clubs of
the 1850s and the early Grange movement, to the National
Progressive Party and the United Farmers of Ontario (UFO).[9]

Its newsletter, *Union Farmer Monthly,* and its quarterly
magazine, *The Union Farmer,*[10] have provided in-depth, consis-
tent evaluations of rural Canada's problems—particularly the
pros and cons of marketing boards and supply-management
marketing. The NFU sees the power of the multinational corporations that control the food industry as the real threat to

family farmers, as well as to consumers, while government is only a danger when it becomes overresponsive to the corporate sector's priorities. The organization's analyses are generally spot-on and well documented, and it tries to put farm problems in the context of wider society.

The union also has a separate associate membership category for urban people who want to actively engage with rural issues, and makes an effort to educate its urban members. It conducts a program—overseen in eastern Ontario by Local 316 president Andrea Cumpson and working in cooperation with the Heifer International Foundation—aimed at training young people who want to embark on careers in agriculture[11]—thus responding to number 5 of the "to-do" list. It also cooperates with local farmers' markets and other direct marketing initiatives, number 8 on the list.[12]

Nevertheless, the NFU's strong farm orientation remains both its greatest strength and greatest weakness. The "single issue" image clings to it stubbornly, and few ordinary urban supermarket shoppers have heard of the organization, let alone read any of its publications.

In fact, in recent decades, consumer groups—responding enthusiastically and with lamentable shortsightedness to a general "cheap food" policy—have actually begun to see farmers as their enemies. Pleading for a high enough farm-gate return on their produce to at least cover their costs of production, farmers have been pilloried as "predatory" by such groups as the Consumers Association of Canada and the Economic Council of Canada.[13]

However, the recent appearance on the scene of the Ontario Landowners Association (mentioned in chapters 1, 5, and 8), and the prospect of its expansion to other provinces, has created a new public relations dynamic. While the

NFU's days of gritty radicalism and street demonstrations, at least at the local level, seem to be long gone (the last major farmer protests in Ontario took place under its predecessor, the Ontario Farmers Union, in 1967),[14] the Landowners Association has exploded upon the scene, full of "piss and vinegar" and willing to take to the streets in a heartbeat. It may have a stronger potential than the NFU not only of attracting media attention, but of uniting disparate rural and urban interests.

Originally launched in 2003 by a handful of farmers and rural residents living near Perth, Ontario, as the Lanark Landowners Association, it advocates a "rural revolution" and has grown by leaps and bounds, quickly becoming a fifteen-thousand-member, province-wide movement and producing its own media star: an outspoken, charismatic scrapper named Randy Hillier. Hillier recently won a hard-fought nomination and subsequent election to become the Progressive Conservative Party's member of Provincial Parliament (MPP) for the riding of Lanark, Frontenac, Lennox and Addington. In many ways, he reminds observers of the French rural activist José Bové,[15] or Poland's Andrzej Lepper,[16] previously mentioned in chapter 1.

Now called the Ontario Landowners Association, the group has begun publishing its own magazine, *The Landowner,* edited by Hillier, Marlene Black, Doug Cully, and Merle Bowes.[17] Like Hillier, the magazine is a pull-no-punches, outspoken vehicle, with a wide network of friends and informants at nearly every social and political level.

Awkward Teenager

However, the Landowners Association is seen by some media observers as a kind of awkward political teenager, physically nearly grown up, at least at the provincial level, but still slightly erratic and unsure of its ultimate goals. One moment radically aggressive, and the next reflective and calculating, it looks as if—like a winning high school football team that catches everyone's attention, but doesn't always know where to carry the ball—it has not yet reached the kind of full maturity that could maximize its impact.

Looks, of course, can be deceiving. Its critics may be underestimating the group, and those who see it, as does writer Helen Forsey, as a dangerous, "demagogic" force "leading people down a trail far to the right," may be judging it too soon.[18]

The NFU still takes part in some public demonstrations, and even sent organizers and demonstrators to some recent international gatherings. NFU national women's president Colleen Ross traveled all the way to Hong Kong as part of a group of protesters at international trade talks. "We go to NAFTA [North American Free Trade Agreement] meetings, we go to WTO [World Trade Organization] meetings," she said. "I was in Hong Kong. I got tear-gassed. We are willing to put everything on the line. But what makes us different is we know exactly why we're there, and why we're doing it."

But the Landowners are in an entirely different category. They are firebrands, truly radical in orientation and willing to fight not only at major national or international gatherings, but also at the grassroots level, property by property, family by family, tooth and nail. And their numerous fights are not limited to farm issues. As the title indicates, they are ready to do battle over any land issue, as well as over perceived injustices to small businesses everywhere.

While the NFU demonstrates at legislatures or international trade gatherings, the Landowners show up at individual homes, shops, and farms, hundreds strong, willing, if necessary, to face down armed police and to go to jail, for a single farmer, or single small business threatened by bureaucratic bullying. Several incidents in which bands of Landowners members flocked to the scene of perceived attacks on rural targets—rallying to the victims' support and often physically blocking government inspectors or police—have already been described in chapter 5.

In another high-profile case, the Landowners even intervened against the attempted deportation of a Canadian farmer to Belgium based on a twenty-six-year-old misdemeanor conviction for shoplifting in his native country. Media reports quoted Hillier:

> We saw this was clearly unjust to do that to a hard working family and we took them in and provided sanctuary for two weeks," Mr. Hillier said. "We had about 150 people show up when we returned the family to their home. They're still there, milking cows. The Canadian Border Services refuses to come near them.[19]

And the Landowners are past masters of the art of mass public demonstration/disruption, at least as fearless as the Algonquins or the Mohawks, and brilliant in their conception and implementation.

In April 2004, hundreds of Landowners, at least ninety of them mounted on tractors or other slow-moving farm vehicles, swung onto Ontario's Highway 417 and paraded from the Carp exit to downtown Ottawa, along the Queensway expressway, tying up traffic for hours.[20] Police blocked off freeway exits while the demonstrators, bearing placards that said "Canadian farmers are on the extinction list—does anyone care?," passed by.

Once in the nation's capital, the Landowners and their supporters converged on Parliament Hill, where they mounted a day-long demonstration, including a live cattle auction, a portable sawmill demonstration, and the tying of effigies of three politicians to the gates of Parliament. Thousands witnessed the events, and three members of Parliament—including then Conservative Party opposition leader (later prime minister) Stephen Harper—addressed the throngs.[21]

In other actions, the Landowners blocked off Canada's busiest highway—the 401—for eight hours, held an illegal deer hunt to protest rules forbidding the culling of nuisance deer that destroy farm crops, and once temporarily shut down the Kemptville, Ontario, offices of the Ministry of Natural Resources and the Ministry of Agriculture and Food. At one demonstration, Hillier himself was arrested for trespassing.

Where the Landowners are concerned, the word "militant" may be an understatement. But members are quick to point out that, much like the Algonquins and Mohawks described in chapters 4 and 5, their protests and acts of civil disobedience have, in the grand tradition of America's Henry David Thoreau,[22] invariably been nonviolent.

"I'm this militant radical, and the most serious offence I've been charged with is trespassing?" laughed Hillier.[23] "All our demonstrations have been peaceful, and done in cooperation with the police," added Landowners cofounder Merle Bowes.[24]

To claim, along with Forsey, that the use of civil disobedience tactics automatically makes the Landowners group "demagogic," one would also have to brand the anti-war demonstrations of the Vietnam era, the civil rights marches of Martin Luther King Jr., or even Mahatma Gandhi's satya-graha (nonviolent resistance)[25] with the same label. This would be unfair. The tactics themselves are only tools.

As for the charge of being "far to the right," this seems based on the fact that a significant number of Landowners members, including Hillier, are Conservative Party supporters, while others, like OLA president Jack MacLaren, have occasionally made public pronouncements that one normally would expect to hear from neoconservative ideologues. At one OLA gathering, for example, MacLaren opined that global warming was a myth.

It also stems from two of the Landowners' major tenets: 1) that government regulation has become abusive, and 2) that property rights are an absolute that must be better protected than they are under current laws. But there are many groups on the left who would support the first position, while the second would not be rejected by centrist parties.

The Tory affiliation of many Landowners can be ascribed to nothing more than rural tradition and social conservatism. Just as most U.S. rural areas vote Republican, and have for generations, most rural Canadian areas have always voted Conservative. Of course, this tendency was given a huge boost when a Liberal Party government brought in the gun registry so universally loathed by farm people (giving rise to the slogan, "It's the guns, stupid"). But for the most part, rural Toryism is more an accident of history and family allegiance than anything else.

Even MacLaren himself—his views on global warming oddly notwithstanding—departs from the stereotypical "diehard Tory" mold.

"I like the Green Party," said MacLaren. "Some of the finest people I've met have been in the Green Party. They came up during the last election and asked if we could talk, and we said, 'Here's what we want and we're not negotiable: property rights, de-amalgamation, less government, and compensation for lost property rights.' They said, 'We have no problem with that,' so I did vote Green. Got my picture taken in the local paper here. I said I supported [local Green Party candidate] John Ogilvy. I think they're gaining ground and credibility."

"We considered voting for the Green Party," said Merle Bowes, who is currently the Lanark Landowners Association's vice president and its delegate to the provincial association. "I and my family do agree with some of their platform. But they've got a long way to go yet.

"Our official position is that we will not play partisan politics. We will support a good candidate no matter what his stripe. My own candidate here for the provincial [Tory] party has been in there far too long and is ineffective."

Even Hillier, though elected as a Tory, is far from what Quebeckers call *"pure laine* (pure wool)"* on the subject. "I don't think there's any party that has a significant and comprehensive enough knowledge of the rural areas to be able to deal with it [farm policy] effectively," he said. "The knowledge base is not there. Generally speaking, ministers, when you go through the evaluation process of who's going to be what, knowledge of the industry or even the ministry does not rank in the criteria at all. In the political level, knowledge is not seen to be important."

Forsey attacks the Landowners because "their public complaints and protests consistently target government, not corporate power...[not] the ever-growing profits of the corporate suppliers, processors distributors and retailers, who divvy up the consumer dollars among themselves and leave the farmer with next to nothing." [26]

She admits that:

> The issues that galvanized the formation of the [Landowners] are real and troubling: the near impossibility of earning a living from a family farm or rural business, the massive burden of red tape imposed on those still trying to do that, the blanket application of urban one-size-fits-all standards to rural institutions, municipal amalgamations that swallow small communities and neutralize rural voices, the withdrawal of rural services and the closing of rural schools and hospitals, and the overall marginalizing of rural people in an overwhelmingly urbanized society.[27]

But people like Hillier, she believes, let the "big fish" get away:

> The property based solutions they propose actually represent a welcome gift to those very corporations. Deregulation and enhanced private property rights are strategies that could have—and quite possibly did—come straight out of right-wing think tanks or political party war rooms. In any case, such schemes are an integral part of the overall corporate agenda of privatization and the undermining of government. The rural revolution's current groundswell of vocal support for these policy directions is a major achievement that the suits must be celebrating." [28]

Yet Hillier doesn't see government in general as inherently evil or undesirable, but only "misgovernment," that responds to bureaucratic or other special interests, and not to "the little guy." He may be closer to Forsey's view than she realizes.

"To read one piece of legislation and fully understand it, to comprehend it and understand the consequences it will place on people, takes a significant amount of time. Take somebody who has no knowledge, dump them in and make them responsible for hundreds of pieces of legislation and thousands of employees. And each one of those pieces of legislation could have maybe three hundred pages of regulations that went with them. We're putting them [government ministers] in a position where they must fail.

"They become beholden to the bureaucracy, and to the lobbyists and special interests for their decision-making. And truly the individual [citizens], their interests and their concerns are not seen or understood at all.

"And there's something a little more nefarious that I'm working on, that I've found out. I don't have all the details, but government has begun to fund lobby groups. This came to light when I took up the battle for [a certain rural industry] back in January. I found out then that [their] association is fully funded by the MNR [Ministry of Natural Resources]. This is supposed to be an industry lobby group. The MNR has full say on who it will pick as director. They have veto powers over any board member, and they've also put in stipulations that the board office must be in Peterborough and the members of the board must live within 30 miles of Peterborough. That's where the head office for the MNR is. It's a big facade, and the real people have no voice whatsoever."

In this case, government bureaucrats appear to be controlling an industry lobby group. In others, industry may control the bureaucrats, at least indirectly. This is the complaint of Forsey, and of many researchers and officers of the NFU. As one of my former professors of political science used to say, "Go around the ring far enough to the Libertarian right and you'll meet a left-wing anarchist coming towards you from the other way."

Government overregulation and property rights are not the only Landowners issues, of course. Another is the question of amalgamation, and the loss of local municipal political powers to the centralized provincial or federal level. In Ontario, amalgamation was a favorite policy of the former right-wing Tory government of ex-premier Mike Harris. The Landowners see it as having been a massive folly, as Merle Bowes insists:

"We're dealing with an amalgamated situation here [in his own riding], with my municipality of Mississippi Mills, which is now a ward [of the city of Almonte]," he said. "Almonte seems to be a bottomless pit for taxpayers' money to flow into. Mississippi Mills had cash reserves. Now everybody's broke. It's the same with the city of Ottawa, which became Ottawa Carleton. You've got a huge rural element to it. But it's governed by, I believe, twenty-three councillors and twenty-one of them are from the urban area. The geographic area makes Ottawa the largest city by far in Canada, and you've got just two people representing the people and the activities that are conducted in this huge rural area." Those two people will always be outvoted by the urban steamroller, he knows, removing rural issues from the control of the very people who know rural conditions best—and who are most directly affected.

"Government by the governed" is as much a Landowners tenet as it was of the original thirteen colonies of revolutionary America.

So is the importance of community, and the concept of rural people as stewards of the environment. On the stewardship idea, Bowes is confident that rural people measure up. "I've been a certified organic grower for many years," he said. "I've done the Environmental Farm Plan. I consider myself a conservationist, and a true one. I've got a few plant species on my property that are designated on the endangered species list. They'll stay there as long as I'm in control of the property. With property rights also come responsibilities. My property rights only go so far as where yours begin."

MacLaren adds: "We need government to acknowledge and respect rural people for being good stewards of the land and good stewards of the environment and food safety."

Sadly, this has not been the philosophy of all OLA members, a fact which has impacted negatively on NFU officers' perception of the organization. The OLA's in-your-face slogan "This land is our land: back off government," offends Colleen Ross. Echoing Ardoch Algonquin co-chief Randy Cota's description of the "seven generations" philosophy, she said:

"Our position as farmers is that it's not our land. We're borrowing it for a time...Landowners members have told me they went in and basically erased all wetlands on their property because they suspected that legislation was going to come down that it was going to become a protected wetland, because of species at risk. They've gone in and tile-drained their wetlands. A Landowner north of Cornwall cut down most of his old maple stand because he said those trees were considered heritage trees and to be protected, and he said, 'Those are my trees and I'll do whatever I want with them.' He got wind that somebody was going to tell him those were protected trees, and he went in and cut them down. To me, that's not a legacy that we want to leave. It's not something we want to be part of.

"We don't have the right to plow up wetlands just because somebody told us not to, or to cut down maple trees or forests because we were told not to. We don't abide by that. We actually find it quite repugnant.

"For [some] Landowners, it's like they just care about themselves. All they want to talk about is their rights as landowners. We're not landowners, we're farmers. We care about land, we care about indigenous people, we're not just in it for ourselves. We care about the future, about our brothers and sisters in the global South."

She admits, of course, that not all Landowners members are as extreme as the two whose actions particularly offended her. She also agrees that the very fact that NFU people are "farmers, not landowners," is one of the union's political weaknesses.

Farmers aren't the only rural people under siege, and they aren't the only people who will suffer if their assailants succeed. Hence, the union's category of associate membership for urban supporters.

Urban Members

The Landowners have come to a similar realization, and have recently begun identifying prospective urban members, whose interests and issues coincide with their rural counterparts—although not all are willing to join the fight publicly.

"There's lots of urban people that are losing their property rights, the same kind of rights we lose in rural areas," said MacLaren. "New legislation came into effect last fall from the Ministry of Agriculture and Food for butcher shops [this point was discussed in chapter 8], that requires them to meet new high standards—which are high-cost, of course. [A woman from the ministry] came into Rob Carpenter's shop in Carleton Place and said to me, 'Well, 90 percent of you smaller operators won't be able to afford this. It's such a high standard it will require you to spend too much.' Rob is in his fifties. He's been a butcher all is life and he's at risk of being put out of business because he can't afford this thing. But he's full of piss and vinegar. He's ready to fight.

"At the same time, there was a butcher in downtown Toronto, been there a long time. A really neat shop. He had a great little business. The community loved it. And this regulation was applied to him. The guy closed his doors. And he'd been there twenty years or more. Randy phoned him to say 'Would you like us to help?' But he said, 'Oh no, we don't want to go public.' He was willing to lie down and die quietly. Rural people tend to be more independent-natured."

Other small urban shop owners—bakers, butchers, and restaurateurs—aren't so shy, and have begun contacting the Landowners.

MacLaren warns all of them: "We can only help people who are willing to fight. And it's stressful. Taking on government, a conflict, is always stressful. It's not fun. But that's what we do, eh? And some of these battles we win, and the laws get changed."

He's right there. Although the Landowners can't claim sole responsibility for some changes, they've certainly had an influence, as one website noted:

The province has reversed its policies regarding the taxing of sugar shacks as industrial sites, has refunded the taxation collected at the end of 2003 from seasonal campground owners, and put a hold on water regulations 170/03, pending a review. The issue around sawdust, which was mentioned by Randy Hillier, is also under review, and the Ministry of Natural Resources has made changes to deer hunting regulations as they pertain to farmers in Lanark, which was one of the original impetuses for the Lanark Landowners in the first place.[29]

Even those city dwellers who don't have property or business interests similar to those of rural people ought to be worried about what happens in the country, Bowes added.

"What's the guy on the sixteenth floor of an apartment building in Toronto to do when the system breaks down, and the food system is really challenged? What's he to do? He's totally vulnerable. First it'll be the people in the rural areas, the most directly and the earliest affected. But ultimately everyone will be affected. The people in the urban areas will be the final sufferers."

Are the activists of the Ontario Landowners Association always right in their analyses? Obviously not.

Are they right-wingers? Sometimes yes and sometimes no. Much like the 1930s-era Roman Catholic supporters of economic "Distributism," which included a strong "back-to-the-land" component,[30] they may find themselves right, left, or center at different times, depending on the individual issue and the individual Landowners member.

They are unquestionably effective, highly visible, and growing. They aren't limited to a single issue. They are open to fresh views and fresh approaches. They have the potential of unifying urban and rural stakeholders. Someday they may go national. There are few others out there at the moment with as much daring and inventiveness—at least, so far.

Will the Landowners and the NFU make common cause?

According to the NFU's Ross, it's not likely, except on one or two individual issues where both share the same stance. "It's not going to happen," she said.

But it's undeniable that urban people must, as soon as possible, begin to make common cause with their beleaguered rural counterparts. Whether Canadian readers prefer the NFU or the Landowners' approach, they ought to support one or both of the only two truly active national or potentially national champions of the rural world standing up to fight. Americans should get behind Farm Aid and the U.S. National Farmers Union.

The all-volunteer members of both groups are already virtually run off their feet trying to keep up with the work of advocacy.

"It's very difficult to run a farm full time and have a full-time, off-farm job, and still do the advocacy work that needs to be done," said Ross. I'm really struggling. I'm trying to support my family, but it's like having way too much bread and not enough butter. We're fighting an uphill battle here, and unless we get a percentage of the Canadian population to start echoing our message, we can't do it. Those many voices have to come from the population outside of the farming community."

There are, of course, other groups out there engaged in these issues, some local and some state or provincial.

For instance, Farm Folk/City Folk, in Vancouver, B.C. (1937 West 2nd Avenue, Vancouver, B.C., v6J 1J2), is actively involved in educating the province's urban consumers about the real issues in farming and food distribution, as is the national organization Food Secure Canada/Sécurité Alimentaire Canada, chaired by Cathleen Kneen. The Canadian Organic Growers Association, mentioned earlier, also works to educate consumers. (Contact addresses for national groups are in the following chapter.)

But in extreme times, times of emergency, what is needed most are activists, fighters, people not afraid to take risks and go beyond normal, everyday discourse. We are living in such times. This is a political fight. We have to go out on limbs, take chances, raise hell.

Or capitulate, and watch our children's future world crumble.

Following Up, Learning More

All words, and no performance.
PHILIP MASSINGER, *The Parliament of Love*

Be not like to horse and mule, which have no understanding.
CHURCH OF ENGLAND PRAYER BOOK, 1662

IN ALL OF PUBLIC life, knowledge without action is useless, while action without adequate knowledge is worse than dangerous. It is foolhardy. Those who may have become sympathetic to the rural cause after reading this book should, it is fervently hoped, be willing to act in support of those groups fighting the good fight. They may also want to learn more about the issues involved than has been presented here.

Organizations

In Canada, the two organizations that have been most active in the battle are:

THE NATIONAL FARMERS UNION, 2717 Wentz Avenue, Saskatoon, Saskatchewan, S7K 4B6, tel. (306) 652-9465, website www.nfu.ca. As already mentioned, there is a separate associate membership category for non-farm supporters. Members receive the magazine *The Union Farmer*.

THE LANDOWNERS ASSOCIATION, P.O. Box 1374, Almonte, Ontario, KOA 1AO, website www.ruralrevolution.com. One need not be a farmer or rural landowner to join. All supporters are welcome. Members receive the magazine *The Landowner*.

Also active nationally, though not engaged in direct political lobbying, or confrontation like that of the Landowners, is Food Secure Canada/Sécurité Alimentaire Canada, chaired by longtime food issue activist Cathleen Kneen. Food Secure Canada, 2746 Cassels Street, Ottawa, Ontario, K2B 6N7, website www.foodsecurecanada.org

In the U.S. the three most prominent organizations are:

THE NATIONAL FARMERS UNION, 400 North Capitol Street NW, Suite 790, Washington, D.C., 20001, tel. (202) 554-1600, website www.nfu.org.

NATIONAL FAMILY FARM COALITION, 110 Maryland Avenue NE, Suite 307, Washington, D.C., 20002, tel. (202) 543-5675, website www.nffc.net.

FARM AID, 11 Ward Street, Suite 200, Somerville, Massachusetts, 02143, tel. (800) 327-6243, website www.farm-aid. org.

All of these organizations would welcome either financial support and contributions, or volunteer support to do the work of political advocacy and public education. Your help is urgently needed.

Farming as a Career

For those interested in farming as a future career, both Canada and the U.S. have numerous universities that offer agricultural majors. Unfortunately, the universities tend to be too dependent on grant money coming directly or indirectly from the corporate, multinational food industry, and their instructors heavily emphasize the industrial, factory farm model as the ideal. Those interested in other types of farming systems should contact:

Canada

The National Farmers Union, listed above. The NFU has an active farmer training program, offering certificates and plenty of hands-on practical experience. National headquarters, as noted, is in Saskatoon. In eastern Ontario, NFU Local 316, headed by Andrea Cumpson has an active program. Contact Cumpson at (613) 353-2260, or www.craftontario.ca.

The Everdale Organic Farm & Environmental Learning Centre, mentioned in chapter 5, also has a program. See their website at www.everdale.org. This farm training center is part of the province-wide Collaborative Regional Alliance for Farmer Training (CRAFT), a network of organic farmer training centers. Contact (519) 855-4859, ext. 104, or visit www.craftontario.ca.

The Canadian Organic Growers Inc., a nationwide organization, has information on organic farm training, and its website, www.cog.ca, includes links to various organizations of interest to prospective farmers.

United States

There are numerous state, local, and regional programs for farmer training outside of the mainstream land-grant agricultural university programs. Unfortunately, some of the local and regional programs are funded or advised by corporate-dominated universities, whose faculties favor the factory farm model.

Programs that emphasize organic methods usually have the word "organic" in their organizational title, such as the California Certified Organic Farmers (CCOF), which conducts a successful Going Organic program. The CCOF can be reached at (831) 423-2263, or at 2155 Delaware Ave., Suite 150, Santa Cruz, California, 95060. Other, similar programs in other U.S. states, too numerous to list here, can be found using Internet search tools and appropriate search terms.

Further Reading

Of course, the more we know, the more effective and targeted our efforts will be. Following is a list of suggested sources of information for those interested in the history, future, and political/philosophical basis of the current rural crisis.

Early Settlement in Canada

Catharine Parr Traill, *The Backwoods of Canada: letters from the wife of an emigrant officer* (Toronto: Prospero Books, 2003).

Originally published in 1836, this account of pioneering in early Ontario has become, like its companion volume by Mrs. Parr Traill's sister (below), a Canadian classic. It vividly describes the trials, tribulations, and successes of the earliest

European farmers in the province, so many of whose hard-won properties—like those of their U.S. counterparts—are today falling to ruin.

Susanna Moodie, *Roughing it in the Bush* (Toronto: McClelland and Stewart, 1989).

Originally published in 1852, this story by Catharine Parr Traill's sister completes the picture of early settlement and the creation of what was once a prosperous rural Canada.

First Nations Land History

Stephen McGregor, *Since Time Immemorial: Our Story. The Story of the Kitigan Zibi Anishinabeg* (Maniwaki, Quebec: Kitigan Zibi Education Council, 2004).

A comprehensive history of the Algonquin First Nation's struggle to protect and maintain its claim to lands it has held in careful stewardship for thousands of years. Available from the council at: 41 Kikinamage Mikan, Maniwaki, Quebec, J9E 3B1.

Sarah Carter, *Lost Harvests* (Montreal & Kingston: McGill-Queen's University Press, 2000).

A history of the Prairie Indian Reserve Farmers, the "story of a people who tried, against all obstacles, to live off the land that belonged to them."

Farm Crisis History

Louis Aubrey Wood, *A History of Farmers' Movements in Canada* (Toronto: University Press, 1975).

Dated, but still the most comprehensive book on the subject.

Paul F. Sharp, *The Agrarian Revolt in Western Canada: A Survey Showing American Parallels* (Regina, Sask.: Canadian Plains Research Center, 1997).

The story of agrarian insurgency in Canada's prairie provinces from 1900 to the Great Depression.

Harry P. Diaz, Joann Jaffe, and Robert Stirling, *Farm Communities at the Crossroads: Challenge and Resistance* (Regina, Sask.: Canadian Plains Research Center, 2003).

The fifty-year struggle for rural survival in Canada's flatlands.

Wendell Berry, *The Unsettling of America* (San Francisco: Sierra Club Books, 1996).

Now recognized as an American classic, this book recounts the steady, deliberate destruction of the American family farm, and its social consequences.

A.V. Krebs, *The Corporate Reapers: The Book of Agribusiness* (Washington, D.C.: Essential Books, 1992).

The late Al Krebs's masterwork, detailing the takeover of U.S. agriculture by the corporate-government nexus, and describing its pernicious effects.

Brewster Kneen, *From Land to Mouth: Understanding the Food System* (Toronto: NC Press, 1995).

The Canadian equivalent of Al Krebs's dissection of corporate farming.

Alexander Ervin, Cathy Holtslander, Darren Qualman, and Rick Sawa, *Beyond Factory Farming: Corporate Hog Barns and*

the Threat to Public Health, the Environment and Rural Commu-
nities (Saskatoon, Sask.: Canadian Center for Policy Alternatives, 2003).

Probably the most comprehensive and graphic account
of this subject, with extensive background material. What
it says about hogs is true of most other factory livestock
operations.

Rev. John McQuillan, Herbert Shove, H. Robbins, Rev. Vincent McNabb, Reginald Jebb, Monsignor J. Dey, K.L. Ken-
rick, George Maxwell, and Rev. H.E.G. Rope, *Flee to the*
Fields: The Founding Papers of the Catholic Land Movement
(Norfolk, Virginia: IHS Press, 2003).

A collection of essays on the so-called Catholic Land
Movement of the 1930s.

Fr. Vincent McNabb, *The Church and the Land* (Norfolk, Virginia: IHS Press, 2003).

A thorough discussion of the theoretical and religious
background of the Catholic Land Movement.

Inspirational/Useful

E.F. Schumacher, *Small is Beautiful: Economics As If People*
Mattered (London: Abacus, 1974).

An international best-seller when it appeared, now
almost forgotten.

E.F. Schumacher, *A Guide for the Perplexed* (New York: Harper
& Row, 1979).

A "survival manual" sequel to *Small is Beautiful.*

Richard Merrill, ed., *Radical Agriculture* (New York: Harper Colophon Books, 1976).

Notable particularly for the chapters contributed by Wendell Berry and anarchist theorist Murray Bookchin.

Helen and Scott Nearing, *The Good Life: Sixty Years of Self-sufficient Living* (New York: Schocken Books, 1989).

Combining both of the Nearings' earlier books, *Living the Good Life* and *Continuing the Good Life*, these texts probably did more than any other source to inspire the 1970s back-to-the-land movement.

Aric McBay and Holly Grinvalds, *From the Ground Up: A Primer for Community Action on Kingston and Countryside's Food System* (Kingston, Ont.: National Farmers Union Local 316 and Food Down the Road, 2007), available from www.fooddowntheroad.ca.

Though local in emphasis, the principles and organizational ideas in this book are applicable as models to be followed by local food advocates anywhere in North America.

A Personal War

*Nobody who could write worth
a damn could ever write in peace.*

MICKEY ROURKE, as "Henry" in *Barfly*

SOMETIMES IT HELPS TO know where an author is coming
from.

Everyone, it seems, has a dream of retiring to the country. My grandfather—ex-boxer, Vaudeville singer, railroad
fireman, and factory foreman Andrew Aloysius Collins—
used to sit on the front porch of his house on Infantry
Avenue, in Detroit in the 1940s, and talk about the chicken
farm he'd start "when our ship comes in." Sometimes it was
in Michigan, out in Chelsea where our cousins had a small
dairy farm, and sometimes it was just across the river in
Ontario, where my great-grandfather (or was it great-grand-
uncle?) came from, after fleeing a famine-ridden Ireland—
whose agricultural policy had been taken over by a ruthless
foreign invader.

Always it was part of that landscape that seems indelibly
colored in green, the Christian symbol of hope.

My dream was no different. It may have begun in the 1950s, on my cousins' farm, where I spent time in the summer working and sharing farm family life. It was a good, healthy, natural way to live, and my cousins seemed to me at the time to be pretty happy people. But I think it had its roots further back than that, in very early childhood, and was reinforced—more accurately, brought to a crisis point—years after those summers working in the hayfields.

The early childhood experience can only be described as a religious one, and one of unusual power to have been remembered so long afterward—even today, when I'm 67. It was the early summer of 1945 or '46, and I was either four or five years old. The key to it was light, a sensation of both warmth and light. Extraordinary light:

It's morning. I step out on the back porch of my parents' house on the West Side of Detroit and look up, around me. I am aware of trees, bushes, and green leaves. Such green! I feel warmth. The air has a quality of whiteness, of light in its purest sense, transparent. I am happy, seeing the leaves, feeling the warmth, *feeling* the light. I feel as if I could some-how step out onto the air, and walk across the light. I don't recall for certain, but I think I may have laughed.

Then it's noon. I'm in the backyard of our neighbor's house, and several card tables are set out on the grass, such exceptionally green grass, for a lawn party. The lawn has just been mown, and there is a fresh-cut smell, like the smell I'd later encounter mowing hay. The sky is beautifully blue, with white, puffy cumulus clouds, and the tablecloths on the card tables are white. They blow in the light breeze, and flap. On the tables are clear glass jugs filled with Kool-Aid, red, yellow, and green colored liquid, through which the sunlight shines. There are beads of moisture, condensation, on the glass. I crawl under the tables, under the flapping tablecloths, and look up at the bright glass jugs, and recognize what I see. It's the same light, the same colors I saw in the morning.

I was, of course, a preschooler, not some kind of religious adept. My notions of anything to do with formal religion were almost completely unformed. But what I think took root that day was a kind of reverence, not for any particular thing, but for *everything*, sight or smell, that was natural and clean.

I felt it again years later, looking out the window of a house in New Hudson, Michigan, at a man on a small tractor, with a tiny, two-bottom plow attached, slowly moving along through a field laying down a furrow where he planned a market vegetable garden. The plow made that characteristic *swishhhh* as it turned the soft earth, and the light was there again.

In that instant, I knew I had to go back to the farm, to the country. It was an almost physical ache. And it wouldn't be for a visit. I knew I had to go there to stay.

Not very long afterward, I did, as noted in chapter 1, joining the 1970s back-to-the-land movement that had grown out of the 1960s counterculture. The move took me first to Quebec and a small farm on the South Shore, near a place called St. Louis de Gonzague, and then to Harrowsmith, Ontario, where I bought a bigger place and went to work for the original, countercultural *Harrowsmith* magazine, reporting on the movement and on rural life in general.

For a while, near the beginning, it was one of the happiest times in my life. Our place had a big, ¾-acre garden, a good barn in which we kept our own twenty laying hens, a maple sugar bush where we tapped trees in the spring, and a big enough woodlot to supply all of the firewood we needed to heat the house all winter. We had a little International Harvester B250 diesel tractor, which ran like a top. I still remember one morning, sitting on that tractor, discing up a plot of land, while the blackbirds and killdeer followed behind, hopping in and out of the furrows looking for insects the disc harrow turned up. It was a beautiful day, and I sat there on the B250, singing at the top of my lungs the same old Irish songs my grandfather had sung. His grandson had seen that "ship come in" after all, even down to the chickens.

There was a river at the end of our road, where the kids swam and fished for rock bass in summer, and where we hunted ducks in the fall. There were good neighbors, a family named Oliver, and the drive to work every morning only took fifteen minutes, along a winding, tree-shaded country road.

At the office, there was good work to do, with good people, producing a magazine that soon became a kind of national institution. It fought for things everyone on the staff believed in: a clean environment, the survival of the family farm, the opportunity for others to live close to the natural world, the idea of community.

And then it all came to an end. The magazine's owners feuded and fought and a legal battle erupted between them. They expected the employees to take sides, and when the smoke cleared the winner of the battle cleaned out all of those perceived to have taken the "wrong," which was to say losing, side. Half the staff were let go, including myself. Not very long after that, the magazine changed hands, bought out by a corporate chain interested only in the bottom line. All of that shining idealism and shared sense of mission vanished, like a puff of smoke. I sued for wrongful dismissal, and eventually won a settlement. But that wasn't until years later.

Meanwhile, unemployment was followed by divorce and family break-up. The farm was sold. We moved away, going separate ways. But the farm in Harrowsmith moved with us, at least with me. Over the next decades the memory of it stuck, at the back of the mind, like a favorite, remembered piece of music.

Until—twenty-two years later—what seemed like a miracle: the chance came to go back.

Research Assignment

I was working at a Canadian university, as an assistant professor of journalism, and managed, after a bout with illness, to negotiate a research assignment. The assignment was to research and write three books, one a journalism textbook and the other two reporting on aspects of agriculture (my research specialty was agricultural journalism, which had been the subject of my graduate dissertation). Some of the sources for these latter two books were in British Columbia, but the vast majority—to my joy—were in eastern Ontario, in Frontenac County (home of the municipality of Harrowsmith), and neighboring Hastings County.

A publisher had already been found, the travel and work parameters were approved by the then dean of arts, and the research budget was allotted. I wasn't ready to retire, but before I left to begin fieldwork an abandoned farm came up for sale in . . . Hastings County. It was the perfect place, when retirement would eventually come, to spend the countdown to the end of things. My son and I snapped it up. It would also make the perfect immediate base for work on my assigned research.

And it did make the perfect base. Most of those who had to be interviewed, and much of the documentary material on which the books would be based, were available within a one- to two-hour drive. They included all of the people quoted in the preceding chapters of this book, as well as the historical museums of Tweed, Kingston, and other towns, and the wonderful research library at the federally owned Central Experimental Farm in Ottawa. It was like being in the middle of a researcher's treasure trove.

Not long after my arrival, I realized that the long-unworked 150-acre farm, which comprised several buildings—including a large, historically significant ten-room former church—could be an ideal location for another project. It could, with backing from a like-minded foundation, or even the university, be developed as a research institute, with room for an on-site library (I had a 2,700-volume personal research collection, with more than 1,000 titles dealing with agriculture, development, and the environment), meeting rooms, and space for outdoor test plots. Bringing it back into production, in the age of global warming, would be an experiment with the new conditions we will face in the coming decades, an experiment whose results could be widely shared. A Community Supported Agriculture (CSA) project could be started, along the lines of the one established by the Center for Agroecology and Sustainable Food Systems at the University of California at Santa Cruz. People could come there for training in ecological horticulture, and in how to set up CSAs in their home communities.

I began, as the late Quebec premier Réné Lévesque used to say, "dreaming in colors."

Within a year, the first two assigned books were completed, and one, *The End of Food* (mentioned and cited in chapter 3), had been published. All seemed well.

The End of Food, which included a harsh critique of the multinational corporate food industry, appeared at the end of June 2006, and within a few months became a Canadian best-seller. Surprised and delighted by this development, I informed the university of it in my regular research reports, but there was almost no reaction. The book began getting reviews in mainstream media, and a series of television and radio interviews followed, several on national networks.

Then, in October, a letter came from the university's manager of pensions and benefits, informing me that, despite protestations from myself, my doctor, and the executive director of the faculty union that no such action was warranted, I was being placed on involuntary, unwanted, and unrequested medical leave. "Sick leave benefits may be payable until January 10, 2007," she wrote.

Then, in December, another letter came, this one from the dean of arts, who had succeeded the previous dean:

> I call your attention to Article 16.1.5 of the Collective Agreement between the university and the Faculty Association. It reads: "The duties of academic staff members are to be performed on campus unless other arrangements are approved in advance by the appropriate dean or equivalent..." I have given no approval for your absence from campus. There is no record of my predecessor giving such an approval.

The dean's predecessor had given just such approval, in writing, and had authorized my travel to Ontario. Terms of the agreement assigning the research were on file in the dean's office, and I had been filing regular reports on my progress, at first to the dean himself and afterward to an associate dean.

Notwithstanding, it appeared that I was being ordered back to campus—which would obviously end my research and curtail my ability to complete the remaining book— this book, *The War in the Country.*

Puzzled and distressed, I sought advice from fellow professors, posting e-mail notes to the university faculty network, explaining the situation, describing the nature of my research in detail, and noting that the university's actions "threaten to curtail a valuable, nationally-recognized research project just as it is nearing completion," by depriving me of income and a research budget. Conducting the required research while restricted to the strict confines of the university campus would have been impossible. "Anyone who may have advice or counsel" was invited to contact me with ideas on what to do to save my project.

One of those who did so was an assistant professor—who was a well-known defender of corporate, factory farm agriculture and who had written extensively on the subject, always from a corporate standpoint. "Will you stop sending us these idiotic e-mails?" he asked. "If you want to vent, talk to your lawyer like everybody else." Recognizing the name, I asked if his view that my post was "idiotic" had "anything to do with your food industry views." He didn't reply, but shortly thereafter, I received notice that "your privileges to post messages to the university e-mail lists are hereby revoked," on grounds that my posts constituted "harassment."

Curious, since *The End of Food* had become a national best-seller, to know how sales of the title were going at the student bookstore on campus, I phoned and asked. "It looks like it's going to be returned [to the publisher]," said the clerk. "You've got to keep rotating your books." I phoned several commercial bookstores in the city and asked if they were rotating the book out. "Why would we do that?" replied one store clerk. "It's a best-seller." A check with the local public library found that demand for the book was strong. To borrow it, one had to put one's name on a long waiting list. I phoned libraries in other cities and provinces. One Ontario library had purchased several copies. All were out. The waiting list had forty-one names.

I asked the faculty association to check into the matter, and received a reply: "No copies of your book were sold" on campus, it said, and the unsold copies were returned to the publisher. Apparently students and faculty had very different tastes than the general reading public.

In January, as promised in the pensions and benefits manager's earlier letter, all income from the university was cut off, including my research budget. I filed for unemployment benefits. Some time before, my son had lost his job, and I found myself trying to stretch the EI cheques to cover not only mortgage payments on the farm, but those on his cottage on a nearby lake (later sold) and his monthly car loan payments as well.

Scrounger's Art

Needless to say, these developments made continued work on the book in progress problematic. The situation called for considerable skill in the venerable art of scrounging.

For example, the popularity of *The End of Food* brought frequent requests from farm and consumer groups to speak, and often the groups would pay expenses, such as mileage. Whenever such a request came from a spot near where I had an interview scheduled, or could do documentary research, I combined the tasks in the same trip. Messages requesting telephone interviews were left at hours when their recipients wouldn't likely be in, forcing them to phone back. Thus the interview would be on their long distance phone bill, not mine.

Near-term hopes of rehabilitating the old farm, and developing it as an experimental site, had by now fizzled. With no income, how could farm equipment, seed, and repairs to the buildings be paid for? It was evident that the university would not be interested in my ideas for a research institute, and I had abandoned the thought of proposing it to them.

Royalties on *The End of Food* were due soon, which for awhile held out hope of at least some financial relief. That is, it did until another letter came in the mail, this one from the U.S. publisher of the food exposé. The letter announced that the publisher had filed for bankruptcy protection under Chapter 11 of U.S. bankruptcy law. Royalty payments from the U.S. publisher were suspended. And, since the title had been published in Canada under license from the U.S. contractor, as primary publisher, that included any Canadian royalties.[1]

It turned out that the family that owned the business had owned a number of other publishing firms in the past, and had twice before filed under Chapter 11.

Then yet another letter arrived in the post, from the federal employment insurance folks. It informed me that my EI benefits, which normally would last for up to ten months, were being cut off prematurely. The university had appealed the original award of benefits, claiming that I had only worked half of the qualifying hours required. This was untrue, and I immediately appealed, winning at the first round. My benefits continued... until the university appealed my appeal of its appeal. The threat loomed that I might be forced, while living on next to no income, to repay the EI benefits I'd already received![2]

Needless to say, this put a considerable financial and emotional strain on daily life, and my attempts to work. Peace of mind became a foreign concept. Finding the confidence and concentration to write was a daily struggle. Into the mix was thrown a problem with my eyes, which required surgery. My son left the farm and moved away.

Overwhelmed by debt and with no one to help with the farm work, I was pretty well obliged to abandon hope of living at the farm when I retired.

The university had already weighed in on this note, informing me that as of June 2007 I would be forced to retire, under its sixty-five-and-out forced retirement policy. Forced retirement had been abandoned in most of Canada, on grounds that it constituted discrimination on account of age, and was thus a violation of human rights. The policy had been outlawed in Ontario, but would not be ended in the province in question until after my retirement date. In June, accordingly, I'd be involuntarily retired.

A legal dispute arose over ownership of the farm, during which I was unable to produce or sell a crop without permission from the respondent. Since I couldn't sell a crop, and had no commercial sales, the tax folks removed my farm property tax status, thus sending my property taxes through the roof.

As I played back the interviews I'd recorded with so many people whose rural livelihoods had been destroyed and whose dreams of staying on the farm had been dashed, I felt obvious empathy.

I myself, like my son, was about to become just another casualty of the war in the country. The light seemed as if it was about to be switched off.

BUT LIKE THOSE of so many other rural people, who at one time or another saw their chances of staying on the land as hopeless, my fortunes unexpectedly changed. The ownership lawsuit was settled. The bank agreed to negotiate a new mortgage with lower monthly payments. I became eligible for pensions, one of which was increased only shortly after qualifying for it. The monthly balance sheet improved markedly.

I contacted several organizations involved in farmer training and research, to broach my original plans, and no fewer than three indicated interest in using my farm property as a training site. The students in these programs—who I intended to include young First Nations people—could supply much-needed farm labor, while learning their trades, and the groups and I could split the profits on the produce raised and sold. A provincial grant for low-income housing rehabilitation was discovered, which could (if obtained) provide funds to retrofit a cabin on the property to house live-in students.

Once again, it became possible to "dream in colors."

At this writing, the dreams keep coming.

I suppose this tale is meant to say to my fellow rural residents: don't give up...at least not yet. It's also meant to explain why this particular author feels so strongly on the subject of *The War in the Country*.

Endnotes

Chapter 1: A Different Kind of Great Dying

1　Edmond Rostand, *Cyrano de Bergerac* (Paris: Le Livre de Poche, 1963), 244.
Translated by the author.

2　Kieren McCarthy, "Why TV News in the US is Utter Rubbish," *The Guardian*,
online edition, www.guardian.co.uk, August 8, 2008.

3　Thomas F. Pawlick, *The Invisible Farm: The Worldwide Decline of Farm News and
Agricultural Journalism Training* (Chicago: Burnham Inc., 2001).

4　Roger Epp, "Beyond Our Own Backyards: Factory Farming and the Political
Economy of Extraction," in *Beyond Factory Farming,* eds. Alexander Ervin, Cathy
Holtslander, Darrin Qualman, and Rick Sawa (Saskatoon, Sask.: Canadian
Centre for Policy Alternatives, 2003), 184.

5　Epp, "Beyond Our Own Backyards," 185–86.

6　National Farmers Union, *The Farm Crisis and the Cattle Sector: Towards a New
Analysis and New Solutions* (Saskatoon, Sask.: National Farmers Union),
November 19, 2008, 1.

7　National Farmers Union, *The Farm Crisis,* 4.

8　Government of Alberta, Ministry of Agriculture, Food, and Rural Development,
"The Aftermath of the Crisis: Rethinking the Chain Approach," *Bacon Bits,*
December 1999, 12.

9　Gary Blumenthal, interviewed by Anna Maria Tremonti for CBC Radio One,
The Current, June 12, 2008.

10　Pawlick, *Invisible Farm,* 32–36; and Thomas F. Pawlick, *The End of Food: How the
Food Industry Is Destroying Our Food Supply—And What You Can Do About It* (Fort Lee,
N.J.: Barricade Books, 2006; Vancouver: Greystone Books, 2006), 165–71.

11　Blumenthal on CBC Radio One, *The Current.*

12　Wendell Berry, *The Unsettling of America* (San Francisco: Sierra Club Books,
1977), 40.

13 Lasting from the early 1500s to roughly 1820 or so, the enclosures consisted of
    rich landowners annexing what had formerly been peasants' common land, then
    fencing it in to raise sheep. Yeoman family farmers, thus deprived, suffered
    destitution.
14 Pawlick, *End of Food*.
15 Helen and Scott Nearing, *The Good Life* (New York: Schocken Books, 1989). Helen
    Nearing first began chronicling the saga of the couple's "60 years of self-sufficient
    living" in 1954, but her original book was succeeded by several others, in several
    different editions, including *Living the Good Life* and *Continuing the Good Life* (1970
    and 1979). My file copy is the 1989 edition, which contains both books.
16 Cover line, *The Mother Earth News* 1 (1), January 1970. My original copy of this
    treasure was bought off the newsstand and was an inspiration to a then–twenty-
    eight-year-old.
17 Claudie and Francis Hunzinger, *Bambois, la vie verte* (Paris: Editions Stock, 1973).
18 Masanobu Fukuoka, *The One-Straw Revolution* (Emmaus, Penn.: Rodale Press, 1978.
    This was a translation of the original *Shizen Noho Wara Ippon No Kakuemi* (Tokyo:
    Hakujusha Co., date unknown).
19 Bill Mollison, with David Holmgren, *Permaculture One: A Perennial Agriculture for
    Human Settlements* (Neutral Bay, NSW: Transworld Publishers, 1978).
20 *Harrowsmith* 1 (1), May/June 1976.
21 Kim Carter and Scott McClellan, "Time is No Friend to Poland's Peasant Farmers,"
    Ceres 23(2), 20–27.
22 Vandana Shiva, *The Violence of the Green Revolution* (Penang, Malaysia: Third World
    Network, 1991), and *Monocultures of the Mind* (Penang, Malaysia: Third World
    Network, 1993).

Chapter 2: How It Used To Be

1   *Wikipedia: The Free Encyclopedia*, s.v. "Supermarket," http://en.wikipedia.org/wiki/
    Supermarket (accessed July 11, 2007).
2   Frank B. Edwards, *The Smiling Wilderness: An Illustrated History
    of Lennox and Addington County* (Napanee, Ont.: The County of Lennox and
    Addington, 2005), 57.

Chapter 3: Great Expectations

1   In 1999, the Conservative and business-friendly government of Ontario passed
    Bill 146, which became the Farming and Food Production Act, commonly referred
    to as the "Right to Farm bill." Coming in the wake of a number of local battles
    between rural residents and newly established ILOs, it reduced the ability of
    citizens to protest against the noxious effects of factory farms, by protecting the
    farms from what some called "human nuisance" and establishing a set of so-called
    "normal farm practices," which would be immune from complaints.
2   Alexander Ervin et al. eds., *Beyond Factory Farming* (Saskatoon, Sask.:
    Canadian Centre for Policy Alternatives, 2003), 80–81.
3   Brian Holmes, "Steps to Take to Prevent Manure Gas-related Accidents,"
    Manure Manager 2(2), 34.

4 Ervin et al., *Beyond Factory Farming*, 82–83.
5 Yves Choiniere and Jim Munroe, "Farm Workers Health Problems Related to Air Quality Inside Livestock Barns," Ontario Ministry of Agriculture and Food Factsheet Order No. 93-003, January 1993, 1.
6 Ibid., 4.
7 Jack Coggins, *The Horseman's Bible* (Garden City, N.Y.: Doubleday and Co. Inc., 1966), 103.
8 Rick Dove, "The American Meat Factory," in *Beyond Factory Farming*, eds. Alexander Ervin, et al. 62.
9 Ibid., 183.
10 Cathy Aker, "Feeding and Managing the Growing and Finishing Pig," Ontario Ministry of Agriculture and Food Factsheet Order No. 88-077, March 1988, 1.
11 Ibid.
12 John Daintith, ed., *Minidictionary of Chemistry* (Oxford: Oxford University Press, 1990), 277.
13 Elizabeth Martin, ed., *Minidictionary of Biology* (Oxford: Oxford University Press, 1990), 201.
14 Janet Vorwald Dohner, *The Encyclopedia of Historic and Endangered Livestock and Poultry Breeds* (New Haven, Conn.: Yale University Press, 2001), 161.
15 Jill Sherrill Smith, "Intensive Hogs Farms: Global Corporations Belly Up to the Rural Trough," a report for Concerned Citizens for Our Community Environments (ccce), posted at www.spcottawa.on.ca/ofsc/bellyup.htm (accessed March 19, 2007).
16 United Poultry Concerns, Inc., *Debeaking*, upc Factsheet, posted at www.upc-online.org (accessed March 25, 2007).
17 *Wikipedia*, s.v. "Roundup," www.en.wikipedia.org (accessed September 13, 2007).
18 Ibid., 3.
19 Ibid., 4.
20 Ibid., 3.
21 Sierra Club of Canada, *Pesticide Fact Sheet*, "2,4-D Dichlorophenoxyacetic Acid," www.sierraclub.ca (accessed September 13, 2007), 1.
22 *Stabroek News*, "eu court bans Gramoxone, Local Use Declining," www.stabroeknews.com, July 13, 2007, 1.
23 *Wikipedia*, s.v. "Paraquat" (accessed September 15, 2007), 2.
24 Treena Hein, "Changes to Federal Animal Transport Regulations," *Small Farm Canada* 4(5), September/October 2007, 15–16.
25 Thomas F. Pawlick, *The End of Food: How the Food Industry Is Destroying Our Food Supply–And What You Can Do About It* (Vancouver: Greystone Books, 2006
26 Ibid., 26.
27 Ibid., 119.
28 For a thorough description of Canada's marketing board system, including its history and the conditions that led to its adoption, see: Thomas Pawlick, "The Cause and Its Effects," *Harrowsmith* vii(2), 1982, 26–36.

29 Fred Tait, "Pork, Politics and Power," in *Beyond Factory Farming*, eds. Alexander Ervin, et al. 40.

30 Tait, "Pork, Politics and Power," 53.

31 CBC Radio One, *The Current*, June 12, 2008.

Chapter 4: The Insurgents and the Surge

1 J.C. Kenny, "'Circle of Command' Halts Pork Plans," *Eastern Ontario AgriNews* (24)7, August 2000, as posted in online edition www.agrinewsinteractive.com (accessed March 3, 2007).

2 Jill Sherrill Smith, *Dreams Collide: Communities and Factory Farms in Conflict*, Beyond Factory Farming Coalition, www.beyondfactoryfarming.org (accessed May 4, 2007), 2.

3 Ibid.

4 Ibid., 1.

5 Ibid., 2.

6 Ibid.

7 Ibid.

8 E-mail from Frank Szarka to Tweed municipal clerk Patricia Bergeron, November 17, 2004 (hard copy provided to the author September 2007).

9 Sue Vander Wey, "The Kinlin Road Hog Factory: Sequence of Events," personal communication, 1.

10 Maril Swan, "FNF Warns Lafarge Against Using Otter Creek Bridge to Deliver Cement," *The Tweed News*, June 2004, 1.

11 Rodger Hanna, "Procedural By-law a Hot Topic," *The Tweed News*, May 26, 2004, 1.

12 Joan Van Meer, "Tweed Electorate is Not a Bunch of Mute Animals," *The Tweed News*, May 21, 2004, 4.

13 Alexander Ervin et al., eds., *Beyond Factory Farming* (Saskatoon, Sask.: Canadian Centre for Policy Alternatives, 2003), 173.

14 OMAFRA Staff, "Nutrient Management Financial Assistance Program," Ontario Ministry of Agriculture, Food and Rural Affairs, October 27, 2005, 1.

15 Shannon Binder Bray, "Tweed Deputy Reeve Denies Hog Farm Expenditures," *Community Press*, May 21, 2004, 1.

Chapter 5: Unwanted in Eden

1 James Boswell, *The Life of Samuel Johnson* (Ware, Hertfordshire: Wordsworth Classics, 1999), 440. Many incorrectly believe the quote to say "The road to Hell is paved with good intentions."

2 For a general introduction to the history of Canadian marketing boards, see: Thomas Pawlick, "The Cause and Its Effects," *Harrowsmith* IV(7), 1982, 26–36.

3 Ibid.

4 A French breed of chicken, a cross between Rhode Island Red and Rhode Island White, and noted for high egg production in the first year. ISA stands for Institut de Sélection Animale.

5 Note: The term *free-roam* means that birds are allowed to run free inside a barn, rather than being kept inside cages. *Free-range* means they are also allowed to

run outside of the barn, either in fenced runs or loose in the barnyard, where they can glean for fresh greens, insects, etc. *Battery* birds are those kept confined in tiny wire cages throughout their lives. Most factory-style poultry operations use the battery system.

6 Ontario Landowners Association, "Finding Profits on Canadian Farms," discussion paper, posted at www.ruralrevolution.com, March 2006.

7 For more information, visit www.everdale.org.

8 CNEWS, "No Assault on Egg Farmer," www.canoe.ca, May 23, 2006.

9 After the story by Czech writer Franz Kafka, in which his Soviet-era protagonist is imprisoned in a huge fortress and spends his life wandering fruitlessly from prison official to prison official, room to room, trying to find out what crime he's been charged with.

10 Diana Henriques, interviewed by Anna Maria Tremonti for CBC Radio One, *The Current*, June 12, 2008.

11 Chris Mercer, "Fischer Boel Rejects EU Milk Quotas," *Food Production Daily*, Decision News Media SAS, www.foodproductiondaily.com, January 25, 2007.

12 Mercer, "Fischer Boel."

13 Valentin Petkantchin, "Dairy Production: The Costs of Supply Management in Canada," Montreal Economic Institute, www.iedm.org, January 2, 2005.

14 Valentin Petkantchin, "Reforming Dairy Supply Management in Canada: The Australian Example," Montreal Economic Institute, www.iedm.org, January 27, 2006.

15 Sylvain Charlebois, Wolfgang Langenbacher, and Andrei Volondin, "The Role and Function of the Canadian Dairy Commission: An Empirical Survey of its Relevance in Today's Civil Society," policy paper at the Saskatchewan Institute of Public Policy, 2006, 14.

16 Ibid.

17 Ibid., 15–16.

18 Ibid., 8.

19 National Farmers Union (Canada), "Farmers Launch Court Challenge over Government Move to Strip CWB of Barley; NFU Takes Lead Role," *Union Farmer Monthly* 57(4), June/July 2007, 2,4.

20 Bill Curry, "Fight Over Wheat Board Not Over Yet, Strahl Vows," *The Globe and Mail*, www.theglobeandmail.com, August 6, 2007.

21 National Farmers Union (Canada), "Ritz Links Arms with Cargill and ADM to Intimidate CWB," *Union Farmer Monthly* 58(1), January/February 2008, 1–2.

22 National Farmers Union (Canada), "Minister Huddles with Agribusiness to Plot Future of CWB," *Union Farmer Monthly* 58(1), January/February 2008, 5.

23 National Farmers Union, "Ritz Links Arms," 2.

24 Aramark, "Company Snapshot," www.aramark.com (accessed February 11, 2008).

25 Amartya K. Sen, "An Aspect of Indian Agriculture," *Economic Weekly*, Annual Number, Vol. 14, February 1962; A.K. Sen, "Size of Holdings and Productivity," *Economic Weekly*, Annual Number, Vol. 16, 1964.

26 Charles Benbrook, Xin Zhao, Jaime Yanez, Neal Davies, and Preston Andrews, "New Evidence Confirms the Nutritional Superiority of Plant-based Organic Foods,"

State of Science Review, Nutritional Superiority of Organic Foods, The Organic Center, www.organic-center.org, March 2008, 42.

Chapter 6: What's Yours Is Mine

1 Ernest J. Sternglass, *Low-Level Radiation* (New York: Ballantine Books, 1972).
2 *Wikipedia,* s.v. "Karen Silkwood," www.en.wikipedia.org (accessed September 27, 2007), 2.
3 Thomas Pawlick, "The Silent Toll," *Harrowsmith* IV(8), 1980, 33–49.
4 Ernest Sternglass, *Secret Fallout: Low-Level Radiation from Hiroshima to Three Mile Island* (New York: McGraw-Hill, 1981).
5 Harvey Wasserman and Norman Solomon, *Killing Our Own: The Disaster of America's Experience with Atomic Radiation* (New York: Dell Publishing, 1982).
6 Robert Leppzer, *Voices from Three Mile Island* (Trumansburg, N.Y.: The Crossing Press, 1980).
7 Albert Bates, Project Director, *Shut Down: Nuclear Power on Trial* (Summertown, Tenn.: The Book Publishing Company, 1979).
8 See, for example, the one-hour documentary *The Greenhouse Effect,* NTSC, TV Ontario Vista (BPN 246001), 1987, script by Thomas F. Pawlick.
9 David Kimble, "Is There Enough Uranium to Run a Nuclear Industry Big Enough to Take Over from Fossil Fuels?" as posted on Austarnet, www.home.austarnet. com.au/davekimble/peakuranium.htm, March 2005, 3.
10 Chris Baltimore and Lisa Lee, "NRG Seeks First US Nuclear Plant Permit in Decades," Reuters News Agency, September 25, 2007.
11 Jason Leopold, "Cheney Pursuing Nuclear Ambitions of His Own," *Truthout,* www.truthout.org/docs_2006/110507A.shtml, November 5, 2007.
12 Unsigned editorial, "A Warming World: No to Nukes," *Los Angeles Times,* July 23, 2007.
13 Ontario Ministry of Energy, "McGuinty Government Delivers a Balanced Plan for Ontario's Electricity Future," press release, June 13, 2006, 1.
14 Nick Trevethan, "UK Nuclear Focus May Boost Emissions—Green Groups," Reuters News Agency, July 12, 2006, 1.
15 Frank Armstrong, "They're Looking for Confrontation," *The Kingston Whig-Standard,* September 15, 2007, 11.
16 Thomas Pawlick, "The Siege of Mud Lake," *Harrowsmith* VI(4), 1982, 32–41.
17 Kathi Avery and Thomas Pawlick, "Last Stand in Wild Rice Country," *Harrowsmith* III(7), 1979, 32–46, 107.
18 Ibid., 34.
19 Thomas Pawlick, "Ben & Leo: A Curious Relationship," *Harrowsmith* III(7), 1979, 48–50.
20 Pawlick, "Siege," 35.
21 Ibid., 34.
22 Ibid., 37.
23 Ibid., 32.
24 Ibid.
25 Ibid.

26 Ibid., 40.

27 Ibid., 40–41.

28 Ibid., 41.

29 Fasken Martineau DuMoulin, "Neal J. Smitheman, Lawyer,"
   www.fasken.com/nsmitheman/ (accessed October 2, 2007).

30 Ibid.

31 Quotations taken from a transcript of the meeting, recorded by Thomas Pawlick.

32 Jeff Green, "Anti-uranium Exploration Activities Entering a New Phase,"
   The Frontenac News, online edition, www.newsweb.ca, September 6, 2007.

33 White was wrong. Emery's 1964 gold was for bobsledding.

34 Pawlick, "Silent Toll," 39.

35 A. Petkau and W.S. Chelack, "Radioprotective Effect of Superoxide Dismutase on
   Model Phospholipid Membranes," *Biochemic et Biophysica Acta* 433 (1976), 445–56,
   and A. Petkau, "Effect of Na+ on a Phospholipid Membrane," *Health Physics* 22
   (1972), 239–44.

36 Thomas Pawlick and Dorrie Matthews, "It Can Happen Here,"
   Harrowsmith IV(8), 1980, 40–41.

37 Ralph D. Torrie, "Uranium Mine Tailings: What the Record Shows,"
   Alternatives 10(2/3), Toronto, 1982.

38 Vivian Graf v. Giuseppe Palu, File No. MA 012-95, L. Kamerman,
   Ontario Mining and Lands Commissioner, October 15, 1996.

39 Gloria Morrison, "Our Story: Uranium Prospecting In Our Backyard,"
   Mining Watch Canada, www.miningwatch.ca, June 12, 2007.

40 See Stephen McGregor et al., *Since Time Immemorial: Our Story* (Maniwaki,
   Quebec: Kitigan Zibi Education Council/Anishinabe Printing, 2004), 140, 165.

41 Jeff Green, "Rally and March Demonstrate Support for Algonquin Mine
   Occupation," the *Frontenac News,* July 12, 2007, 1.

42 Julius Strauss, "Stakes are High as Miners and Natives Square Off,"
   The Globe and Mail, 22 February 2006, 1.

43 Steve Bonspiel, "Big Trout Lake First Nation Faces $10 Billion Lawsuit,"
   Nation (Beesum Communications), June 23, 2006, 1.

44 Sylvio Ventures Inc., "Sylvio Ventures Inc. Announces Agreement to Acquire
   Frontenac Ventures Corp.," press release via www.hostopia.com, May 30, 2007,
   accessed from StockHouse.com, www.stockhouse.com/news/print_news.
   asp?newsid'5538561.

45 Chinese Investment Club Inc., "Pangeo Pharma Inc.," as posted at
   www.nafinance.com/Listed_Co/English/pangeo_e.htm, April 24, 2007.

46 In the matter of The Securities Act, R.S.O. 1990 C.S. 5, as amended and in
   the matter of Pangeo Pharma Inc., Order (Section 144), December 21, 2005,
   Ontario Securities Commission, www.osc.gov.on.ca/Regulation/Orders/2006/
   ord_20060120_221_pange, 2.

47 CBC News, "Pangeo Pharma Restructuring Under Bankruptcy Protection,"
   www.cbc.ca/money/story/2003/07/10/pangeo_030710.html, July 10, 2003, 1.

48 In the matter of Pangeo, as above.

49 Ibid.

50 Ibid.

51 Ibid.

52 Ibid. 3.

53 In the matter of The Securities Act, R.S.O. 1990, Chapter S.5, as amended, and in the matter of Silvio Ventures Inc., Order (Section 144), October 27, 2006, Ontario Securities Commission, www.osc.gov.on.ca/Regulation/Orders/2006/ ord_20061110_222_silvio.j, 2.

54 Bullboard discussion forum comment titled, "Direction," Stockhouse Bullboards, www.stockhouse.ca/bullboards, May 7, 2007.

55 Note: A "shell," according to *Wikipedia* (www.en.wikipedia.org/wiki/Shell_ corporation), is "a company that is incorporated, but has no significant assets or operations." Such companies are perfectly legal and, if they are listed on the stock exchanges, are often used by non-listed companies to raise venture capital by getting their own initial public stock offering (IPO) before investors. *Bushed,* of course, had no way of knowing whether Silvio had significant assets or operations, but was making a wild guess.

56 Bullboard's discussion form comment, titled "Siv.h," May 8, 2007.

57 Ibid., "What the insiders think it's worth," May 8, 2007.

58 Ibid., "SIV.H solid buy & rising," May 10, 2007.

59 Ibid., "Uranium property," May 25, 2007.

60 Ibid., "uranium.com," May 26, 2007.

61 Ibid., "Finally the news comes out," May 31, 2007.

62 Ibid., "Finally the news comes out," June 3, 2007.

63 Ibid., "Future" June 4, 2007.

64 Ibid., "Does anyone know," July 18, 2007.

65 Ibid.

66 Bill Curry, "Non-natives Support Algonquins' Mining Rallies," *The Globe and Mail* online edition, www.theglobeandmail.com, July 14, 2007, 2.

67 Bonspiel, "Big Trout Lake," 2.

68 Ibid.

69 Mike Oliveira, "Development of Platinum Mine Near Northern Ontario Reserve Leads to $10 Billion Suit," Canadian Press, www.money.canoe.ca/News/Sectors/ Mining/2006/05/28/1602528-cp.html, May 28, 2006, 2.

70 Frank Armstrong, "Sides in Uranium Dispute Seek Truce; Judge Asks for Compromise to be Found Until Trial Starts in September," *The Kingston Whig-Standard,* www.thewhig.com, July 31, 2007, 1.

71 *The Kingston Whig-Standard,* "Aboriginals and Anarchy," editorial, www.thewhig.com, September 4, 2007.

72 Julie Koch Brison, "North Frontenac Council Takes a Stand on Uranium Mining," *The Frontenac News,* September 13, 2007, 1.

73 Jeff Green, "Mr. Kittle Goes to Ottawa," the *Frontenac News,* September 13, 2007, 1.

74 Silvio Ventures Inc., "Termination of Agreement with Frontenac Ventures Corp," press release posted on the Marketwire website, www.marketwire.com/mw/ release.do?id'771197, September 18, 2007.

75 Ibid.

76 Bullboards, "Big deal—we lose," October 3, 2007.

77 Ibid., "Update from Toronto *Star*," October 16, 2007.

78 Unsigned article, "Mine Protester's Plea Doesn't Sway Premier; McGuinty Says Hunger Strike by Sharbot Lake Site Opponent Endangering Her Health," *The Kingston Whig-Standard,* online edition, www.thewhig.com, November 28, 2007.

79 "Council Endorses Mining Moratorium," *The Kingston Whig-Standard,* online edition, www.thewhig.com, November 22, 2007.

80 Knights on Guard, www.knightsonguard.com/home.htm, as retrieved by Google on October 24, 2007.

81 "Group Slams Fining, Jailing of Protester," *The Kingston Whig-Standard,* online edition, www.thewhig.com, February 19, 2008.

82 Scott Reid and Randy Hillier, "A Message of Support for Robert Lovelace," news release published through Randy Hillier's legislative offices at Queen's Park, Toronto, February 21, 2008.

83 Michael Valpy, "Archbishop Issues Stern Rebuke on Jailing of Natives," *The Globe and Mail,* online edition, www.theglobeandmail.com, March 25, 2008.

84 Joan Kuyek, Mining Watch Canada, www.miningwatch.ca, "Ottawa City Council All But Unanimously Passed the Following Resolution Today," e-mail to membership February 27, 2008.

85 Michael Oliveira, "Jailing Aboriginal Protesters 'Too Harsh,' Appeal Court Says," Canadian Press, as published in *The Globe and Mail,* online edition, www.theglobeandmail.com, July 7, 2008.

Chapter 7: Since Time Immemorial

1 John Johnson, "Letter to Colonel Darling, Military Secretary to the Earl of Dalhousie, Commander in Chief of British Forces in Canada, November 5, 1824, *National Archives of Canada,* NAC RG10, Vol. 494 (Ottawa), 31027–31032.

2 Tyson Yunkaporta, "Wangkumarra, Native Title, Mining," *Suite101.com,* October 23, 2007.

3 ACSA Inc., "ACSA Challenges Senator John McCain's Legislative Record on Dineh-Navaho," *Advances Magazine,* www.acsa.net, August 12, 2008.

4 CBC News, "Panel Rejects Northgate's Kemess North Mine Project," www.cbc.ca/money/story/2007/09/17/kemess.html, September 18, 2007.

5 Stephen McGregor et al., *Since Time Immemorial: Our Story* (Maniwaki, Quebec, Kitiganzibi Education Council/Anishinabe Printing, 2004), 256.

6 Ardoch Algonquin First Nation, "Ardoch Algonquin First Nation Manomin Heritage Center," press release posted at www.aafna.ca/community.html, (accessed December 6, 2007), 3.

7 David Rose, "Re: More Meetings at Pine Lake," the *Frontenac News,* online edition, www.newsweb.ca, December 21, 2006.

8 Tim Naumetz, "The Algonquin Claim: What's At Stake, Who's Involved," *The Ottawa Citizen,* online edition, www.canada.com/ottawacitizen, July 8, 2007.

9 Jeff Green, "Elections Intended to Rejuvenate Land Claim Process," the *Frontenac News,* online edition, www.newsweb.ca, April 28, 2005.

10 Ottawa Algonquin First Nation, "Summary—Algonquin Negotiation Process,"
    Ottawa Algonquin First Nation website, www.ottawaalgonquins.com (accessed
    December 6, 2007).

11 Samantha Craggs, "Supporters Rally to Free Shawn Brant," *The Belleville
    Intelligencer,* online edition, www.intelligencer.ca, August 25, 2007, 1.

12 Bruce Bell, "Mohawk Land Protest Closes Road, Business," *The Belleville
    Intelligencer,* online edition, www.intelligencer.ca, January 10, 2007, 1.

13 Jamesr, "Interview with Tyendinaga Warrior Shawn Brant," Common Cause
    website, www.linchpin.ca, November 26, 2007.

14 Dominik Wisniewski, "Mayor Optimistic About Land Claim Process,"
    The Regional Beaver, December 28, 2007, 2.

15 Jamesr, "Interview with Shawn Brant," 1.

16 Jonah Gindin, "Stone by Stone, Rail by Rail," *Briarpatch Magazine,*
    online edition, www.briarpatchmagazine.com/2008/06/09stone-by-stone-rail-by-
    rail, June 9, 2008.

17 Michael Oliveira, "Mohawk Supporters Protest at Queen's Park,"
    The Globe and Mail, April 24, 2007, A9.

18 Michael J. Brethour, "Native Protestors Angry About MNR Snub," *The Shield,*
    April 13, 2007, 1.

19 Dale Morrisey, "Quarry Occupiers Block Rail Lines," *The Napanee Guide,*
    April 27, 2007, 3.

20 Michael Oliveira, "Impact of Protests Worry Band Council," Canadian Press,
    as published in *The Kingston Whig-Standard,* April 24, 2007, 7.

21 Ibid.

22 Gindin, "Stone by Stone."

23 Joshua Clipperton, "Lawyer Wants Fantino Suspended," Canadian Press, as
    published in *The Globe and Mail,* online edition, www.theglobeandmail.com,
    July 19, 2008.

Chapter 8: None of Your Business(es)

1   Sometimes attributed to China's Chairman Mao Zedong, or to various people
    responding to him. Mao actually wrote "The Peoples' Army is a school of fish
    that swims in the ocean of the people," a phrase probably itself inspired by
    V.I. Lenin's comment at a party congress on March 22, 1922: "In the sea of people,
    we are after all but a drop in the ocean." Numerous writers on counter-insurgency,
    from the Vietnam War era to former U.S. Secretary of Defense Donald Rumsfeld,
    have responded with the idea of "draining the ocean," or more pejoratively,
    "the swamp," in order to rid it of such fish… or mosquitos.

2   Rick Neilson, "Locals Stand Up to Inspection Officials," *Small Farm Canada,*
    May/June 2007, 6–7.

3   National Farmers Union Region 3 (Ontario), "Comments to the Ontario Meat
    Inspection Review," April 6, 2004, 3.

4   National Farmers Union, "Comments on the Saskatchewan Meat Inspection
    Review," December 9, 2005, 2.

5   Ibid., 3.

6   Ibid., 4.

7   Tamsyn Burgmann and Joan Bryden, "Health Officials Tie Listeria Outbreak to
    Maple Leaf Meats," *The Globe and Mail*, online edition, www.theglobeandmail.com,
    August 24, 2008.

8   Caroline Alphonso, "Windsor Death Raises Listeria Outbreak Toll to 15," *The
    Globe and Mail*, online edition, www.theglobeandmail.com, September 11, 2008.

9   Tu Thanh Ha, Bill Curry, and Anne McIlroy, "Inspectors Failed to Adopt More
    Rigorous U.S. Measures," *The Globe and Mail*, online edition,
    www.theglobeandmail.com, August 27, 2008, 1.

10 Ann Lukits, "Regulations Grate on Cheesemakers," *The Kingston Whig-Standard*,
    online edition, www.thewhig.com, September 26, 2008.

11 Ibid.

12 Ibid.

13 Non-Canadian readers may be unaware that the province of Ontario, which
    borders Quebec, has a fairly sizeable French-speaking minority, for whom French
    instruction is seen as a matter of cultural survival.

14 Ronald Zajac, "Boundary 2020 Foes Buoyed by Decision to Appoint Facilitator,"
    The Recorder & Times, online edition, www.beta.recorder.ca, August 5, 2008.

15 "Upper Canada School Board Plows Ahead with Boundary 2020,"
    The Landowner Magazine, 3(1), June/July 2008, 44.

16 *The Kingston Whig-Standard*, "Our View," editorial August 14, 2008.

17 Chinta Puxley, "Hot Time in the Small Towns," Canadian Press,
    as published in *The Globe and Mail*, online edition, www.theglobeandmail.com,
    August 20, 2008.

18 Ibid.

19 Nick Gardiner, "Group Thinks McGuinty to Charge Well Owners,"
    The Recorder & Times, April 10, 2007, 3A.

20 Anthony S.C. Hampton, "University of Guelph Surveys Well Owners,"
    Napanee Guide, September 19, 2008, 9.

21 Jim Barber, "County of L&A to Conduct High-Speed Internet Survey,"
    Napanee Guide, September 19, 2008, 9.

22 Jeff Esau, "Rural Ontario: Will the Government Cure It or Kill It?"
    The Landowner Magazine, February/March 2007, 18, 38.

Chapter 9: A Missing of Minds

1   Canwest News Service, "Agriculture Census Highlights,"
    www.canada.com, May 17, 2007.

2   Brent Cameron, "A Rural Requiem," *The Landowner Magazine*, 3(2),
    August/September 2008, 42–43.

3   John Duffy, "The First North American Election?" in *The Globe and Mail*,
    online edition, www.theglobeandmail.com, September 12, 2008, 2.

4   Ibid.

5   *JM from Realityville*, Letter to the Editor responding to Brodie Fenelon,
    "More Youths Using Guns in Violent Crime: Statscan," *The Globe and Mail*,
    online edition, www.theglobeandmail.com, February 20, 2008.

6   For an example of the real danger such groups pose, see: Gloria Kim, "Saving Animals, They Hunt Humans," *Maclean's* magazine, online, www.macleans.ca, March 20, 2006, or Steve O'Neill, "Animal Rights on the Rise," *Farm & Country News* online, www.agpub.on.ca, December 4, 2007.

7   Justine Hunter, "Six Men Can't Pry Bear Off Victim," *The Globe and Mail*, online edition, www.theglobeandmail.com, September 10, 2008, 1.

8   Thomas Pawlick, "Queries & Quandaries: Whole (Pet) Foods," *Harrowsmith* IV(7), April 1980, 115–16.

9   John Mallam and Steve Parker, *Encyclopedia of Dinosaurs and Other Prehistoric Creatures* (Bath, U.K.: Parragon Publishing, 2002), 16–17.

10 Peter Tompkins and Christopher Bird, *The Secret Life of Plants* (New York: Perennial Library, 1989).

11 Ibid., 3.

12 Ibid., 22.

13 *Wikipedia*, s.v. "Jainism," www.en.wikipedia.org, (accessed March 5, 2008), 8.

14 Tompkins and Baird, *The Secret Life*, 8.

15 Robert Brightman, *Grateful Prey: Rock Cree Human-Animal Relationships* (Regina: Canadian Plains Research Center/University of California Press, 1993).

Chapter 10: A Wider Alliance

1   That is, reform in the original, *Oxford Dictionary* meaning of the term, "to make or become better by the removal of faults and errors," rather than the new definition neo-conservative, corporate spin doctors have given it in recent years, namely "to eliminate or destroy" (as in "reform" publicly funded health care by eliminating it).

2   Bill Curry, "Native Leaders Demand Campaign Attention," *The Globe and Mail*, online edition, www.theglobeandmail.com, September 28, 2008.

3   *Globe and Mail* Update, "Is it Time for the Tories to Release a Platform?" *The Globe and Mail*, online edition, www.theglobeandmail.com, September 26, 2008.

4   Liberal Party of Canada, "Richer, Fairer, Greener: An Action Plan for the 21st Century," Section 4, "Strong Rural and Northern Canada," Liberal Party website, www.liberal.ca, September 2008.

5   Omar El Akkad, "NDP platform Pledges Billions for Child Care," *The Globe and Mail*, online edition, www.theglobeandmail.com, September 28, 2008, 1.

6   Green Party of Canada, "Looking Forward: A Fresh Perspective on Canada's Future, Section 3, Create Healthy Business," Green Party website, www.greenparty.ca, September 2008.

7   National Farmers Union in Ontario, "The History of the NFU," as posted on the NFU website, www.nfu.ca, September 27, 2008, 8.

8   Geri Kamenz, "Premier Continues Valuable Tradition of Greeting Farmers," *Napanee Guide*, September 26, 2008, 24.

9   Two excellent summaries of this history are: Louis Aubrey Wood, *A History of Farmers' Movements in Canada* (Toronto: University of Toronto Press, 1975), and National Farmers Union in Ontario, "The History of the N.F.U.," as posted on the NFU website, www.nfu.ca/on/misc_files/History.htm, March 6, 2008.

10 National Farmers Union, *Union Farmer Monthly,* 2717 Wentz Ave., Saskatoon, Sask. s7k 4b6; *The Union Farmer,* Terry Pugh, Editor, 2717 Wentz Ave., Saskatoon, Sask. s7k 4b6.

11 Anthony S.C. Hampton, "New Program to Promote Farmer Training," *Napanee Guide,* August 15, 2008, 8.

12 National Farmers Union Local 316 and Food Down the Road, "From the Ground Up: A Primer for Community Action on Kingston and Countryside's Food System," October 1, 2007, available online at www.fooddowntheroad.ca.

13 Pawlick, "Cause and Its Effects," 27.

14 National Farmers Union in Ontario, "History of the N.F.U.," 12.

15 For an interview with Bové, see: *YaleGlobal Online,* "Food Should Be Left Off the Free Trade Table," www.yaleglobal.yale.edu, April 6, 2005. A good outline of the conditions that prompted Bové's movement is: Philip H. Gordon and Nicolas de Boisgrollier, "Why the French Love Their Farmers," YaleGlobalOnline, www.yaleglobal.yale.edu, November 15, 2005.

16 *Wikipedia,* s.v. "Andrzej Lepper," www.en.wikipedia.org/wiki/Andrzej_Lepper, October 25, 2007.

17 *The Landowner Magazine,* 6588 Fallowfield Road, Stittsville, Ont., k2s 1b8, e-mail: marlene@dilkie.com. Six issues per year.

18 Helen Forsey, "Betting the Farm: The Lanark Landowners Association Has Staked the Future of Rural Ontario on the Fall of Big Government," *This Magazine,* www.thismagazine.ca, March 6, 2008.

19 John Campbell, "Landowners Group Sounds War Cry," *The Independent,* online edition, www.indynews.ca, February 8, 2006, 2.

20 Graham Hughes and Kelly Roesler, "Angry Farmers Storm the City," *The Ottawa Citizen,* April 9, 2004, 1.

21 Ibid., 3.

22 See Henry David Thoreau, "Civil Disobedience," an 1849 essay originally published as "Resistance to Civil Government," as posted at www.eserver.org/thoreau/civil.html (accessed March 17, 2008).

23 Roy MacGregor, "This Country: Ontario Votes a Knuckle-dragging, Mouth-breathing Redneck Hillbilly, A Militant, Radical, Gun-toting Nut," *The Globe and Mail,* September 13, 2007, A1.

24 Forsey, "Betting the Farm," 3.

25 For a good exposition of the principles of satyagraha, see: M.K. Gandhi, *Collected Writings on Non-Violent Resistance* (New York: Schocken Books, 1970).

26 Forsey, "Betting the Farm," 3.

27 Ibid., 2.

28 Ibid., 3.

29 Land O'Lakes NewsWeb, "Leona Euchres Lanark Landowners," www.newsweb.ca, March 31, 2005, 1.

30 Two good sources on this subject (slightly marred by tinges of religious bias) are: Fr. Vincent McNabb, *The Church and the Land* (Norfolk, Virginia: ihs Press, 2003), and Mgr. Richard Williamson et al., *The Rural Solution* (Moyne, Ireland: The Traditionalist Press, 2003).

Appendix: A Personal War

1   A year later, while the bankruptcy proceedings were continuing in U.S. courts, I received a single royalty check, for $1,500.

2   Eventually, Canada Revenue Agency, which adjudicates such matters, ruled that I had in fact worked 2,706 hours during the year in question, or more than fifty hours a week, which constituted full-time employment and qualified me for benefits.